BREAKING WINDOWS

How Bill Gates Fumbled
the Future of Microsoft

DAVID BANK

THE FREE PRESS

NEW YORK LONDON TORONTO SYDNEY SINGAPORE

*f*P

THE FREE PRESS
A Division of Simon & Schuster, Inc.
1230 Avenue of the Americas
New York, NY 10020

THE FREE PRESS and colophon are trademarks of Simon & Schuster, Inc.

For information about special discounts for bulk purchases,
please contact Simon & Schuster Special Sales:
1-800-456-6798 or business@simonandschuster.com

Designed by Karolina Harris

Manufactured in the United States of America

10   9   8   7   6   5   4   3   2   1

Library of Congress Cataloging-in-Publication Data

Bank, David, 1960–
    Breaking Windows: how Bill Gates fumbled the future of Microsoft / David
Bank.
        p.   cm.
    Includes bibliographical references and index.
    1. Microsoft Corporation.   2. Computer software industry—United States.
    3. Gates, Bill, 1955–   I. Title.
HD9696.63.U64 M5326   2001
338.7'610053'0973—dc21   2001033034

ISBN 0-7432-0315-1

FOR LEONORE,
WHO HAS TAUGHT ME
ALWAYS TO BELIEVE AND NEVER TO REGRET

The cloud laughed at the rainbow
  saying that it was an upstart
    gaudy in its emptiness.

The rainbow calmly answered,
  "I am as inevitably real as the sun himself."

—*Rabindranath Tagore*

Contents

Prologue: The E-mail Trail

AT A SMALL party in downtown Seattle in the spring of 2000, Tod Nielsen was introduced to an affable young man who said he was a paralegal at a local law firm. Nielsen mentioned he worked at Microsoft.

"I know," the paralegal said. He was familiar with Nielsen's shifting assignments, his promotion to vice president, and his upbeat tone. "You have always seemed like a really nice guy."

"Excuse me," Nielsen said. "Have we met before?"

"No," the man explained. "But I'm the guy who reads your e-mail."

The paralegal was far from the only person reading Nielsen's e-mail, or that of dozens of Microsoft's midlevel managers and top executives. With the company's business practices under legal scrutiny for most of the past decade, the collection and review of the company's internal communications had become as routine as the specials in the employee cafeterias. Once a month or so, a company lawyer contacted Nielsen's assistant and arranged to arrive at a time when Nielsen would be out of his office. With a technician, the lawyer downloaded the e-mail archive from the hard disk drive of Nielsen's computer and copied any new Word files or PowerPoint presentations. Nielsen's hard copies of charts and presentations were taken down the hall to be photocopied and returned to his office. Nielsen could hardly tell anyone had been there. The drill was the same for all the key employees working on major projects, such as Windows, Office, Internet Explorer, and tools for outside software programmers.

Each round of newly collected documents was added to e-mail records copied straight from the caches on Microsoft's central computer servers. Each printout was stamped with an identification number and, in a bit of wishful thinking, the word Confidential. A courier delivered the documents to one of several outside law firms. There, the piles of paper were divided among dozens of paralegals, who over time developed familiarity with the people on their particular lists of Microsoft executives.

Paralegals spent their days reviewing the huge volume of everyday electronic correspondence that coursed through the networks of the world's largest software company. The bulk of the material was mundane. But if the subject matter appeared to be covered by any of the dozens of subpoenas and "civil investigative demands" issued in the legal actions against Microsoft, the documents were pulled for further review by lawyers. Under legal orders, Microsoft's attorneys then turned over the relevant material to prosecutors from the antitrust division of the U.S. Department of Justice, or to lawyers for Sun Microsystems or the other companies waging private lawsuits against Microsoft. By introducing the e-mail into evidence in the courtroom, the opposing parties made the documents public, and later posted them on sites on the World Wide Web. On a smaller scale, a similar effort was underway at Microsoft's competitors, such as Sun, Oracle, Netscape, IBM, and AOL, in response to legal demands from both the government and Microsoft.

Most of Microsoft's e-mail was collected long before the most sensational snippets began to appear in the press. But even after they must have realized the potential ramifications, Microsoft employees continued their running dialogues in writing. The collecting of e-mail became part of the white noise of a day in the office at Microsoft and was easily forgotten. So were the pro forma warnings from the legal department advising against the use of incendiary language in written communications. And the company's defense lawyers dutifully continued to turn over the transcripts of these in-house dialogues, providing their legal adversaries with some of their most valuable evidence.

Beyond the damaging snippets, the record of internal communications provided an unprecedented glimpse into the strategic debates and internal decision-making processes of a company that had long restricted outside access to its insular corporate culture. The leader of the emerging information age was turned inside out by a powerful tool of that new age, electronic mail.

IN THE FALL OF 1998, a courier delivered three heavy boxes full of paper to the downtown San Francisco offices of the *Wall Street Journal*, where I was the reporter assigned to the Microsoft beat. A legal effort by the *San Jose Mercury News* and several trade publications had convinced the judge to unseal most of the evidence in the federal civil lawsuit against Microsoft by Sun Microsystems, filed in 1997, in which Sun charged Microsoft with violating the terms of its license to use Sun's heavily hyped Java software technology.

With my colleague, Don Clark, I took over a conference room and began tagging and sorting the photocopies of the e-mails and other documents. The most interesting parts, to us, had little to do with the specifics of the legal cases. We read each e-mail thread from the beginning, and tried to understand the often arcane technical discussions. It required considerable effort to sort out the players and the plots. But by arranging the documents in chronological order and constructing an organization chart, we began to assemble a picture of Microsoft's internal debates and personal rivalries. What emerged was a cast of characters, known by their e-mail screen names, who had played parts in a grand opera set in the dramatic early days of the digital revolution.

Some players were familiar. "Bradsi" was Brad Silverberg, the senior vice president who had delivered Windows 3.1 and Windows 95 before forming Microsoft's Internet division to wage the "browser war" against the upstart Netscape Communications. "Jimall" was Jim Allchin, now the head of Microsoft's Windows division and the champion of its new Windows 2000 operating system. "Paulma" was Paul Maritz, effectively the company's third-ranking executive and the one to whom both Silverberg and Allchin reported. "Steveb" was Steve Ballmer, then the head of Microsoft's sales force and later its CEO. Over much of the e-mail hovered the presence of "Billg," Bill Gates, Microsoft's chairman and cofounder, who had created a company that remained uniquely a projection of himself.

Other e-mails came from the ranks of programmers with whom reporters rarely came into contact. There was a February 1997 message, for example, from Andrew Layman, a member of Microsoft's own Java team, that concluded, "We appear to have a clash between what Bill says we should be doing and what we . . . are in fact doing." The response from his colleague Russ Arun: "Yup, there is a disconnect with Billg."

I had already gotten hints of such a conflict. In an interview earlier in 1998, Allchin had criticized the embrace of Java by others at Microsoft. He considered Java a flawed technology that handed an advantage to Sun. "Even at Microsoft, there were some people who drank the Java Kool-Aid," he told me. Separately, over dinner in Seattle, a midlevel Microsoft manager had described what he called a "come to Bill" meeting in the spring of 1997. The meeting stood out even among Microsoft's knock-down drag-out reviews: Gates had been merciless in lacerating the Java team for failing to pay sufficient attention to protecting Windows, the company's crown jewel.

"Why don't you just give up your options and join the Peace

Corps?" my source quoted Gates as shouting. "Hasn't anybody here ever heard of Windows? Windows is what this company is about!"

Now, as I culled through the documents in the Java lawsuit, I came across a series of e-mails from March 1997 that appeared to refer to the internally infamous meeting. The leader of the Java team, Ben Slivka, or "Bens," was responding to a colleague who had tried to comfort him for the shellacking he had received from Gates.

"It is disappointing that Bill chooses to flame like that without giving me a chance to educate him," Slivka wrote back. "Bill is convinced my group is trying to kill Windows, and I clearly haven't said the right things to show him otherwise."

It was a rare crack in Microsoft's monolithic public image. With the climactic meeting as an anchor, I reconstructed the debate over Java and the future of Windows. Microsoft's Java efforts had foundered in part on technical grounds, but the e-mail record revealed a more fundamental split between Silverberg and Allchin, both members of the eight-man executive committee that steered the company's strategy. Allchin emerged as a hardcore "Windows hawk," fiercely protective of the revenue stream and competitive leverage Microsoft gained from Windows, its flagship product. Silverberg was the leader of Microsoft's "Internet doves," pushing the company to develop a new platform for software development in order to capture the new opportunities opened by the Internet.

Allchin prevailed. By the time the story appeared on the front page of the *Wall Street Journal* in February 1999, on the day Allchin took the witness stand in Microsoft's antitrust trial, he appeared to have been vindicated. Windows had become more wildly popular than ever, driven by ever-falling PC prices and the popularity of the Web. Through the end of that year, Microsoft's already staggering profit margins expanded and its stock market value soared even higher.

Allchin and Gates had only bought Windows some time. Over the next two years it became clear that Microsoft's internal splits underlay much of what happened—the courtroom debacle in the antitrust trial, the exodus of many of the company's most talented employees, and Gates's own fall from grace as a corporate leader and technology visionary.

BY THE SPRING OF 2000, as the two-year antitrust trial neared its conclusion, the cycle of dialogue and disclosure had become a recursive loop. Microsoft's lawyers were collecting, reviewing, and turning over e-mails written during the course of the trial itself. The newly released e-mails revealed the state of affairs inside Microsoft in early 1999, not long after Allchin and other executives had testified.

The past was catching up with the present, most notably in a long e-mail exchange between Silverberg and Slivka that had taken place on a cold, cloudy Sunday afternoon in February 1999. Slivka, who had refused to talk with me for the article on the rivalry between the Windows hawks and the Internet doves, mentioned to Silverberg that he had agreed to have an off-the-record dinner now that my article had been published.

"Hmm, David Bank. He's not exactly on my Xmas card list right now," Silverberg wrote back. The article about the earlier battle hadn't helped his current position inside the company or his mood. After a long leave of absence, Silverberg was back at the company part time as a consultant to Ballmer. He was weighing Ballmer's offer to return full time to take command of all of Microsoft's consumer efforts. He thought the account made him appear soft on Sun, which he wasn't, and that his support for a new platform could appear as disloyalty to Windows. He didn't trust me, he said. Silverberg complained that I had disregarded the explanations he had provided in a lengthy off-the-record e-mail and that I had fallen for what he called the "superwhipped spin" fed to me by other Microsoft executives. "What I sent him was accurate," he wrote. "Yes, a little sanitized, but still accurate, and 100 times more accurate than what he got from Microsoft."

Slivka promised to be circumspect. "Sounds like I'll be having a coy little dinner with Mr. Bank," he said.

But Slivka and Silverberg were anything but circumspect in this e-mail exchange. Their dialogue made clear that in the two years since Gates's tirade at the Java strategy meeting, the divisions inside Microsoft had only grown deeper, the disenchantment more profound.

The spark was Slivka's analysis of the company's Internet strategy, which he had sent several days earlier to Gates and Ballmer as well as Silverberg. "I fear very deeply that trying to win the Internet using Windows is a losing strategy," he wrote. Slivka had the temerity to suggest Microsoft had fallen into what Harvard Business School professor Clayton Christensen described as the inability of even well-managed companies to embrace innovation that threatened their successful franchises. Christensen's 1997 book *The Innovator's Dilemma* had become a manifesto for many Microsoft employees.

Silverberg agreed. What followed was off-the-cuff, but represents one of the most explicit critiques ever of Gates's leadership of Microsoft. The criticism was all the more credible because it came not from the company's critics or competitors, but from one of its own most senior executives.

"I simply do not want to spend my life in meetings struggling with the internal issues, getting pissy mail from Billg," Silverberg wrote to Slivka. "Or hearing from people who want me to do unnatural and losing things to 'protect' Windows."

This e-mail exchange was released by Justice Department prosecutors in May 2000, attached to a brief prepared to bolster their claim that Microsoft could feasibly be split into two separate companies. Silverberg insisted he had meant no such thing and was embarrassed that his personal frustrations had been used to hurt the company. But once again, the e-mail was less interesting for its legal implications than for its confirmation of the dissatisfaction and division in Microsoft's executive ranks over the company's direction.

"I simply do not believe in the path the company is pursuing right now," Silverberg had written. "I think Steve [Ballmer] feels totally overwhelmed right now. He does not know how he's going to solve the problems and he doesn't know who he'll be able to count on."

In preparing this book, I found little enthusiasm at Microsoft for revisiting the internal debates that have so riven the company. The participants have, as they say, moved on. However, in the written record, they have left behind fascinating fragments that made it possible to reconstruct parts of the Microsoft story that otherwise might never have been told. It is Microsoft itself that provided the trail to follow.

1

Track the Inevitable

THE LAST PAJAMA PARTY

If we were under surveillance, we never knew it. We slipped around the side of the main house, down the circular driveway, past the empty security station, and around the tennis courts. Cutting between the cabins on the wooded path toward the water, we found ourselves under the screened porch of our host's cabin. We heard his murmured conversation with his aides. Not wanting to eavesdrop—rather, not wanting to get caught—we hurried to the dock. We stood quietly as the water lapping at the pilings kept time with the creaking planks and looked up at the starry Northwest night.

A half hour earlier, after wine, shrimp with caviar, barbecued salmon, leg of lamb, more wine, and dessert, we had allowed our hosts to go to bed. Pairs of roommates, determined earlier by names drawn from a hat, made their way to their sleeping quarters. Not me. There was no way that I was turning in without scouting the property. My cabin-mate agreed. Who knew when we would have another chance to prowl the grounds of Gateaway? Who knew whether we would ever again be overnight guests of Bill Gates?

In August 1997, Gates, the chairman of Microsoft Corporation, and his best friend and number two, Steve Ballmer, invited a dozen business and technology reporters and editors to spend a night at the Gates family's summer compound on the Hood Canal southwest of Seattle. Beginning in 1996, the "pajama party" was becoming an annual event, an attempt to satisfy journalists' incessant demands for access to Gates. As it turned out, the tradition lasted only two years. After 1997, Bill Gates hasn't been much in the mood to play host to unruly reporters.

That afternoon, a van picked us up from the lobby of Building 18 on Microsoft's campus in Redmond. We chattered excitedly, like Scouts going to summer camp, on the short drive to Gates's house in Medina. Gates still lived in the gray Cape Cod with graceful trellises near the landing on the eastern shore of Lake Washington, where ferries once arrived from Seattle. Locals considered the house, which Gates had bought for $8 million from Jack Sikma, a former center for the Seattle Supersonics, one of the prettiest in town. He had already sold it to Gerald Grinstein, an airline executive, who planned to raze it and build an Irish country mansion. In two weeks, the Gateses were moving into their new place, the $50 million bunker up the road that had been under construction for five years.

We waited on the lawn in front of the guest house down by the lake. A half hour later Gates arrived, wearing green trousers and a plaid shirt, carrying his own overnight bag.

Two chartered seaplanes, Turbo Beavers, taxied to the dock. I maneuvered into Gates's group; Ballmer rode in the other plane. The pilot handed out earplugs as we climbed into the sheet-metal cabin with school-bus seats. In an era of private Gulfstream G5s, a lumbering, noisy seaplane seems a modest perk. But in the watery Northwest, a seaplane is more useful than any corporate jet. The last DeHavilland Beaver rolled off the assembly line in 1967, but the plane is still the reliable workhorse of Kenmore Air, the charter service. The original 450-horsepower Pratt & Whitney piston engines have been replaced with turbines; the things really move. With thick wings for lift and oversized floats that turn them into a boat on the water, Beavers are remarkably safe. Still, I couldn't help thinking that the rest of us would be minor afterthoughts in the front-page newspaper accounts if either plane were to go down.

We climbed above Seattle's crowded freeways and into the sparkling sky. The afternoon sun had burned off the morning fog, and the view was clear out to the Olympic Range. Gates sat in the back. The roar of the motor made conversation tough, relieving Gates of most of his small-talk obligation. As we banked west, he showed us the construction cranes that were still hovering over his high-tech Xanadu, and the lakeside mansions of Seattle's nouveau riche. He pointed out the white modernist house of Charles Simonyi, an early star at Microsoft, who had designed his structure to be approached by helicopter. The curved bank of windows of Simonyi's place resembles the waving Windows flag, though the house was conceived before the logo. As we left Seattle, Gates showed us the snow-capped Hurricane Ridge and the shipping route from the Pacific, through the Strait of Juan de Fuca, into Admiralty Inlet and southwest down the Hood Canal, where Gates has spent summers since he was a child.

We landed on the water about forty minutes later. The setting is serene, with blue herons swooping low. For Gates, the Hood Canal is comfortably familiar. In his childhood, his family rented summer cabins at Cheerio, a rustic resort nearby. In Microsoft's early years, he took his "Think Week" retreats at his grandmother's house on the canal. After she died, he built Gateaway. For years after Microsoft's initial public offering in 1986, Gates hosted friends and employees at Hood Canal for the annual Microgames, echoing the summer tournaments of his youth at Cheerio. The shores of the placid cul-de-sac are dotted with the summer getaways for Seattle's comfortable class. Gates's neighbors include members of the Nordstrom department store family and Jeff Raikes, another of Microsoft's top executives. In economic terms, Raikes probably made the right choice in leaving the family farm in Nebraska for the software industry.

There are four cabins—houses, really—on the three-and-a-half-acre property. Before Mary Gates, Bill's mother, died in 1994, the Gates family came out together to Hood Canal more often. Now the place serves mostly as a Microsoft corporate retreat center, and it feels like it. Still, when they visit, Gates's sisters Libby and Kristi and their families each have their own cabin. Another cabin is for Gates, his wife Melinda, and their daughter Jennifer and son Rory, born in 1999. The biggest house, with the main kitchen and a big open-timber living room with an imposing fireplace, is for Gates's father, known as Bill Sr., and his second wife, Mimi Gardner Gates, the director of the Seattle Art Museum.

In the lodging lottery, I drew one of the bedrooms in sister Libby's cabin and dropped off my bag. The buildings, painted a dull tan, are more suburban condo than hunting lodge. In the bathrooms, plastic frames hold printed instructions for disposing of used towels and charging long-distance telephone calls. Maybe the warm, lived-in environment the Gateses enjoyed had been scrubbed anecdote-free in anticipation of our arrival. Maybe, in several generations, Gateaway will be regarded as the ancestral summer retreat of one of America's great families, the Northwest equivalent of Hyannis Port or Kennebunkport. But it's hard to imagine.

We are told Gates does his best thinking out here. His "Think Weeks" are staples of Microsoft legend. In preparation for those weeks, Gates's assistants collect long memos from Microsoft developers and new software from Microsoft and its competitors. Gates works his way through three cardboard boxes of material, away from meetings and e-mail and public appearances. His strategy memos, such as "Information at Your Fingertips" and "The Internet Tidal Wave," as well as his first book, *The Road Ahead*, were all hatched or completed at Hood Canal.

At the first session that afternoon, the trade-magazine reporters scribbled furiously as Gates and Ballmer provided minor details about new software features and the likely release dates for products. It was banal stuff for a company at the peak of its power in the most dynamic industry in the world. At the first pajama party in 1996, Gates gloated about how he had "crushed" competition from Borland, once a powerful rival. This time, Gates watched his tone. In the fall of 1997, there was too much at stake for Gates to openly discuss the real challenges he faced.

After less than a year as the Microsoft beat reporter for the *Wall Street Journal*, I was still struggling to comprehend Microsoft's story so far. In 1986, Microsoft was a promising start-up that had just gone public. In 1992, it was breaking out of the pack of PC software makers, but was still a small-fry compared to the technology industry giants. By 1995, many people wrote Microsoft's obituary when it seemed that the company had missed the technology shift toward the Internet. Now, the media spin cycle had turned again. Microsoft 97 was a juggernaut and a threatening one at that.

The company's numbers were staggering. Windows and Office were the two best-selling software products in history. To have both at the same time was like a movie studio with the two biggest blockbusters of all time, year in and year out. Like a hit movie, best-selling software has a huge payoff—once the initial development costs are recovered, every additional unit sold is nearly pure profit. Movie producers crow about films that gross $100 or $150 million. By June 1998, the Windows desktop platform pulled in annual revenues of nearly $5 billion, and the Office desktop applications grossed more than $6 billion. Microsoft's double whammy was a cash machine: Operating profits swelled dramatically to more than fifty cents out of every dollar in revenue. The company was piling up cash faster than it could spend it. By 1997, Microsoft's stock had already risen 180-fold since the initial public offering. That gave the company a higher market value than General Motors, Exxon, IBM, and Coca-Cola, second only to General Electric. All for a company that produced nothing but ethereal strings of 1s and 0s that under even the best of circumstances would be obsolete in no more than three years.

On a languid summer afternoon, it was easy to imagine Microsoft's success was permanent. The company's strategic position had never been stronger. Microsoft had all but beaten Netscape in the "browser war" and appeared to be containing the threat from Sun Microsystem's Java technology. The company was counting on a new version of the more powerful Windows NT operating system to be the next stage of Microsoft's growth rocket. After dispatching its PC rivals, Microsoft was finally ready to take on the big boys of computing: IBM, Oracle, and Sun Microsystems.

The only dark cloud on the horizon was the pesky U.S. Department of Justice, which once again had been nosing around in Microsoft's e-mail archives. The company had been under investigation throughout the decade. In 1995, it had averted an antitrust trial over its Windows marketing practices with a negotiated settlement. Now, the focus of the new investigation was the company's tactics in the browser war. While we were at Hood Canal, news had leaked that the feds were broadening their investigation. But Microsoft's lawyers were confident that in the end the Justice Department lawyers would come to their senses and back off. Microsoft attorneys explained the company's position to the investigators again and again: Bundling the Internet Explorer Web browser with Windows was no different from what Microsoft had been doing for sixteen years, integrating additional features into the operating system.

Put that way, it seemed benign enough. But nobody inside Microsoft was confused about the practice: Any outside product used by half of Windows users was a sure bet for inclusion in the next release of the operating system itself. Any product that popular represented a potential threat to the Windows platform because it could become a platform itself. Integration was Microsoft's weapon for disabling the threats to Windows. That was simply how Microsoft did business.

As the summer afternoon turned into evening, two helicopters fer-

ried in a half-dozen more top executives for drinks and dinner, served
on the deck. The buzz was about Microsoft's deal with Apple Computer, which had generated an avalanche of coverage as an historic
rapprochement between the winner of the desktop-computing battle
of the early 1990s and its vanquished rival. The man of the hour was
Greg Maffei, Gates's newest best buddy. Maffei had worked out the
deal with Steve Jobs, Apple's sort-of chief executive, as Jobs walked
barefoot through the streets of Palo Alto. It was Maffei who engineered the telephone conversation between Jobs and Gates on the
eve of the announcement. "You're making the world a better place,"
Jobs told Gates. The quote appeared on the cover of *Time* magazine;
Jobs, a master of image-management, had arranged to have a reporter standing nearby.

As a religion major at Dartmouth, Maffei had thought he might
become a lawyer or a journalist. Instead, he went to Harvard Business
School. Brash and articulate and meticulously prepped in every aspect of Microsoft's business, Maffei was relentless and tough at the
negotiating table. Maffei brought Wall Street savvy to Microsoft for
the first time, fascinating Gates with complex financing mechanisms
such as put warrants and preferred stock offerings that netted Microsoft billions. The winnings stoked Gates's passion for gambling.
Maffei encouraged him to place bigger bets, arguing that they were
risking only the house's money. Maffei helped Gates see Wall Street
as a huge equation to be solved and Microsoft's spectacular balance
sheet as a unique strategic advantage. His office in Building 8 was a
hundred feet from Gates's suite, giving Maffei easy access to discuss
deals and dealmaking.

The brinkmanship required to close the Apple deal had challenged even Gates and Maffei. To force a resolution, Microsoft
threatened to discontinue its Office software suite for Apple's Macintosh computers, a potentially lethal blow for Apple, which had already lost many of its outside software developers. In the end,
Microsoft invested $150 million and ponied up another $100 million
to head off Apple's threat of a major patent infringement suit. Apple
agreed to adopt Microsoft's Internet Explorer browser. Two days
after he left us at Hood Canal, Gates told those who attended a Microsoft executive staff meeting that his real goal was to keep Apple
split from Sun, particularly on Java technology. "He doesn't care that
much about being aligned with Apple," reported one person at the
meeting. "He just wants them split from other potential allies."

Maffei wasn't the only executive who was flush with power. Bob Muglia, a bland, ambitious vice president, had been remarkably blunt in negotiating a deal with RealNetworks, the streaming video start-up. As described in a memo by Bruce Jacobsen, then Real's president and a Microsoft veteran, Muglia said Microsoft considered not only browsers but even words and numbers to be part of the operating system. Surely video was merely a feature of Windows. Microsoft had to control that franchise, Jacobsen said Muglia told him. Anyone who competed against Microsoft's platform lost. Microsoft had obliterated any company with such pretensions. The only exceptions were Sun and Oracle, Jacobsen quoted Muglia as saying, and they were next.

Other executives were similarly confident in their ambitious strategies. Brad Chase, the Microsoft marketing chief who had quarterbacked the browser market share drive, had Netscape on a treadmill. He planned to turn up the speed until the upstart fell off, exhausted. Pete Higgins, the boyish-looking chief of Microsoft Network and the rest of the interactive media division, had an impressive golf handicap and hundreds of millions of dollars to burn to take on America Online. MSN was far behind, but Higgins was a veteran of the Office business, where Microsoft had once trailed competitors such as WordPerfect and Lotus even more badly. Microsoft had caught them and quickly left them in the dust.

Craig Mundie, somewhat older and more battle scarred than the other Microsoft executives, was Gates's point man on interactive television. He had come from the minicomputer industry, and had experienced the attack from less expensive and increasingly more powerful PCs. The lesson: In the computer industry, the threat always comes up from below, from something smaller, simpler, cheaper. Now, Mundie was acting on that lesson to blunt a threat to PCs themselves. He had Microsoft's billions at his disposal to push a stripped-down version of the Windows operating system, Windows CE, for television set-top boxes, handheld computers, and other electronic devices. The mantra that every executive chanted was the same: We know how to win.

Their huge success put the executives in thrall to a cult of personality. Not only Gates's, but Microsoft's, and their own. Here was a company, a big company, where smart people ruled. Hierarchies and chains of command didn't matter. Overt aggression was cultivated, not tamed. Any midlevel manager felt free to tell a senior vice president that his ideas were brain-dead. Some newcomers couldn't take it, and like a transplanted organ rejected by the host, they were soon cast out. But for those who could play the game, the meritocracy was thrilling. The company hired the smartest people and let the best ideas rise to the top. The best people rose with them. These executives had risen to the top; by definition, they were the smartest and the best.

Almost entirely male, most were about to turn, or had just turned, forty years old. They went to college in the 1970s. It was an auspicious time. They were young enough to be largely unscarred by the social and political wars of the 1960s but old enough to internalize the baby boomer sense of their own unlimited potential. According to the theorists of their generation, ideology was ending, postindustrial society was emerging, and a "new class" was rising. The power of the new, educated elite flowed from the manipulation of language and symbols. In that, software was a pure play, a field in which one-time outcasts derided as nerds could attain unheard-of wealth.

The Apple deal capped a stunning series of investments. Microsoft bought tiny WebTV for $425 million and invested $1 billion in Comcast, a major cable operator. In one day, the company bought into the three streaming-media companies, including RealNetworks. The avalanche of deals all raised a fundamental question: What does Bill want?

The obvious answer was: everything. "The common wisdom is that the person to worry about the most right now is Bill Gates,"said Walt Disney's Michael Eisner. "Everybody in the communications business is paranoid of Microsoft, including me," said Rupert Murdoch. Declared Barry Diller: "Beware Bill Gates."

Gates pulled a neat hat trick—scaring the daylights out of three major industries in the single month of April 1997. At the convention of the National Association of Newspapers in Chicago, he advised publishers not to get "overly paranoid" about Microsoft's ambitions in the news business. It was too late. Bob Ingle of Knight Ridder called Microsoft the "master of the big lie technique" after Gates told publishers that Microsoft was not going after newspapers' classified advertising when it plainly was.

Gates's plans also riled broadcast television executives at the National Association of Broadcasters in Las Vegas. Microsoft, along with Intel and Compaq, was pushing technical standards that would favor PCs over TVs as the broadcast industry switched to digital transmission.

And when the heads of all of the nation's major cable television systems had dinner with Gates in Redmond, he offered to underwrite much of the software for their new digital systems. All he wanted in return was a cut of the new businesses that would result from putting digital services, running on Windows, into the living rooms of 65 million cable households. The cable operators coveted the cash but were wary of giving Gates a lock on the future of their business; they suspected he might have a clearer view than they did of the size of the future revenue streams. Gates had no takers, except for Brian Roberts of Comcast, who accepted the $1 billion investment but refused to make any commitments. Time Warner's Gerald Levin called Gates's cable proposal "overreaching." John Malone, of Tele-Communications Inc., perfected the art of bringing in Microsoft's competitors explicitly to keep the giant in line.

The only three issues that mattered to cable operators, Mundie told me, were economics, execution, and control. Microsoft had a compelling story on the first two, but it couldn't get over the third hurdle. "Why do people love to pick on Bill Gates and Microsoft?" he said. "It's all about control."

As we mingled with Microsoft executives out on the deck, I began to realize that Microsoft's ambitions were both more benign and more audacious than had been generally realized. Microsoft was bluffing, using fear to drive software demand. Like Mr. Big in a protection racket, Microsoft was perfecting a one-two punch for driving demand. By threatening to enter new markets, Microsoft speeded up the pace of technology spending in industry after industry. Then, as a dominant software provider, Microsoft collected a sizable share of the increased spending.

"Scaring people is okay if it gets them to invest," explained Charles Stevens, a Microsoft vice president who assigned teams to target every major industry, from utilities to health care. "We say, 'There's a great opportunity. If no one's going to do it, we're going to do it.'

"We come in and the big guys start looking over their shoulder. They say, 'I'm the one with the customer assets. I have much more content and advertising. I have a whole distribution system. I don't want to compete with Microsoft on tools and infrastructure. I should use their technology . . .'

"We'll get the newspapers, the banks, the cable guys working on our platform," he predicted.

The real opportunity, Gates knew, went far beyond mere product sales to individual companies. He strategized at the industry level, looking for a way to secure a stake for Microsoft. The company hoped to get its "fair share," as Microsoft executives put it with a wink, of the new revenues as major industries restructured themselves for the Information Age. In each sector, Microsoft was looking to pick off a key "strategic partner" to place its foot firmly in the door. Gates didn't need to own it all as long as Microsoft was integrated, enmeshed, and partnered in it all. Once Microsoft was implanted in the economic organism, the revenues would flow.

When the executives boarded the helicopters to return to Microsoft, Gates watched intently from his chair on the deck, closing down the questioning around the table as the helicopter pilots revved their engines. Only after the helicopters had cleared the dock did Gates snap back his attention.

After dinner, he moved the conversation indoors. He stood in front of the massive stone fireplace with a glass of wine, characteristically rocking, front foot to back, and holding court for nearly two more hours. I was surprised by his calmness. He had figured out a model perfectly adapted to ride all of the major trends in technology and the economy. Microsoft was just a giant science fair project, so Gates could prove that he had been right.

When Gates finally left, so did everybody else.

A half hour later, John Markoff of the *New York Times* and I had nearly completed our surreptitious circumnavigation of the Gates compound. We stood chatting at the end of the dock above the flat, dark water. Looking back, we watched Gates in his cabin, backlit by a lamp.

It was hard for me to see then that the seeds of Microsoft's fall from grace in the next three years were already being planted. In the months following our night at Hood Canal, Gates made a series of crucial decisions that set Microsoft on a very different path from the one that seemed most likely to me then. I didn't know the depths of the ideological and personal divisions splitting Microsoft. I didn't know the extent of the difficulties the company was facing in delivering key products and penetrating important markets. I certainly did not anticipate the ferocity with which the U.S. government would attack the company that seemed to be leading America's economic resurgence. Most important, I didn't understand how the strengths that had served Bill Gates so well had become his greatest weaknesses, and how the mistakes he most sought to avoid would be the very ones that he would ultimately make.

BEDTIME STORY

William Henry Gates III could have told himself a reassuring story as he prepared for bed that night. Once upon a time, a nineteen-year-old boy had a very, very good idea.

The essential truth about Microsoft flows from Gates's big idea, a single, searing insight so powerful that it had already obtained for twenty-two years. In Gates's view, it would take perhaps another twenty years before the idea was fully played out.

Sometimes, as Gates liked to say, people just don't track the inevitable.

As Gates approached middle age, he had become increasingly fond of reaching back to the founding vision to reassure himself that he remained on the right historical trajectory. He was always careful to give credit to his 36 percent initial partner, but when Gates began speeches and discussions with phrases such as "When Paul Allen and I founded Microsoft . . . ," it was his own original idea that he was really talking about. Gates has led Microsoft for its entire life; the company is singularly a projection of him—and his idea.

Later, when Microsoft came under attack by the Department of Justice, Gates would say that his biggest regret was that he didn't tell his story more effectively. "It's clear that the whole story of Microsoft, the whole story of the PC was missed here," he would say.

"It all goes back to the founding principles of the company," he explained to me in an e-mail exchange a few weeks after the pajama party. They all come down to one idea: As hardware gets cheap, software gets valuable. Software is the bottleneck. Computer software will always be in shortage because what people want to do with computers is always increasing.

"We wrote down 23 years ago that:

"1. Software (is) the key to unlocking exponential improvement in the power of computers.

"2. Software should be separate from hardware because the way you manage and attract great people is different.

"3. Software should be separate from hardware because you allow customers to choose whatever hardware they think is best.

"4. Software will eventually make computers totally natural and easy to work with.

"5. Selling software in volume allows for low prices even while spending increasing amounts on research and development.

"I don't see any change that makes me think something is wrong with these principles."

Microsoft's founding vision can be stated in four words: software separate from hardware. Paul Allen, in Microsoft's early days, wanted the company to build computer hardware as well as software, but Gates insisted Microsoft adopt a software-only strategy. The wisdom of creating software separate from hardware proved out magnificently. Moore's Law, attributed to Intel cofounder Gordon Moore, holds that the number of transistors that can be squeezed onto a chip seems to double about every eighteen months, halving the price. On the surface, the observation seems to be a prediction about advances in computer hardware, a rough guide to the amount of computer power at a given price that will become available over time.

As chip power per dollar increases exponentially, computer hardware falls rapidly in price. Suppliers become nearly interchangeable providers of processing power. MIPS—millions of instructions per second—become commodities, like pork bellies and bushels of corn. Just as farmers face falling prices when they have a bumper harvest, chip makers have had to adapt to a bumper crop of computer power. The price of processing fell a million-fold in the last twenty years and may well fall a million-fold more in the next twenty years.

Historically, computer companies stayed ahead of falling prices by selling their customers ever more powerful machines. Computer companies were "vertically integrated" organizations. Everything from the chip to the operating system to the applications to the services came from a single vendor. Most computer companies were organized the same way, whether they were mainframe makers such as IBM; or the mini-computer companies such as Digital Equipment Corporation, which first challenged IBM; or the new wave of workstation makers, such as Sun Microsystems, which based their offerings on the Unix operating system; or even Apple Computer, which developed the much-loved Macintosh operating system to differentiate its computers from lower-priced PCs. The hardware makers bundled software programs with their computers. But the purpose of the software was to enhance sales of the hardware, the real source of the companies' revenues. Because the proprietary software could not run on rival hardware, the companies effectively locked in their customers, creating cozy and profitable hardware accounts the companies could milk for years.

Microsoft's software-only approach helped open the lock. By creating a common software platform that ran on hardware from many competing suppliers, Microsoft helped free customers from the clutches of the proprietary hardware makers. The rise of the "PC model" was the single biggest change in the computer industry before the advent of the Internet.

The real coup in the 1981 deal that Gates, Allen, and Ballmer struck with IBM wasn't that they licensed a disk operating system they didn't yet own to IBM for use in the first PC. It was the clause in the contract that left Microsoft with the right to license DOS to IBM's competitors. That was the moment software was liberated from hardware; it was the moment the triumph of the PC model became inevitable.

"When we were doing the revolutionary work in previous phases, we knew something that no one else knew," Gates told me. "The vision alone was a unique asset. We understood that the PC model would succeed and that people were underestimating the value of the PC and of the tool and where that would go. The vision alone put us way out in front."

The king was dead; long live the king. By licensing its operating system software to many hardware makers, Microsoft seized the key tollbooth in the reorganized industry. With hardware no longer the gatekeeper, first DOS and then Windows became the new chokepoint. On one side of the chokepoint, hardware makers competed furiously to increase features or decrease prices for computers that all ran identical software from Microsoft. On the other side of the chokepoint, creators of application software targeted their product at Microsoft's platform, not the particular products of the hardware makers.

The establishment of DOS, and then Windows, as the common software "platform" that worked on many makes of hardware radically restructured the computer industry. Microsoft didn't need to produce computers to get exactly what it needed: more and powerful machines, nearly all of them based on Microsoft's platform. The fierce competition delivered innovations in hardware far faster than Microsoft ever could have on its own. Instead of vertical companies that delivered complete systems, the industry reformed around its horizontal components—chips, hard drives, operating systems, application software, consulting services, and so on—with different companies dominating each layer. In the new PC model, Intel and a few competitors made the chips; companies like Dell and Compaq and Hewlett-Packard slugged it out in the ferociously competitive market for assembling and distributing the PCs themselves. Microsoft supplied the operating system. Later, Microsoft came to also dominate the fundamental productivity applications, such as the word processor, the spreadsheet, the presentation program and, eventually, the browser, e-mail, and calendar software.

Gates can claim a large measure of credit for the inexpensive PC. The PC model is responsible for harnessing Moore's Law to the real world of selling computers, unleashing ferocious competition and investment. Microsoft can claim a large share of credit for whatever social benefits that has brought. The industry ships more than 100 million units a year, at prices that at times have dipped as low as $399. Gates is right when he claims that the price-slashing nature of the PC model is the reason competitors who rely on high prices and low volume hate Microsoft so much. The markup on even a $2,000 PC box is a fraction compared to the fat profits computer companies once enjoyed on million-dollar mainframes and high-end servers.

The old-model, vertically integrated vendors retreated to higher ground, pushing more powerful computers that could still command high prices. In Gates's mind they were irreversibly on the defensive. For Microsoft it was all upside—as chips got more powerful and Microsoft invested more in its software, PCs would just eat and eat and eat their way up the computing food chain.

What the PC model cut in profit margins, it more than made up for in total volume. High volume, not high prices, is the key to Microsoft's high profits. No other product matches software when it comes to what is called operating leverage. The first copy of a new software program may cost hundreds of millions or billions of dollars. The second copy costs pennies. Volume is what enabled Microsoft to spend as much developing Windows 2000 as Boeing spent developing the 747—and yet sell the product for less than $150.

Volume doesn't just happen. Microsoft attacked the chicken-and-egg problem by investing heavily in a network of partners—distributors, resellers, consultants, training programs, technical education, and developer support. Microsoft put itself at the center. Gates didn't have to be greedy. Every time any of Microsoft's partners landed a customer, they served to drive the platform forward. Microsoft received its cut. A small and growing slice of a huge and growing pie trumps a large slice of a shrinking pie any day. Microsoft generated huge profits by aiming not at profits but at market share.

With the PC operating system market secured in the late '80s, Microsoft began formulating a far more ambitious strategy for becoming the dominant platform provider for the entire information infrastructure. The digital revolution will transform the bulk of the global economy, presenting possibly the greatest commercial opportunities in history. To capture it, Gates's plan was Windows Everywhere.

"Everything I do is long term, optimized for having the best software company 10 and 20 years from now," Gates said in our 1997 e-mail exchange.

In a sanitized form, the Windows Everywhere strategy was prefigured in Microsoft's longtime motto, "A computer on every desk and in every home." The extended version, chanted by new employees at orientation sessions led by Microsoft veterans, was even more apt: "A computer on every desk and in every home, running Microsoft software." (Company lore has it that even before Microsoft's legal problems, the company's lawyers nixed the longer version because of antitrust concerns.) Employees pass along the story that for years, senior executives privately repeated the real mantra: "A computer on every desk and in every home, all running Microsoft software *exclusively.*"

Total World Domination, as Microsoft employees jokingly translated the company's mission statement, wasn't an evil plot. In Microsoft's view, domination by a single firm was simply the inevitable result of the positive feedback cycles that are part of the fundamental economic dynamics of software.

The Windows Everywhere plan, officially known as "Windows Scalable Architecture," was to extend the economics of high-volume software both up and down from Microsoft's core PC market. Windows would become the single software architecture for everything from the smallest handheld devices to the most demanding corporate enterprise systems. Microsoft's dominance on the desktop would give it a leg up in the new markets. The same virtuous circle that had worked so well in PCs would thus be re-created for the much larger sphere encompassing everything from huge back-end databases to the wide world of entertainment.

The insight was so fundamental that Microsoft was really only a vessel for its execution. "Not only has the PC model succeeded, the PC specifically has succeeded," Gates said. "Is it inevitable that PCs will dominate the high end of computing? It's absolutely inevitable.

Microsoft could make every mistake and disappear and still the PC model will dominate high-end computing. That will happen. That's guaranteed to happen. Companies have to adjust to that reality, or not adjust to that reality, and they'll be measured accordingly."

"Sometimes," he said, "it seems like people just don't track the inevitable."

The key to success was capturing the hearts and minds of software developers. Simple economics propelled most developers in the direction of the highest-volume outlet for their applications. Like Microsoft, other software developers depended on high volume to spread their upfront costs over more units. With Windows Everywhere, Microsoft would offer the highest-volume platform in history by letting developers use the same set of tools and target the same software interfaces for pocket-sized devices, television set-top boxes, desktop machines, powerful workstations, or large servers on corporate networks. Microsoft would hide the difference in the internal workings of each device behind a uniform set of programming interfaces. Once a developer knew how to create programs for Windows PCs, he or she would know how to create programs for big corporate systems or tiny handheld devices.

Microsoft's "platform" then would no longer serve only as the crucial interface between PC hardware makers and PC software developers, but between all hardware and all software.

Stoking Gates's passion for Windows Everywhere was Nathan Myhrvold, the eclectic big thinker who through much of the early 1990s was Gates's best tech buddy. Ballmer, of course, was Gates's undisputed best friend, the reliable rock who kept Gates grounded and disciplined and could always be trusted to do what was best for him and for the company. Gates and Ballmer were like a married couple; Myhrvold provided a more adventurous romp.

Gates and Myhrvold hit it off quickly in 1986, after Microsoft bought Dynamical Systems Research, the Berkeley software start-up Myhrvold had founded with some fellow physics Ph.D.s from Princeton University. Myhrvold's prescient trend-spotting in the late 1980s earned Gates's respect. His internal memos came to define the genre, such that any long diatribe sent around for discussion became known as a "Nathan spawn." Myhrvold's long memo to Gates on the threats to MS-DOS convinced Gates he needed a "Unix killer," the concept that evolved into Windows NT. As the champion of Windows Everywhere, Myhrvold also helped get Microsoft started on a stripped-down Windows for handhelds and cell phones. Of the people he liked to consult with on technology, Gates said, "Nathan is by far the most important on that list."

Gates liked Myhrvold's ability to make sparks fly in conversation, even if many of his ideas turned out to be half-baked, overblown, premature, or just plain wrong. Myhrvold's visions had run Microsoft into a number of dead ends. He was the patron of Microsoft's interactive TV efforts in the heyday of the digital convergence hype of the early '90s; some of the technology was later salvaged for parts for Internet products. Myhrvold helped Gates with *The Road Ahead*, his first book. He took his share of grief for the fact that the first edition, which appeared in 1995, scarcely mentioned the Internet, arguably the most important feature of the road ahead.

Myhrvold was also a champion of Microsoft's ultimately unsuccessful quest to collect a transaction fee, or as Myhrvold colorfully called it, a "vig," on every credit-card purchase on the Internet. A vig, or vigorish, is the fee bookmakers collect for bringing bettors together.

Microsoft's quest for a cut of e-commerce transactions was an underappreciated factor in the June 1995 meeting with Netscape that later figured prominently in Microsoft's legal problems. A few months before the meeting, Barb Fox, part of Myhrvold's team, reported, "We DID get the per transaction deal we wanted" from Visa. Netscape was seeking a similar deal from MasterCard. At the meeting itself, Fox and others tried to enlist Netscape in a united front to "steamroller" the credit-card associations into giving the software companies a cut of every Internet transaction. "This seems to be the grail that we all lust for," wrote Thomas Reardon, one of Microsoft's representatives at the meeting. Ultimately, neither Netscape nor the credit-card alliances went along with Microsoft's plan. After Microsoft's critics seized on the company's quest for a "vig" on Internet transactions as evidence of its supposedly predatory ambitions, Myhrvold backed away from the term and said he doubted it would be possible for any software provider to broadly collect such fees.

It was easy to see why Gates found Myhrvold amusing. When reporters, including me, trod the well-worn path to Myhrvold's office, they were apt to be distracted by the model of an Anomalcaris, a lobsterlike creature with a radial mouth that was the biggest predator of the Cambrian period, about 500 million years ago. Or by Myhrvold's description of sex between dinosaurs or his French-cooking class or his work with physicist Stephen Hawking. Myhrvold slipped easily into the role of broad-minded scientific raconteur, serving up clever quips and gesticulating madly. Later, he often feigned frustration that his attempts to hold forth on more serious subjects were generally ignored in favor of, as he said, a "few random sound bites on other topics."

Myhrvold wasn't shy about claiming credit for the Windows Everywhere strategy. "I had this radical idea in '86 or '87 that you could have a scalable software system for little handheld computers . . . and servers," he boasted in a 1998 interview. "No one had ever had that idea. We made $50 billion in market value on that idea. We nailed it." The idea, he said, "is worth another $50 billion or $100 billion before we reach its crest."

Frustrated that Microsoft wasn't effectively explaining the dynamics of its success, he spent a summer weekend in 1993 ghostwriting an article, "Telling It Like It Is." He suggested that the article go out under Gates's name to a publication such as the *Harvard Business Review*. To illustrate the power of technology standards, Myhrvold recounted the battle between the VHS and Betamax formats for videocassette recorders. VHS was initially of lower quality, but for a variety of reasons—VHS offered two hours of recording time on each tape, enough for a full movie, versus one hour for Sony; Japan Victor Company licensed the VHS format to multiple manufacturers, whereas Sony didn't allow any Betamax clones—VHS pulled ahead. That meant a larger market for VHS-format videos in video stores. The availability of titles fueled demand for VHS-based VCRs, which further increased the market for titles. Betamax effectively disappeared. To Myhrvold, the episode was a classic example of a positive feedback loop.

"The laws of positive feedback economics dictate that there could only be one winner," he wrote.

Similarly, he explained that the software company that succeeded in setting the standards and establishing the dominant platform would reap outsized rewards, a percentage of profits far in excess even of its percentage of market share.

"The historical situation is that the market share leader in systems software takes about 90 percent or so of the market, the runner-up takes about 90 percent of what is left, and so on," Myhrvold explained.

Microsoft exploited positive feedback masterfully in the market for PC operating systems. The more users of a platform, the more attractive the platform becomes to outside software programmers, who thus create more software for the platform, which in turn further increases the platform's appeal, beginning another cycle of the positive feedback loop.

Each round of the game was all-or-nothing. "The inexorable pull of positive feedback cannot allow a situation where there are several equal competitors sharing the limelight," Myhrvold wrote, "except in the brief moment when a newcomer on the way to the top passes the former champion on the way down."

Gates also believed in the "singularity." Like a black hole in outer space, successful execution of the positive feedback strategy sucked everything into the center. The incumbent couldn't get lazy about innovation or greedy on price; the positive feedback loop worked for challengers as well as for incumbents. But if the winner kept expanding his domain, it would be harder for competitors to mount a serious challenge.

Track the inevitable.

In Gates's view, it was inevitable that a common software platform would take hold in televisions, handheld devices, and other consumer electronics. The horizontal model would separate the hardware makers from a software provider, just as it had in the PC business. Positive feedback loops would dictate that there would be a single winner.

If Microsoft succeeded with its Windows Everywhere strategy, it would be an unprecedented achievement. Software operating systems had historically been incompatible. A decade ago, it was difficult just to exchange documents and spreadsheets between Windows-based PCs and Macintosh computers. It was hard to even think how the same operating system could work on a handheld device and a PC, much less how either could function as a network operating system that served up documents stored in central filing systems or as the guts of a set-top box for interactive TV. With Windows Everywhere, they would all look and feel the same, for both users and developers. The total volume would dwarf the PC market, and the integration between all the parts would make Microsoft's position virtually unassailable.

Windows Everywhere looked like a winner. In the PC market, the Windows platform was the undisputed winner. Starting in 1995, Windows 95 drove a huge positive feedback cycle for Microsoft. Microsoft took advantage of the PC industry's transition from 16-bit chips to more-powerful 32-bit processors to finally put Microsoft's user experience nearly on a par with Apple's Macintosh. The new 32-bit Windows platform came to be known as Win32.

Now, Microsoft was applying the high-volume, low-price PC model to the market for the more powerful computers that functioned as servers on corporate networks. Windows NT was moving up on Sun Microsystems, Hewlett-Packard, and IBM, each of whom clung to the old vertically integrated model, selling their own operating systems with their higher-priced hardware.

In consumer devices, Windows CE had gotten off to a slow start. But Gates believed customers, such as the cable television operators, would come around, even without Microsoft's investments of billions of dollars. If cable companies were going to deploy millions of low-cost units for digital television and interactive services, they would realize they needed a common software layer, just like the PC makers had. "It could take five or six years for all of that to happen, but that will happen," Gates told me.

The grip that the Windows Everywhere idea had on Gates's imagination was so strong that he nearly missed the Internet. Even before the Windows 95 hoopla ended, another software product was generating a positive feedback loop even more powerful than Windows. Soon after it was introduced in October 1994, Netscape's Navigator Web browser shot to more than 80 percent market share. Netscape's surge was amplified by Java, a technology from Sun Microsystems that promised to become a new common software layer, sitting on top of Windows as well as other operating systems. Netscape and Sun were doing to Microsoft what DOS and Windows had done to the old hardware makers. If Sun and Netscape could establish their platform as the industry's new chokepoint, Windows would be reduced, in Netscape cofounder Marc Andreessen's famous phrase, to a "partially debugged set of device drivers."

The challenge kept Gates awake at night. At 3 A.M. on a rainy Monday in April 1995, Gates declared in an e-mail to his top lieutenants that the "Internet is destroying our position as the setter of standards." Gates worried that the Internet was undermining the company's campaign to supply Windows software to cable television operators for what at the time was called the Information Superhighway. "I admit I find it hard to focus lots of resources on (technical) trials and things when the Internet is taking away our power every day and will have eroded it irretrievably by the time broadband is pervasive on the course we are on right now."

In his "Internet Tidal Wave" memo a month later, Gates recognized in the Internet a phenomenon he had seen before. The Internet was riding the curve of declining telecommunications costs just as the personal computer had ridden the curve of declining processing costs. The Internet was already generating positive feedback loops, just like the personal computer—the more the Internet attracted users, the more content producers were publishing on the Internet, attracting more users.

"I have gone through several stages of increasing my views of [the Internet's] importance," Gates wrote. "Now I assign the Internet the highest level of importance."

Gates personalized the threat to Netscape, a "new competitor 'born' on the Internet." Netscape's overwhelming market share gave the company the power to dictate the evolution of Internet standards. Those standards worked on many different operating systems. As Netscape's standards became more important than Windows', Gates wrote, Netscape's browser would "commoditize the underlying operating system."

Over the next year, the threat became even more dire. In September 1996, Adam Bosworth, a veteran developer in whom Gates had considerable confidence, laid out the full scope of the Java threat in a long Think Week memo to Gates.

"This scares the hell out of me," Gates wrote after reading Bosworth's analysis. "It's still very unclear to me what our [operating system] will offer to Java [programs] that will make them unique enough to preserve our market position."

NOW, in the summer of 1997, Microsoft appeared to have successfully turned back the twin challenges. In his second book, *Business at the Speed of Thought*, Gates wrote, "As an act of leadership, I created a sense of crisis about the Internet in 1994 and 1995." The fire drill worked. In the two years since December 7, 1995, Gates had returned the fight to Microsoft's own turf—the PC operating system. By absorbing the Internet into Windows, Microsoft succeeded in slowing the pace of innovation. All the talk about the Internet force being bigger than even Microsoft was hooey.

In Microsoft, Gates had created an adaptable organism designed to perpetually absorb new threats and turn them to its own advantage. Everybody, from the hardware dinosaurs to the minicomputer insurgents to the PC software wannabes to the dot-com flash-in-the-pans to the giant telecom-cum-entertainment-cum-broadband play-ers—they all wanted what Gates had: long-term customer accounts with growing and recurring revenues and, most important, strong and defensible barriers to entry that kept prices high. Critics might criticize the derivative quality of the company's software, but it was increasingly clear Microsoft itself was a unique innovation.

Microsoft was once again riding an unprecedented positive feed-back loop: growing market share in software; a growing software market as the world switched to knowledge work and digital enter-tainment; and a knowledge economy generating far faster growth than was previously thought possible. Faster growth was fueling heavy investment in the new digital systems and networks of the global economy, further fueling software demand.

"I don't think anybody has been in this powerful a position in the world economy since the world began," Alfred Chandler, professor emeritus of business history at Harvard University, told me not long after the pajama party. "In the age of information, which is software, you have to go through Bill Gates."

Bill Gates could again sleep well that night in August 1997. The PC model, he believed, was still the biggest thing happening in the computer industry.

DOLLARS PER DESKTOP

On the second day of the pajama party, we woke up to juice and bagels and a briefing by Ballmer that offered a considerably more down-to-earth tour of what he called Microsoft's "opportunity map." The difference between talking about the software business with Gates and with Ballmer was the difference between going to a base-ball game as a kid with your mother or your father. Same ballpark, same ballgame. But you're likely to see and learn different things.

Gates made no secret that he considered Ballmer a weak technol-ogy strategist. He told aides there was little chance Ballmer would become Microsoft's chief executive; the role of a CEO at a large soft-ware company simply required somebody with deeper technical knowledge, he said. But there was no doubt about Ballmer's organi-zational and operational strengths. Since he joined the company in 1980, Ballmer had tinkered constantly with Microsoft's organiza-tional chart to get the right people working on the right things.

As executive vice president for sales and marketing, Ballmer ran the eleven thousand employees who closed the deals and made the numbers that fueled Microsoft's growth. Five years earlier, he had reluctantly agreed to take over Microsoft's sales and marketing organization. The goal was to get more knowledge of Microsoft's product strategy into the sales team, but he worried about losing touch with the technology strategy, the heart and soul of the company. He went to Jon Shirley, who remained on the board after retiring as president of Microsoft. If you want to be president someday, Shirley told him, you've got to take the sales job.

For all Gates's professed concern for customers, it was Ballmer who was in closest touch with the people who actually used—and paid for—Microsoft's software. That gave Ballmer a meat-and-potatoes view of the business.

The law of large numbers meant Microsoft had to add ever more billions in new revenues each year to sustain its growth rate. Gates dissembled on the subject, dismissing any notion that growth was a concern. "I don't wake up in the morning thinking about growth," he wrote me in our e-mail exchange in 1997. "Growth is not a goal I have or give to anyone in the company."

Ballmer had no such luxury. He knew that Microsoft was a machine built for growth. Just as software standards create a "virtuous circle" for Microsoft's product, revenue and earnings growth created a virtuous circle for Microsoft itself. The rising share price helped Microsoft attract the computer industry's most talented individuals, who further improved Microsoft's performance. As long as the share price rose, stock options aligned employees long-term interests with the company's. Microsoft pulled off the nifty trick of sharing more wealth with more people than any company in history while letting the stock market pick up most of Microsoft's employee compensation costs. Microsoft was one of the earliest and certainly biggest users of stock options, the quintessential new economy-financing mechanism.

Ballmer loved to take apart Microsoft's numbers. As a kid, Ballmer's father, who never went to college but worked as an accountant for thirty years at Ford Motor Company, explained to the young Steve the minute details of business arcana like domestic international sales corporations, identifying tax savings, and other opportunities. Ballmer likewise prided himself on mastery of the details.

The metric that obsessed Ballmer was "dollars per desktop," Microsoft's annual revenue for every installed personal computer, new or old, anywhere in the world. "Everything I do is global!" he thundered in one of my interviews with him. Ballmer ran Microsoft's global sales operation by the "yellow book," a loose-leaf binder with a page of results for every one of Microsoft's more than two dozen foreign subsidiaries. In 1994, Brazil generated about $40 in Microsoft revenue per new computer; three years later, that had increased to more than $90. India was about two years behind, going from less than $17 per PC to nearly $30. The U.S. number was about $110, but some foreign markets supplied even more—Australia's contribution for each new desktop PC was $135.

Ballmer's goal: to increase Microsoft's revenues from the 250 million personal computers in use around the world to an average of $200 per year. "Units! It's all about units!" he exclaimed.

The only customers who were giving Microsoft the dollars per desktop that Ballmer was aiming for were the largest corporate customers, who signed up for annual subscriptions at $200 per PC per year for essentially all the software Microsoft released. Those ranks were growing, but taken as a whole, the ten thousand largest corporate customers, with 33 million PCs, spent only $80 and $90 a year per PC on Microsoft software. Small businesses, with about 70 million computers, spent an average of $27 per PC with Microsoft. The home market was the toughest to crack. The bulk of home consumers, using the 70 million home computers worldwide, spent under $10 a year on Microsoft software after purchasing their PCs.

The major problem: Microsoft was in an upgrade business in which the original product never wears out. Home consumers, even more than businesses, seemed to have little trouble resisting the company's suggestions for constant software upgrades, preferring to stick with current versions of software that continued to work just fine, thank you. To the extent this year's product is good, it's that much harder to make a compelling case for buying next year's. How good does a word processor need to be?

The company planned to get around that by expanding the annual licensing program to more businesses and laying the groundwork for consumer subscriptions to a steady stream of upgrades, add-ons and services. Instead of software as a packaged good, sold once and then used forever, Gates wanted to turn software into a utility, billed annually if not monthly. Gates referred to the services as "Windows dial tone," or Wintone. He had told Wall Street analysts in the summer of 1997, "Somebody signs up for twelve months to get all the bits we can send, all the support we can send—we see that as the future of the business."

The long-term strategy was to make software from Microsoft Corporation as universal as electricity, water, and telephone service—and much more valuable. The company was laying the foundation for a Windows-based "digital nervous system" for the entire economy.

During a break in the session at Hood Canal, I tried out my arithmetic on Ballmer. At $200 a computer times 250 million computers, that's $50 billion in revenues. Microsoft's revenues in the 1997 fiscal year that had just ended were only $11.4 billion. Ballmer caught Gates's sleeve as he walked by us on his way back into the house. "Hey, Bill, David thinks we're a $50 billion company, heh, heh, heh," Ballmer told him. Gates just smiled.

It wasn't just me. The share price—the market's best guess of Microsoft's future value—assumed a five-year growth rate that would push revenues to more than $50 billion and make Microsoft the first company to top $1 trillion in market value.

Of course, Ballmer took every opportunity to talk down the share price. Three weeks before the Hood Canal retreat, for example, Ballmer tanked Microsoft's stock for a day by musing in an interview with me that the high price was "not healthy" for Microsoft's shareholders.

"Is our company really worth $180 billion?" he said. "It's beyond my imagination spectrum. I don't think it's true. . . . This is a fine company and a fine business and we're doing a fine job. But we're maybe not worth $180 billion yet." The story ran the day Microsoft hosted hundreds of Wall Street analysts in Seattle at its annual conference. The stock fell sharply at the opening, sending the analysts scurrying for the phones.

Indeed, the skyrocketing share price was becoming Microsoft's biggest problem. The market was raising the value of Microsoft's shares far faster than the company could conceivably increase its revenues or profits. A significant slowdown in growth that triggered a prolonged slump in the share price could turn the virtuous circle into a vicious cycle: slowing growth, slumping stock, higher compensation costs, lower earnings, further stock slides, difficulty recruiting and retaining employees, slower and lower-quality products, falling market share. Like a shark that must keep swimming to stay alive, Microsoft had to keep growing.

Gates hated such talk. "What he hates is to have to say the thing has to grow all the time, that you always have to beat what you did today tomorrow," Maffei told me. "What Bill objects to is that the market is demanding it and that if we don't keep growing the stock falls. That doesn't give you a lot of room to breathe."

The more Microsoft's stock climbed, the more nervous Gates seemed. The company's market value represented an expectation of future success so unprecedented that Gates was no longer sure he could fulfill it. The market value gave Gates no credit for what he had done so far; everything depended on what he did in the future. Baked into the market value was the assumption that Microsoft's revenues would go to the moon. After all he had accomplished, they still wanted more. He had created more wealth than anybody else in the history of the world, and it wasn't enough. The market is always asking: What are you going to do for me next year? A company's market value is the assimilation of all knowledge, crunched into a number that represents the expected value of the company's earnings out into the future, discounted back to the present.

That put Gates on a treadmill running faster and faster. He can never escape. When Jack Welch of General Electric announced his retirement, he was hailed as one of the greatest chief executives in history. If GE goes into the toilet under new CEO Jeffrey Immelt, nobody will blame Welch. But Microsoft will always be Bill Gates's company. How can he ever leave a winner?

INNOVATOR'S DILEMMA

An industry leader faces its greatest danger at the peak of success. On the surface, the insight seems profound. Sears was a "retailing powerhouse" just as the shift to discount retailing and home centers left it lurching. As recently as the 1970s, it was IBM that was the monolithic overlord of the Information Age.

For all its dramatic value, Gates knew the notion is at best a tautology. If a company is at its peak, by definition its downhill slide has begun.

At one executive meeting, Gates grandly announced, "The company has never been under more stress, never been in more danger."

"When hasn't that been true?" Myhrvold snorted.

Gates thought for a second. "Never." The laughter broke the tension in the room.

In Gates's view, the company has from nearly the beginning been on borrowed time. What the company was attempting had never been done before. Certainly not this way, all in software, pure, digital, intellectual property. That kind of property could too easily walk out the door in the form of talent, or too easily be stolen in the form of pirated copies. In Microsoft's early days, it was the rare venture capitalist who would even consider investments in pure software companies. The financial leverage in software is huge, but so are the risks. Your competitor can flood the market just as easily as you.

In addition, the complexity of code made the engineering required something beyond the scope of anything that had existed before. In the early years, Gates argued passionately that no software company could grow beyond about $10 million in revenues a year—the teams would get too big, the complexity would become overwhelming. Then it was $100 million, then $1 billion. All through Microsoft's history, Gates predicted far less success than Microsoft in fact achieved. On the eve of Microsoft's initial public offering on Wall Street, Gates advised his father to sell his shares in the company at the stock market's opening bell the next morning. "These Goldman Sachs guys have wildly overvalued us," he told him.

Gates never tires of telling audiences that Microsoft carries no guarantees. Gates knows there are next to no significant instances in business history in which the first company in a new industry leads that industry twenty years later. Despite its success, Gates in 1997 believed the chances that Microsoft would be the leading software company in twenty years were fifty-fifty at best.

"One day, somebody will catch us napping," he wrote in *Business at the Speed of Thought.* "One day, an eager upstart will put Microsoft out of business. I just hope it's fifty years from now, not two or five."

The eager upstart is the canonical agent of change in the technology industry, the David who slays the Goliath of the previous era. It is a commonplace in the computer industry to say there are no examples in which the company that led one era of technological development remained on top in the next era. To Gates, that piece of conventional wisdom is also a tautology. A new era is proclaimed only when a new leader displaces the former winner.

The myth of the eager upstart recalls nostalgically all those long nights tinkering in the garage, the camaraderie of the early days, when everybody did everything. Gates himself is nostalgic for Microsoft's early years. "I get to review every line of code and interview every person," he remembers. "In terms of excellence per person or output per person, you just can't beat that phase. You know everything."

If ever there was an eager upstart from central casting, Netscape was it. But by the summer of 1997, the entrenched incumbent had beaten back the threat. Microsoft had stalled Netscape's advance and scratched its way to nearly 30 percent market share. It was now only a matter of time before the market tipped decisively in Microsoft's direction. That was a profound blow to the New Economy gurus flitting around Silicon Valley, who desperately wanted to proclaim the birth of a new Internet era and did, loudly.

Microsoft had dominated the character-based era with DOS; Windows had become the dominant "graphical user interface"; and Internet Explorer was on its way to becoming the dominant Web browser. Few other companies had achieved repeat successes. Microsoft had pulled off a three-peat. Microsoft dominated the valuable user interface of all three eras, so how could they really be separate eras after all?

Gates was at his most mocking in sympathizing with the pundits' plight. "Now they have to say, 'Gee, when the Internet era started, that was supposed to kill all those companies. Why are they still around?' he said. "It's not a pretty thing."

MICROSOFT'S ability to flawlessly fire successive stages of a growth rocket raised the question "Is Microsoft the most successful commercial enterprise in history?" Before it was vilified as a predator, Microsoft was widely praised as a pathbreaking pioneer of a new kind of business organism that was uniquely adapted to the Information Age.

John Porter, managing partner of Fidelity Investments, one of the largest institutional holders of Microsoft shares, told me, "At some point you have to say 'Game over.' " Microsoft's unchallenged market dominance, the scope of its opportunities, and its flawless execution made it likely Microsoft would be recognized as the greatest success story ever, he said in 1998. "They certainly have the best timing I'm aware of, in terms of seeing a market and getting there ahead of everyone else."

Jonathan Cohen, an analyst then with Merrill Lynch, said, "Microsoft has been singularly successful and appears almost perfectly positioned to continue that success. I'm not aware of any company this century that has generated as much profitability as efficiently in as short a period of time and has come to so dominate its market as Microsoft. And it dominates not just in market share but in terms of strategy, in the way that what it does influences everything else."

The evidence introduced in the antitrust suit paradoxically served to ratify Microsoft's clout. If companies such as IBM, Intel, and Compaq bent to Microsoft's will, the thinking went, the company must have real power.

Gates wanted no part of the all-time champion discussion. "I'm shy, reluctant, whatever, to take a moniker like that and apply it to Microsoft in any way," he said. "It's a curse for anybody who gets that moniker. Then every article in the future will be about how their leader sat there and basked in superlatives, not realizing that in a very competitive businesses like ours, particularly ours, none of the products last."

Gates knew well the classic examples that give rise to that kind of superstition. Ken Olsen, the legendary founder of Digital Equipment Corporation, was a distant god of Gates's computer geek youth. Olsen pioneered the small computer market in the first place, creating the minicomputer industry and building DEC (later more commonly called "Digital") into the anchor tenant of Route 128 in Boston's tech heyday of the 1970s. "Instead of paying the millions IBM wanted for its 'Big Iron,' a buyer could get one of Olsen's PDP-1's for $120,000," Gates recounts in *The Road Ahead*. It wasn't as powerful as a mainframe, but it was good enough for many tasks. IBM waited eleven years to enter the minicomputer market.

Two decades later, Olsen repeatedly dismissed the personal computer as a passing fad. "Olsen's vision faltered," Gates writes. "He was brilliant at seeing new ways of doing things, and then—after years of being an innovator—he missed a big bend in the road." Gates noted the irony that Digital in 1998 agreed to be acquired by a PC company, Compaq Computer.

Digital wasn't alone. Gates noted that most of the computer companies noted for their nimbleness in Thomas J. Peters's *In Search of Excellence* faced serious problems in the years since the book was published in 1982. IBM, for example, insulated its skunk-works PC effort from the stultifying effects of IBM's corporate imperatives but was nonetheless unable to change its fundamental nature as a company that makes its money by selling hardware.

IBM's problem, in Gates's view, was that it split its bets. It could never fully embrace the model that its software should be set free to commoditize the underlying hardware. Thus it was always at odds with the fundamental dynamics of the new, horizontally layered PC industry. IBM couldn't help but shackle its PC software effort by trying to use it to pull along its mainframe business. IBM continued for two decades to see PCs through the lens of its larger computer systems.

"IBM would not admit failure and back off. The strategic control that they thought it might give them in hardware margins was too alluring to give up," Gates wrote. "This view distorted and slowed its response to a fundamental technology shift."

One of the most sobering examples of an incumbent that failed to adapt came not from computers but from the icon of American industry himself, Henry Ford. For a time, Gates hung a framed photo and autograph of Ford above his desk and referred to his predecessor as the world's richest man simply as Henry. With the innovation of the paced assembly line, Ford perfected the high-volume, low-priced model in the auto industry. In 1908, the entire auto industry produced 65,000 cars. By the early 1920s, Ford's Model T production topped 2 million a year and prices had fallen sharply. With a high minimum wage that complemented his mass-market approach, Ford was a classic bootstrapper of his own virtuous circle. In 1920, Ford had 90 percent of the low-priced car market.

For Gates, however, the photo of Ford represented not a kindred spirit but a Ghost of Microsoft Future. Ford never adapted to the dynamics of the modern automobile industry. Gates's favorite business book is *My Years with General Motors,* by Alfred Sloan, the legendary corporate executive who outflanked Ford. Sloan dissects Ford's mistakes with merciless precision. In 1925, Ford's sales held even, but as the market grew, his market share declined from 54 percent to 45 percent, a "sign of danger, if Mr. Ford had chosen to read it," Sloan wrote. By the 1920s, the rising supply of used cars undercut Ford at the low end. For a slightly higher price, Chevrolet offered more features. Rising incomes and installment plans let Americans stretch for higher quality. The marketing of "model years" created an appetite for constant improvement. All of that overwhelmed Ford's concept of a static-model utility car.

By the time Ford realized he needed an upgrade, in 1927, he had to shut down his great River Rouge assembly plant for nearly a year to retool. The delay effectively ceded the market to Chevrolet and Plymouth, then an eager upstart.

"The old master had failed to master change," Sloan wrote. "Don't ask me why."

In *Business at the Speed of Thought*, Gates uses the Ford example to argue for creating a culture in which bad news travels fast and middle managers are able to act quickly on negative information. "Somebody at Ford saw the changes coming in the 1920s," Gates wrote in his book. "An engineer who came up with a new design was fired for his temerity. The senior leadership didn't listen."

So it wasn't that Gates didn't understand deep in his bones the notions that Harvard Business School professor Clayton Christensen popularized in his book *The Innovator's Dilemma*. The book asks the question: Why do bad things happen to good companies? Companies that do all the right things, like innovating rapidly, listening to customers, and investing in the future, still fall prey to fundamental market and technology shifts. His answer: Well-accepted and highly successful management practices are destined to miss the threats posed by what he calls "disruptive technologies." Such failures, far from being the result of arrogance or blindness, are rather the result of rational decisions by executives genuinely seeking to enhance profitability and shareholder value.

In Christensen's schema, a disruptive technology starts as an untested product with an unknown business model or one that offers lower profit margins. Most significant, few customers even seem to want the new thing. Any rational manager would stick with the old approach and brush aside the threat from a product at best suited for marginal, niche markets. At the same time, constant improvements in the traditional technology make it all the more valuable and seemingly invincible—giving rise to breathless accounts of a company at the peak of its power. By the time the disruptive technology makes the jump to the mainstream and undercuts the incumbent with a "good enough" product at a markedly lower price, it's usually too late for the incumbent to recover.

Christensen's book refines a theme that has made the rounds of business school professors for years. James Utterback, in *Mastering the Dynamics of Innovation*, is truly gloomy about the prospects for change, noting the "disturbing regularity with which industrial leaders follow their core technologies into obsolescence and obscurity." Firms that ride an innovation to the heights of industrial leadership more often than not fail to shift to newer technologies, he wrote.

What accounted for the pattern of failure? "The habits of mind, commitments and strategy, or patterns of behavior of the organization's elite," Utterback wrote. "Established firms with massively profitable businesses are almost invariably more conservative and risk-averse than are fledgling competitors with none."

Gates understood the risks. "Companies can get caught in a negative spiral, too," he wrote in *The Road Ahead.* "A company in a positive spiral has an air of destiny. One in a negative spiral operates in an atmosphere of doom. If a company starts to lose market share or delivers a bad product, the talk turns to, 'Why do you work there?' 'Why would you invest in that company?' 'I don't think you should buy from them.' The press and the analysts smell blood and start telling inside stories about who's quarreling and who's responsible for mismanagement. Customers begin to question whether they should continue to buy the company's products. Within the sick company, everything gets questioned, including the things the company is doing right. Even a fine strategy can get dismissed with the argument, 'You're just defending the old way,' and that can lead to more mistakes. Then down the company spirals."

Indeed, Microsoft faced a special form of the Innovator's Dilemma—the Monopolist's Dilemma.

Like any rational actor in its position, Microsoft was structurally compelled to defend the old model. It is worth almost any amount—up to the net present value of the monopoly in perpetuity—to defend a monopoly. That's why economists say monopolies distort the economy and retard innovation even if they might lower prices in the short term. In the long term, they are a conservative force against innovation.

The scope of Microsoft's dominance set it apart, as did the rest of the company's outsized numbers—for profits, margins, growth, cash. Microsoft, almost alone, had been able to command substantial revenues from desktop software. Microsoft had real and substantial franchises, and Gates was not about to let them be destroyed.

Two years earlier, Gates and his competitors agree, the Internet presented a fundamental threat to Microsoft revenues. The new model of software development and distribution appeared destined to undercut Microsoft's traditional franchises and replace it with a model that demanded heavy investment, with the promise of profits only in the long term, if ever. Microsoft's competitors didn't expect the company to be able to respond to the lower profit margins presaged by the Web. Oracle, for example, hoped to strip Microsoft of its desktop profits with low-cost network computers. For Sun, Java was a loss leader that helped give it cachet and possibly boosted its hardware business. Netscape's browser was effectively free client software intended to drive corporate demand for Netscape's more expensive server software.

"If Microsoft is going to wage this war on the desktop, they're going to sacrifice their monopoly," Ray Lane, then Oracle's president, told me.

Gates's antipathy to free software is legendary. While still a student at Harvard, he wrote his "Open Letter to Hobbyists," in which he complained that pirated copies of the BASIC computer language he and Paul Allen had adapted for early PCs were being passed around by users. "As the majority of hobbyists must be aware, most of you steal your software," Gates wrote. "Who cares if the people who worked on it get paid. . . . What hobbyist can put 3 man-years into programming, finding all bugs, documenting his product and distribute it for free?"

The Internet brought all of that back. In 1994, when Microsoft was pursuing interactive TV pilot projects, David Marquardt, a Microsoft board member, suggested that most of what Gates was envisioning already existed in rough form as the Internet. "That's the stupidest thing I've ever heard," Gates snapped at Marquardt. "Nobody can make any money on the Internet. Everything is free."

He was still shaking his head in March 1996. "It's one of the most unusual markets that there has ever been," he said. "It's all free software."

Yet, instead of dooming Microsoft, the Internet fueled demand for ever-cheaper PCs as a way to gain access to the Web. Since nearly every one of those PCs included a copy of Windows, the Internet pushed Microsoft to an unexpected surge of growth.

The brilliance of Gates's jiujitsu is that he appeared singularly able to turn back the Internet's inexorable pull toward commoditization, falling prices, and disappearing profits. Even Intel, which for years succeeded in holding PC prices steady at around $2,000 by offering improved performance, was forced to adapt to the new market of sinking PC prices, first below $1,000 and at one point as low as $400. Microsoft, in contrast, seemed to be succeeding in claiming even more "dollars per desktop" by shifting customers from Windows 95 and 98, which brought in about $50 per copy for Microsoft, to Windows NT, which fetched about $100 per copy.

Software pricing remained a dark art. Marginal costs offered little guidance, since with digital reproduction, such costs approached zero. Gates knew there was no direct mapping between value and price. Instead, price was a function of competitive dynamics. "The software industry in the past, in many cases, has been able to capture some of the value they've created in the financial model, but there's no guarantee," he told me. "I have a certain faith that by doing good tools, there's some value that will follow out of that. But there's no guarantee."

In December 1997, Joachim Kempin, Microsoft's tough-as-nails vice president in charge of sales to PC makers, wrote a stunningly blunt memo on Microsoft's threats and opportunities. "We believe that we ducked the bullet for 15–18 months. . . . While we have increased our prices over the last 10 years other component prices have come down and continue to come down."

Kempin defined his goal clearly: to get the highest possible fee for each copy of Windows, balanced only by the need to prevent PC makers from changing their practice of pre-installing the operating system at the factory. Negotiations with Compaq, which alone paid Microsoft about $750 million a year in licensing fees, were turning into a major fight over Compaq's demand that Microsoft offer a price break for sub-$1,000 PCs. "The answer here has to be 'no' for all people involved." As for Windows prices, he advised, "As long as we gain [market] share we should not lower them."

Kempin had firm advice for Gates, Ballmer, and Maritz: "Defend current model."

Gates liked to present himself as detached from the imperatives of Microsoft's money matters, but he was intimately aware of where Microsoft could squeeze harder and the weak spots that might undermine its revenues. "This document basically points out that the move to NT and volume increases are our ONLY upsides for the near future," Gates wrote in response to Kempin's memo. "I agree that for the next 2–3 years this is the best plan."

Gates listed the threats: the "excitement" of outside software developers for Java, potential clones of Windows, and the explosion in the number of "non-PC devices," such as handheld digital assistants like the PalmPilot and a new generation of digital devices for playing music, video, and games. On his last trip to Japan, Gates had been surprised by how fast such devices were catching on. "The high price of Windows for $500 machines does make these non-PC devices more attractive," Gates wrote. On the horizon, Gates spotted another potential price-buster that was still so distant he didn't even have a clear sense of how to spell it: "low-cost Unix systems, LUNIX in particular."

Gates guarded the profitability of Microsoft's assets extraordinarily carefully. "Bill always wants to know 'How are you going to make money?,' confirmed Paul Maritz, effectively Microsoft's third-ranking executive before he left the company in September 2000. "It's a good thing to keep asking that. Because if you don't have that, you're going to go out of business."

"Bill is playing a tough game," Maffei agreed. Gates wasn't going to sacrifice the success of Microsoft's business model without a fight. "Bill would be the first to say, 'I could throw it all out and do great whizbang free software and I'd destroy more shareholder value in a day than I created in twenty years.' "

Microsoft had not only beaten back the challenge from the Internet, but had done it without being forced to lower prices in response to competitors' massive giveaways.

Thus, to Gates, Microsoft's victory in the set-piece battle that came to be known as the Great Browser War of 1995–1997 was not simply a victory over Netscape. It was a victory over the Innovator's Dilemma itself.

Gates thinks Christensen's Innovator's Dilemma thesis is plain wrong. For starters, he says, Christensen chose to study the wrong industry for his thesis. In the disk drive industry, Gates says, "Every breakthrough in disk drives—every single one that really counted—was done by IBM." In the boom and bust world of providing for the massive storage needs of digital systems, IBM has retained the edge in both technology and profitability. The new guys come in and go out, but IBM remained the leader.

"The large organization, that took the long-term approach, that did the R and D, they won every time," Gates said. "Every single time."

The bigger problem with the *Innovator's Dilemma* book, Gates says, is that it doesn't say what large companies should do. "Yes, a company needs to pick some revolutionary thing and bet its life on those things," Gates said. "That's all you get" out of Christensen's thesis, he said.

Microsoft faced a stream of so-called disruptive technologies. The successful long-term players don't let fads define them. "You can't completely—" Gates cuts himself off. "Well, some fads are completely empty. But in the world of technology I can't even think of any. Every fad has had some germ of truth in it." The trend du jour was always cast as a disruptive technology.

"If there's a single sentence—" Gates sputtered at the end of our most recent conversation. "Anybody who tells you there's a single sentence, like 'Trying to preserve the old is a bad thing. . . . ' Anybody who says there's one sentence that provides the guidance for making the choices about organizing new projects, taking risks, staking out pilot projects, setting timetables, integrating organizations and technologies to put together"—he took a deep breath and kept on going—"anybody who says there's a single sentence that determines the answer to those questions, they just don't get it. They don't get that"—he paused.

"It's more fun from the outside to think that there is. Company XYZ failed because of—One Sentence Description," he said. "No. Unless there are a bunch of morons running that company, that is not what is happening."

2

Hawks and Doves

TEAMS

Gaining respect and commanding influence at Microsoft is an extreme sport. People airlift their Porsches to Europe for the summer race circuit, check ice hockey opponents with full body slams, jump from helicopters to snowboard down glaciers. They keep meticulous count of who made the right calls and who made the wrong calls on every market and technology trend, forever.

But the ultimate way to gain respect at Microsoft is to ship software. Nearly every office has a shelf for the Plexiglas plaques awarded to team members to commemorate the date when a software project finally crosses from the realm of development into the reality of the marketplace, where millions of people will use it—or won't.

Gates chose Jim Allchin to deliver the goods for Windows Everywhere.

James Edward Allchin drives his software teams with the same intensity he plays electric guitar in the Southern rock style of the Allman Brothers, Eric Johnson, and Stevie Ray Vaughan. He is lean and efficient in movement and speech. The phrase "does not suffer fools gladly" is part of nearly every description of him. Allchin's hair went completely white by his late twenties, and he projects the steely seriousness of someone for whom software is an early religious calling. As the massive effort to deliver the software that would be called Windows 2000 reached a crucial milestone, he called the effort a "way of life."

The software army under Allchin's command was one of the greatest ever assembled. More than five thousand programmers and testers worked around the clock six and sometimes seven days a week to crank out 29 million lines of code. They wrote tens of millions more lines of code just to test the product code. Even before Allchin took over the project, the first version of Windows NT consisted of 6 million lines of code, required a team of 250 developers, and cost $150 million, making it one of the most complex engineering feats in human history. Dave Cutler, the creator of the original version of Windows NT, explained breathlessly, "No one mind can comprehend it all."

Allchin's latest upgrade, Windows 2000, is more than five times as complex. The new operating system was touted as the product that would finally fulfill marketing buzzwords like "rock-solid" and "scalable," as well as "cheap," because it ran on industry-standard Intel-architecture PCs. Before it was done, development costs would total more than $3 billion, making Windows 2000, as Gates liked to say, more expensive than the design of the Boeing 747. It would be a stunning engineering achievement, perhaps the last great piece of huge system software to be brought forth from scratch by the brute-force efforts of thousands of developers within a single corporation. Gates often pointed out that unlike most corporate executives, he couldn't offer guests photo-opportunity tours of assembly lines and plant floors. But in Allchin's Personal and Business Systems Group, he certainly had a software factory.

The massive investment, and Allchin's mandate, was to bring forth the long-awaited "unification of the code base." Since the collapse of Microsoft's ill-fated collaboration with IBM on OS/2 in the early 1990s, the company had been on an epic quest to base all of its operating system on a single architectural foundation, a single operating system "kernel." It was a matter of engineering efficiency. Microsoft's two code bases meant two sets of device drivers, two toolkits for developers, and two marketing messages. Unification meant Microsoft would finally kill off the underlying funkiness of DOS, which still lay at the heart of Windows 95 and 98 and even the Windows Millennium Edition, fatally compromising reliability and security.

The replacement was to be New Technology, ever after known as NT, a new operating system built from scratch. The goal was to get not only new users, but every one of the 200 million current PC users running one of the earlier versions of DOS-based Windows, to adopt the new software. NT represented a forced obsolescence of the old product, a huge upgrade cycle that presented a rare opportunity for a major price hike. Microsoft planned to roughly double the price of Windows, from the $50 wholesale price for Windows 95 to $100 for NT.

Allchin wrote to one aide, "I can't tell you how important it is to make the switch to NT (aka higher priced system)."

Even more fundamentally, each copy of NT represented a "socket" to plug in the rest of Microsoft's software line, a reliable foundation for all of Microsoft's future plans. The pressure on Allchin was immense. Windows 2000 is the "most important release Microsoft will do this decade," Allchin told me in September 1997. "We're obviously betting the company on it."

Managing the upgrade of Microsoft's customer base from classic Windows to NT without losing market share was a tactical business maneuver of the utmost delicacy. For all the advantages of NT, the old products, Windows 3.1 and Windows 95, were the ones that ran more than 90 percent of all PCs. The prospect of swapping out the code base for the PC market's entire "installed base" opened a major vulnerability to competitors. The trick was to require all applications to work on both and then gently drop the old system. If the handoff worked, Microsoft's nearly decade-long strategy would rank as one of the most skillful maneuvers in business history.

By mid-1998, Gates was already claiming success. "That dual strategy worked perfectly, absolutely perfectly," Gates told me. "The precipitous thing would be to say we'll immediately switch to [NT]."

Allchin, with a deep sense of responsibility and a super-serious de-meanor, was anything but precipitous. Success had done little to ease his deeply ingrained fear of being run over, losing everything, going broke. To him, "The way you avoid bad times is to know there can be bad times. To not get carried away with expenses. And to think about the business, think about the business, think about the business. Many people here haven't seen bad times."

Allchin knows bad times. He was a baby when his father moved the family from Grand Rapids, Michigan, where warehouse work was crushing him, to a farm near Keysville, Florida, a highway crossing east of Tampa. Allchin and his brother Keith grew up poor. Even so, Allchin has happy memories of the tin-roof shack his father built for the family. It was so small there was no room for doors inside. He and Keith, three years older, went to school barefoot. Sometimes cash was so short that his mother and even his father had to take jobs off the farm. Jim and Keith worked before and after school, earning a nickel a tree for hoeing weeds in the orange orchard until a series of late freezes in the early 1960s wrecked the citrus crops and shattered the farm's shaky finances.

Allchin rebuilt engines of go-carts and tractors on the farm and was particularly fascinated by electricity. "I love building things," he says. Once, he found instructions in a book for making an electrical transformer. He wrapped a wire around a core from a piece of farm equipment. When he plugged it into an outlet, smoke poured out, wires melted, and the coil burst into flames.

He got fired from his first computer job, as a high-school intern at a payroll-processing company in Winter Haven. His job was to carry the punch cards from the backroom to the attendant running the Burroughs mainframe computer. Once, when the attendant was away, he loaded the deck himself, interrupting another run in progress. He ruined hours of work on the computer and was asked not to return. He did manage to write his first program, determining the day of the week from the date, in Burroughs assembler language.

Allchin entered the University of Florida to study electrical engineering but dropped in and out of school to play music. He told his mother he needed to find out whether he could make a living with music and went on the southern music circuit, playing roadhouses and clubs. His bands—with names like Rain, Tudor Rose, and Red White and Blue—sometimes rented out halls and sold tickets on their own to keep more of the take. He ate a lot of cereal and even went on food stamps for a time. In the end, he didn't like the road. Too many guitar legends growing old flat broke, too many drugs. He went back to school and graduated as one of the first majors in Florida's newly created computer science program.

At Texas Instruments, he teamed up to build a new operating system with Dick Kiger, a former professor who had no problem with Allchin's moccasins and long hair. In 1976, Allchin followed Kiger to Wyoming to start a company that used telecommunications and Wyoming's central location to run computer services for businesses around the country—and then to Dallas to start another company together.

Computer networking hooked Allchin even more strongly than electricity had when he was a kid. "It's just cool to have things that are autonomous talk to one another," he says. Soon he was restless to go back to school. He had earned his master's degree at Stanford, but his research assistant's salary didn't cover living expenses in pricey Palo Alto, California. Georgia Tech, already deep into the computer science of networking, offered him a full fellowship.

At Georgia Tech, Allchin pursued one of the holy grails of computer science, an operating system for "physically decentralized and logically centralized" computing. Clouds, a prototype for such a "distributed" system that would work reliably across a network, never fail, and automatically send computing tasks wherever resources were available, became a marker for his lifelong dream. His 1983 Ph.D. dissertation starts with a section titled "A Perfect World." His first line was "Programming a computer system that never fails and in which there is no interference between competing processes is truly a programmer's dream."

"I never really got excited about big multiprocessor machines that seemed all complex and couldn't scale," Allchin told me. "But things that were autonomous, working in concert to do something, that has always been exciting to me. I liked to see machines talking to each other. It's a little like humans cooperating together to get things done. That just seemed cool. I also believe, longer term, that's the way to get more intelligence. You can get great intelligence by having things talk together."

Before the networked world settled on the Internet's TCP/IP as the global standard, other networking approaches vied for dominance. Allchin was recruited by Dave Mahoney, a veteran of the minicomputer maker Data General, who with several members of his team had started Banyan, one such networking company. Banyan built a pioneering system called Vines. Allchin was still finishing his thesis at Georgia Tech, sleeping all day and working all night in order to get time on the university's computer. Allchin told Mahoney he had no time to meet; he didn't even wake up until 5 P.M. Mahoney convinced Allchin to meet him at the Atlanta airport at six o'clock. He hired him on the spot.

Allchin started as an engineer, but Mahoney soon put him in charge of all of Banyan's software development. "When he gets into the mission, he's the most passionate person you can have on your team," Mahoney said. Allchin's rhythm was thirty-six hours of work, then sleep, then another thirty-six straight hours. "I really wanted to crank code," he said. "I had really missed cranking code. It's a serious habit."

Banyan faced a serious strategic choice. Before the Intel 386, widely available computers weren't powerful enough to run Vines. To ensure performance, the company assembled its own hardware boxes and sold them bundled with the software, for prices upward of $30,000. Long-term, it was clear there was no way to compete with the prices of standard PCs. The company needed to make the transition back to software only—as Microsoft had understood from the beginning. Software was where the long-term profits were, but Banyan had become reliant on the short-term hardware revenues. As a result, it took several years for Banyan to dump the hardware business.

"When you've got a revenue stream that's funding all the employees, and a certain profit level—the transition from hardware to software is incredibly complex," Allchin says. "They made the transition. Unfortunately, I think it killed the company because they didn't do it faster." Allchin pushed for the change, sometimes brashly, arguing, "We need to get to be a software company and do it now and take the lumps."

The parting of Allchin and Mahoney was contentious, but Allchin still lights up when talking about Banyan's technology. After an open lecture at Microsoft where he talked about Vines, a Microsoft engineer approached him. "I've always wanted to meet you," he told Allchin. "I installed Vines servers all around the world. You just plug it in, answer a few questions and you never go back.'" Then he paused and asked, "When are you going to do that here?"

It took a year for Gates to recruit Allchin. Microsoft was talking with Mahoney about acquiring all of Banyan but was put off by its reliance on hardware revenues. After studying the deal, Gates and other executives decided they didn't want Banyan. They wanted Allchin.

Allchin was skeptical. In 1990, Microsoft's software was an industry joke. The first time he saw MS-DOS while still at Georgia Tech, Allchin remembers saying, "It sets computer science back by a decade. It was such a pathetic little thing." Scarcely better was OS/2, the successor to DOS that Microsoft was still developing jointly with IBM. "OS/2 was just garbage," he says, "a dead whale they were trying to kick down the beach." Windows he dismissed as a "nice toy."

"It wasn't that I didn't think I could help change it," he says of Microsoft's software culture. "It was that I didn't know if the desire was there to change it, if the understanding that it was bad was even there," he says. "The question was, 'Did they have the desire to really do the right thing?'"

Allchin found a kindred spirit in Dave Cutler, a veteran of Digital Equipment, who transplanted his earlier success with Digital's VAX operating system to launch the NT effort. Cutler, obstreperous and equally dismissive of Microsoft's efforts to date, seemed to Allchin to share a common religion. That made it easier to believe Gates's protests that he really was committed to reliable, high-quality software. "He was older and he really wanted to build reliable things," Allchin says.

Gates's winning argument was simple volume economics—Microsoft could afford to throw more engineers at the challenges than anybody else. "Really, the stuff going back to his thesis . . . he's getting the chance to make that a world standard," Gates told me. "It's perfect for him to be here and make that a reality."

Within a month of arriving at Microsoft in 1991, Allchin ruffled feathers. His first move was to dismantle Microsoft's networking effort, known as LAN Man, short for Local Area Network Manager. The group "was on a total losing strategy," he says. "I walked in and said, 'This is never going to work. You have to shut it down. Shut it down. Take the whole thing down.'" The group employed more than 300 people. "I said, 'We have to blow it up.'"

So it goes at Microsoft. The company's organizational structure is a shifting collection of teams, grouped into products, managed in divisions that correspond to Microsoft's major product lines. Developers and marketing specialists have remarkable freedom to plot their own careers, joining and leaving teams as Microsoft's priorities and their own interests change. Reputation is the coin of the realm. Reorganizations are constant, as markets shifts and new initiatives require additional resources. Vice presidents, like coaches during an expansion draft in professional sports, protect their stars and raid other teams for specialized expertise. Command of a hot new effort gives the head coaches the ultimate recruitment edge—the whiff of success.

Soon after he arrived, Allchin experienced a heady taste of what it meant to be at the center of Gates's and Microsoft's attention. Gates put Allchin in charge of Microsoft's most ambitious project ever, a future successor to NT code-named Cairo. Cairo was to deliver on Gates's promise of "Information at Your Fingertips," first made in speeches and strategy papers in the early 1990s—an Internet-type vision of connected information but based entirely on Microsoft's technology. Cairo was to be designed to be network-savvy from the inception, and able to handle all types of data, from text to video to programming code itself.

Cairo was pegged as a full-blown version of Windows, eventually slated for release in 1996. As the company's center of gravity swung away from the classic Windows of the past, the Cairo project attracted many of Microsoft's best and brightest developers. *Fortune* magazine devoted a large part of a 1995 cover story to explaining why Cairo was vital to Microsoft's ambitions. Gates described Cairo as the most complex software program ever, one-upping even NT.

Among the teams that Allchin recruited to Cairo was the Windows "shell" team, with responsibility for the primary user interface seen by nearly every computer user. The user interface, or UI, is the screen display that lets users navigate the rest of the operating system and their applications. In technology terms, it's called a "shell," because it wraps around the underlying code and provides a way for users to take advantage of particular features. A shell is not highly sophisticated software code, but it is highly strategic. Once users become accustomed to a particular way of accomplishing tasks on their computer, they are loathe to change.

As part of Cairo, the new Windows shell was to be "object oriented," a technology direction that became another of the computer industry's holy grails. The idea was to make the shell more flexible and adaptable. By tapping Allchin to guide the next revision of the Windows shell, Gates effectively conferred responsibility for maintaining the dominance of Microsoft's computing platform.

Allchin staffed Cairo generously, but many of the developers he recruited had little experience shipping successful software at Microsoft. In Microsoft terms, the project was not "converging" on a shipment date. The complexities had become overwhelming. Critics cited a proverb: "Don't try to boil the whole ocean."

"It was an ambitious set of work, some of which was overreaching at the time, and we backed off," Gates explained to me.

Members of the team have fond memories. "Some of the best work I ever did," remembers Brian Fleming, who served as Gates's technical assistant and later joined the Cairo team. "Of course, the majority of the stuff I did never shipped."

Allchin's own verdict on Cairo is mixed. "All of the concepts, barring one, have shipped in one form or another. Maybe not in the way we envisioned, but we made some really great traction," he says.

But he knows almost doesn't count. "Cairo didn't ship," Allchin says. "Microsoft is a ship-it company, a product company. This failed."

With the demise of Cairo, Allchin was put in charge of the NT project, taking over from Cutler, who had shipped an earlier version of the new operating system. NT was still the booster engine for the next stage of Microsoft's growth rocket, the market for "enterprise" software for large corporate customers. But it was still too difficult and too complex for home computer users.

Gates was forced to put the Windows unification plan on hold once again. In order to hold onto its consumer base, Microsoft would have to continue its parallel Windows and NT development efforts a little longer. More powerful chips would soon make it possible to move from 16-bit processing to 32-bit processing, giving programs better graphics and a slicker feel. To avoid being left behind, Gates revived an effort to use the old DOS code base one more time. Gates anointed an updated version of Windows 3.1, code-named Chicago, as the company's next major version of Windows. A pattern had been established. NT was the anointed heir to the Windows throne, but Microsoft continued to rely on "classic" Windows, repeatedly finding new ways to patch over the old MS-DOS code.

Chicago, of course, became Windows 95, the blockbuster that sealed Microsoft's dominance.

That victory is credited not to Allchin but to Brad Silverberg, like Allchin a senior vice president. Silverberg had led the group that delivered Windows 3.1. To reflect the parallel Windows efforts, Silverberg was in charge of "personal" systems and Allchin ran "business" systems. When it worked, the rivalry between Microsoft's two top developers created a kind of creative tension inside Microsoft. In the absence of effective outside competition, that kept alive a semblance of natural selection in operating system development. But with two strong-willed executives on a collision course, nobody should have been surprised when they collided.

BRAD ALAN SILVERBERG was a history major before he switched to computer science. He was particularly partial to the French Revolution. But at the turn of the millennium, the revolution was happening in computer technology. His history lessons were useful nonetheless. There's no better way to command attention at Microsoft than by harnessing the power of a software revolution.

Silverberg grew up in Beachwood, a Cleveland suburb of small-business people, lawyers, and doctors, like his father. In high school he turned his favorite subjects, political science and history, into a team sport, debating world affairs in "model United Nations" competitions. Silverberg's team won Georgetown University's model UN, the biggest of them all with twelve hundred students. He liked math but didn't see how he could make a living at it. He hated science. He chose Brown University in part because it had no math or science requirement. He expected to become a lawyer.

"By chance, I decided to take a programming class freshman year," he says. "It really was a fluke how I signed up for that class. The first few weeks I struggled and was ready to drop it. But I didn't give up." One day, it all clicked. "I finally understood what I was doing and how the computer worked. And I was hooked."

Silverberg continued for a while as a modern European history major, but he had a hunger for computers that he didn't feel for the law. It is a measure of how much things have changed that he felt guilty about his new path. "It felt self-indulgent to be at an Ivy League school, costing my parents a lot of money, and not having a real plan for a career."

Silverberg didn't want to work for a big company like IBM, but there weren't many fun computer companies to work for when he graduated in 1972. "I am not a big-company person," he said. "I don't exactly conform to authority well." So he earned a master's degree from the University of Toronto, spent a winter as a ski bum in Park City, Utah, and then started at SRI International, formerly Stanford Research Institute, a think tank in the heart of what was just becoming Silicon Valley.

It was a time when the legends of the computer industry were not yet legends. SRI was one of the first sites on the Arpanet, the Pentagon project that evolved into the Internet. Xerox's Palo Alto Research Center, where early PC technologies such as the graphical user interface and the mouse were invented (but not successfully commercialized), was just up the road. Silverberg roomed with an old Brown classmate, John Crawford, the architect of Intel's 386 chip and later the 486, Pentium, and forthcoming Merced chips as well.

"Here I was, in the middle of the new revolution," he said. "I wanted to be part of it," he says.

Silverberg joined Apple Computer. He worked on the Lisa, the first widely available graphical user interface for a personal computer. A few years later, he was one of the first people hired at Analytica, a software start-up soon acquired by Borland International. Silverberg became the right-hand man to chief executive Philippe Kahn.

Kahn, an outspoken Frenchman who was obsessed with Microsoft, made Borland an early contender for dominance in the nascent PC software market. When Microsoft developers began wearing T-shirts that said "Delete Philippe," Borland printed some of its own that read "Be a Billy Clubber." Kahn was delighted every time Borland won the reviews in head-to-head competition but frustrated by the leverage Microsoft could exert as a result of its control of the operating system.

Each side raided the other for talent. Gates came calling for Silverberg in early 1989, offering a job running Microsoft's database and spreadsheet application efforts. Silverberg kept the discussion going for seven months but eventually turned Gates down. Databases and spreadsheets were not as interesting to him as operating systems and platforms. He wanted to help Borland get through its initial public offering in the United States, and he harbored an instinctive distrust of Microsoft. Complicating matters even further, the Silverbergs' newborn daughter was diagnosed with a heart condition and they didn't want to have to find new doctors in Seattle.

By the end of the year, Silverberg's thinking changed. His daughter's condition had miraculously corrected itself. Silverberg tested early "beta" versions of Microsoft's new Windows software and thought, "This could be big."

In November 1989, Silverberg called Gates. He was interested if the right job was available. This time, Gates offered the chance to run Microsoft's MS-DOS and Windows effort. "I knew it was the opportunity I had spent my career preparing for," Silverberg says.

The advent of the "graphical user interface," with its metaphor of a "desktop" and the ability to point and click at file folders and program icons, was a turning point in the history of information technology as pivotal in its day as the arrival of the Web browser nearly a decade later. In 1990, the PC industry was captivated by the idea of Windows. With DOS and most other early operating systems, computer users controlled the functions of their computers by typing commands in text form on a dark screen. Gates wanted to match the more refined graphical user interface of the Apple Macintosh, introduced five years earlier, and bring it to cheaper and more widespread IBM-compatible hardware.

It was the execution that was weak. Silverberg took over marketing of Windows 3.0 and quickly discovered the product's limitations. He reluctantly decided to develop Windows 3.1, "basically Win 3.0 done right," he says.

But Silverberg was looking to make an even bigger bet on Moore's Law with a new operating system that would take advantage of more powerful chips to integrate Windows with DOS and offer a new user interface more similar to Apple's Macintosh. Chicago, later renamed Windows 95, was what Silverberg really came to Microsoft to build.

He nearly didn't get the chance. The Chicago project was officially canceled in 1992. Microsoft had decided to put all its efforts into NT. Silverberg kept some of the work going under other budgets. He had a hunch that NT was still not ready for the mass market. He knew the pendulum would eventually swing back. Windows 95 aimed for compatibility with old applications written for DOS and earlier versions of Windows. The NT team's goal was "rock-solid" reliability, even if compatibility suffered. And he knew that consumers demanded compatibility.

With the revival of Chicago, Silverberg was once again in charge of Windows and the next iteration of the Windows user interface. He reclaimed the critical shell team from Allchin's Cairo group. "That's the most advanced thinking we have," Allchin recalls Silverberg arguing. "We've got to have that."

Control of the direction of the Windows shell had become a weather vane for determining the way Microsoft's internal political winds were blowing. Giving up control of the shell put Allchin's NT team in a frustratingly dependent position. "They would make changes without consulting us," complained Moshe Dunie, Allchin's chief deputy on the NT project. "That would create work for the NT team which had to change code to make it compatible."

For most of the 1990s, Allchin and Silverberg defined the yin and yang of Microsoft. If Allchin represents Microsoft's future as a supplier of serious big-system software to large corporations, Silverberg represents its roots as a company that ran end runs around companies' formal procurement policies by appealing directly to computer end-users. If Allchin's team were buttoned-down veterans of serious systems companies, Silverberg's recruits were from college campuses and Silicon Valley's brash upstarts and saw themselves as gung-ho "pirates" dedicated to creating "cool" new features. If Allchin is a computer science purist, a stickler for getting the technical architecture right, Silverberg jumps in first to find out what users want and gives it to them. If Allchin is more technically pure, Silverberg is more marketing oriented. If Allchin's model is top-down, Silverberg's is bottom-up.

In different circumstances, Allchin and Silverberg might have been close allies. Both knew what it meant to deliver huge, multiyear projects that consumed hundreds of millions of dollars and thousands of developer-years. Both were overachievers driven by inner doubts that made failure both terrifying and impossible.

The conflicting objectives of the parallel Windows and NT development efforts inevitably created friction.

"It was maybe not a crosstown gang rivalry, but definitely a crosstown football team rivalry," says David Cole, one of Silverberg's top lieutenants on Windows 95.

Ben Slivka, another leader on Windows 95, was more blunt. "The teams hated each other," he says.

Internal power struggles at Microsoft were different than at many other corporations, where backbiting, gossip, politicking, and maneuvering are part of the blood sport of corporate intrigue. At Microsoft, they were technical and bloodless, fought out by engineers passionate about their beliefs, outspoken in their language, quick to denounce brain-dead ideas, but reluctant to make personal attacks.

The prevailing view of the Windows team was "Those NT guys don't understand end-users."

"That was a hack you did. That was garbage,' " the NT team apt to respond. "You couldn't code your way out of a paper bag."

"Yeah, but we're faster,' " came the response from the Windows team.

To the public, Microsoft appeared to be competing with rivals such as Apple, IBM, Novell, and Sun Microsystems. But for much of the 1990s, the biggest competition was inside Microsoft itself, between the operating system that commanded more than 90 percent of the market and the one seeking to displace it.

Silverberg accepted the terms of the competition. The job of the NT team was "to kill Windows 95," he wrote later. "They are heads-on competitors and [we] should not expect any cooperation or dependencies between the two."

The launch of Windows 95 was an event the likes of which the PC industry had never seen. Jay Leno hosted the event at Microsoft's Redmond campus. The company licensed "Start Me Up" by the Rolling Stones to be the new product's theme song. Consumers lined up outside computer stores to buy the new software as soon as it went on sale; newspapers and television stations provided saturation coverage of the "midnight madness" inside.

But inside Microsoft, the completion of Windows 95 set off a different kind of madness, the kind that sets in when it becomes clear that the challenge is not over but has just begun. Even before the launch, memos and e-mail were flying as Microsoft executives began to grasp how far they had fallen behind on the Internet.

EMBRACE AND EXTEND

On the day of the Windows 95 launch, a dazed Adam Bosworth wandered through the bedlam that reigned on the Microsoft campus. He was just back from a two-month sabbatical in Fiji, Tahiti, and the Cook Islands. He had been completely cut off from computers and news. While he was gone, his team had moved to a new building. When he finally located his office, it was filled with hundreds of pounds of sand, a miniature swimming pool, and a huge palm tree and decorated like a scene from *South Pacific*, a typical Microsoft welcome-home stunt.

Bosworth, bearded and gruff, is a veteran engineer of the classic, early-Microsoft sort. He was a contemporary of Gates's at Harvard in the mid-1970s, but he had only a vague awareness of Gates; Gates hadn't heard of Bosworth at all. But the PC software industry of the early 1980s was a small community. Bosworth had founded Analytica; Silverberg had been his first hire. Like Silverberg, Bosworth had joined Borland after the acquisition but grew frustrated as the company was repeatedly outmaneuvered by Microsoft. One missed opportunity so demoralized Bosworth that he switched sides and joined Microsoft several years before Silverberg did.

At Microsoft, Bosworth helped vanquish Borland. He built Access, which started as the scrappy underdog to Borland's Paradox and dBase from Ashton-Tate. By 1995, Access had a 95 percent share of the market, just like the rest of Microsoft's desktop software applications.

When he dug out his office and got caught up with colleagues, it began to dawn on him that almost everything he and Microsoft were doing was about to be wrong. Within a couple of months, Bosworth laid out his new thinking in a long e-mail diatribe he called the "Internet Applications Manifesto."

Bosworth commanded considerable respect as both a thinker and a doer. Others knew his views could command Gates's attention. "My memos tended to have impact, if only to annoy people," Bosworth says.

In his memo, he argued that global Web connections changed the rules about how to write software. The new rules would spawn new forms of organization optimized to take advantage of them. Microsoft got as close as anybody ever had to 100 percent of the market, but even it had not gotten there. The Web was bigger. As the Web was becoming a massive worldwide database, the way to make data accessible was very different from the way data systems worked inside corporate networks. "Open" was no longer just a utopian vision or an abused marketing label, but the new coin of the realm, the next evolutionary adaptation.

Why does the Web work? he asked.

He distilled four answers. First, the Web is simple. "Since no one is in control, people vote with their feet and more people will vote for simple than hard," Bosworth told me.

Second, the Web is flexible and forgiving. "If you put things in there that shouldn't be there, the browser just ignores it. That's very different from the binary models we had built before, which were like this finely engineered German machinery, which either fit perfectly or not at all."

Third, the Web is heterogeneous. In computer terms, that means it works on all computing platforms, not only on Windows. As a result, there was no longer a reason to think the computing world would converge on Windows. Gates's cherished "singularity" was obsolete. Interoperability would win out over integration.

The fourth point was the most subtle: The Web is "loosely coupled." Most previous computing architectures required tight integration between the "server" program that stores the data and the "client" program that manipulates it. In contrast, there's no need to upgrade a Web browser every time a Web publisher changes a site. Server and client are loosely coupled. This is crucial on the Web, where servers need to be accessible to every browser and browsers need to work with every server. Only then is it possible to quickly deploy applications that are available around the world. "The whole world can talk to you, and you can't possibly know the whole world," Bosworth explained.

With those four guideposts, Bosworth said, most of the software architecture Microsoft had developed was of little use on the Internet.

Instead, Bosworth made the argument for open, public protocols as a new way to do business. His manifesto "wasn't received with enormous enthusiasm," he says. Microsoft, like the old proprietary hardware makers and most other software companies, strives to gain a lock on its customers. The goal is to find something that customers like and use and then make it difficult for them to leave. The Internet threatened that.

"The idea that something is simple is not regarded as a good thing" at Microsoft, Bosworth said. "Simple things are easier to clone. Microsoft has a clear idea of their business. It's an idea that has served them very well. It relies on the fact that you can't commoditize them."

At about the same time, John Ludwig, one of Silverberg's top lieutenants on the Windows 95 effort, hosted a group of outside Web developers at Microsoft's campus to discuss the company's future plans. "We got slaughtered," Ludwig says.

"Wow, there's a whole class of developers who we don't understand anymore," he realized. "We've lost their attention. They may be with small companies, but there are a set of guys for whom the traditional Windows messages don't fly. They think we're morons."

Microsoft relied on "independent software vendors," known in the industry as ISVs, to write Windows applications and thus make the underlying platform attractive to consumers. Microsoft evangelized developers to use Win32, the Windows platform for 32-bit systems. Windows' sagging popularity had become common knowledge. "We all know we have lost the attention of the leading edge of the ISV industry and that is spreading throughout the ISV industry," Ludwig wrote in a 1995 e-mail.

It was as if Microsoft had forgotten its own history. Was Windows' success a result of its elegant design or its stunning technical advances over other operating systems? Even inside Microsoft, the answer was no. Instead, software developers adopted Windows because it provided a great opportunity. With millions of machines running Windows, developers who wrote applications for the Windows platform could sell lots of copies. Microsoft bootstrapped the process, cajoling early developers and seeding the market. At "critical mass," it all took off. Microsoft cemented the loyalty by spending hundreds of millions of dollars each year to subsidize Windows developers with training, conferences, technical information, and forums to exchange information. With such inertia, Windows was likely to remain dominant for years to come.

"But when you start to lose the hearts and minds of the bleeding edge of developers, that's a warning sign that we don't get it," Ludwig

says. "For a large generation, Windows was not a compelling product. It didn't solve their problems. We just didn't have anything to
say."

It was becoming clear that the Internet was even bigger than Windows. Outside software developers wanted to know what Microsoft
was offering. Tod Nielsen, the gregarious evangelist for the Windows platform, was finding it increasingly difficult to keep the loyalty
of the developers.

"I want to write my user interface in HTML," the industry-
standard Web markup language, the developers told Nielsen.

"Write to Win32," Nielsen responded.

"That doesn't work," they told him.

Microsoft was facing the "lowest 'customer satisfaction' period
ever for Windows," Rich Tong, a veteran marketing vice president,
wrote in a memo. "We have a huge amount of work to fix the reputation Windows currently suffers from."

Allchin himself acknowledged the problems with Windows and
laid out the basics of a plan to fix the shortcomings. "From a perception level it's just not cool any more," he wrote in an e-mail to Gates.
Among the reasons: "Windows is viewed as old. . . . Windows is
viewed as complex. . . . Developers wonder if they can make money
on Windows."

Allchin found a fan at Waggener Edstrom, Microsoft's outside
public relations agency. He forwarded his plan to an account executive, Catherine Merten, and signed the cover note "Your Jamie." She
wrote back, "God, you are so good at what you do!" Allchin and
Merten were married a month later.

BY THE STANDARDS of university labs or the Silicon Valley start-
up scene, Silverberg may have been a late adopter of the Internet, but
he knew a software revolution when he saw one. He quickly seized
the opportunity and scrambled to recoup. Even before Windows 95
shipped, he assembled a crack Internet team at Microsoft. The Internet needn't undermine Windows, he thought. It could save it.

The last-minute effort to add a rudimentary Web browser to Windows 95 fell to Ben Slivka, a manic programmer known for wearing
shorts and Hawaiian shirts even in the coldest weather. Slivka also
had a reputation as one of Microsoft's most outspoken agitators. In
May 1995, he circulated a memo proclaiming "The Web is the next

platform." The popularity of the Web, he predicted, would soon rival, and even surpass, Windows. "If we don't quickly become the supplier of choice for Internet technology, the Internet will grow and change under someone else's influence, and we risk losing the standard-setting role [with the attendant profit margins] we have come to enjoy with MS-DOS and Windows [and Office]."

Other members of Silverberg's team put together a marketing blueprint for winning the browser war. Chris Jones and Thomas Reardon sent their sixteen-page memo, "How to Get 30% Share in 12 Months," to Gates to read during one of his Think Weeks. It was an audacious goal; at the time, Microsoft's share of the browser market barely registered in surveys.

Once again, 30 percent was the magic number. At that point, any Web developer would have to target Microsoft's browser in addition to Netscape's or risk forgoing a sizable chunk of the potential audience. Netscape would no longer be able to unilaterally dictate the direction of Internet standards.

The first task: cloning, or copying, Netscape's features through reverse-engineering. "Get serious about cloning Netscape," Silverberg's team proposed. "We must have a plan to clone all the features they have today, plus new ones they will add before our next release."

Next, they advocated aggressive tactics to drive adoption of Internet Explorer's unique features. "We should be prepared to write a check, buy sites, or add features—basically do whatever it takes to drive adoption," the memo said. Most important, Microsoft needed to enlist online services like America Online to integrate Microsoft's browser into their offerings. The memo even appeared to suggest hampering the performance of other browsers. "The Internet is part of Windows. We will bind the shell to Explorer, so that running any other browser is a jolting experience."

At the same time, Microsoft had to drop ambitions to drive its own standards in competition with the Internet. "We say we are open but we are still pushing proprietary formats in our Internet authoring tools," the team wrote. "Currently we are perceived as promoting our own agenda instead of trying to make the Internet easier for our customers."

Instead of pushing entirely separate standards, Microsoft would "embrace and extend" existing Internet standards. "Embrace and extend" was quickly derided by competitors as a euphemism for "engulf and devour." But it represented a shift for Microsoft. The old "lock-in" model had served its purposes, but now it was becoming a liability in the marketplace. Customers didn't want to get locked into proprietary approaches that limited their future choices.

Gates endorsed some but not all of the strategy proposals in his Pearl Harbor Day declaration of December 7, 1995. He made no apologies for Microsoft's efforts to clone Netscape's features. Cloning was a common industry tactic, he explained. Microsoft had cloned the Lotus 1–2–3 spreadsheet to create Excel. Word had mimicked every feature of WordPerfect. And Microsoft itself had faced clones of MS-DOS.

Gates treated his audience to a remarkably frank lesson in software economics. "There are always businesses that start up to build clones of that software," he said. "If they catch up, then the value of the software becomes zero." Now Microsoft would clone Netscape's browser, and when it did, Netscape's advantage would evaporate. "And so you get the interesting question: Will it be a case where everybody's tied in doing these things, in which case you've got about zero value?" Gates asked. "Or will one party or another be ahead on this?"

Gates showed a prototype of future Web technology that represented a new direction for the Windows user interface. The classic Windows desktop, with its icons and folders, was to be radically reinvented. The desktop would become more like a Web page, uniting information contained on a local computer's hard disk with all the information on the Internet.

Since the Windows UI was going to become more like the browser, rather than the other way around, responsibility for the Windows shell was left with Silverberg's browser group rather than moving under Allchin with the rest of the old Windows 95 team. But Gates was clear the new Internet direction did not imply a new organizational structure. "We're not forming an Internet division. To us, you know, it's like having an electricity division or a software division. The Internet is pervasive to everything that we're doing."

If Gates's declaration that day represented a stake in the ground, the Professional Developers Conference four months later was when Microsoft began to deliver on its Internet promises. For software developers, Microsoft's developers' conferences were the equivalent of papal encyclicals. Thousands of programmers gathered to find out in what direction the overlords from Redmond would take them.

On the eve of the developers' conference, two opposing camps inside Microsoft were still debating that question. On one side, the Internet "doves," led by Silverberg, argued for a faster and more complete embrace of the Internet. On the other, the Windows "hawks," led by Allchin, feared that approach would undermine the value of Windows. Silverberg had flouted Gates's public statement that Microsoft didn't need an Internet division and was leading more than twenty-five hundred employees in Microsoft's new Internet Platform and Tools Division, coining the division's name and circulating it publicly before anybody could object. The division claimed "overall strategy, development and marketing responsibility for Microsoft's Internet platform." Now the doves wanted to market their Internet technology as Microsoft's Active Platform, to play off of the ActiveX technology, a set of tools for creating more sophisticated Web sites.

The use of the "P" word was explosive. A platform is more than an operating system. It's a foundation for software development, including tools, interfaces, system services, and other features that programmers use to create and run their software. Control of a successful platform puts a company in the middle of a network of exponentially increasing returns; as developers create popular applications for a platform, demand for the platform grows, attracting more developers, driving more demand.

The Windows hawks objected to the introduction of a new platform, arguing that the offerings should be called simply a "framework," not a platform. Microsoft already had a platform: Windows. Allchin's goal of Windows unification depended on Win32 as a single development platform for both Windows 95 and NT. If Silverberg got his way, Microsoft would be sanctioning a new platform, an Internet platform.

That's what Silverberg wanted. To match Microsoft's competitors, who were boasting that they were making Windows obsolete, Silverberg had his own plan. "Let's obsolete Windows with Windows + ActiveX," read a slide from his presentation kicking off the new division. Bob Muglia, who under Silverberg oversaw nearly eight hundred employees creating tools for software developers, defined the new goal: "Reposition developer priority from Win32 to ActiveX."

On the day of the event, the company made a stunning series of announcements. First, Microsoft completed a deal with Sun Microsystems at 4:45 A.M. on the first day of the show to be able to announce that it had licensed Java, the computer language sweeping the industry.

Then Steve Jobs, the cofounder of Apple and at that point the chief executive of Next, came on stage to bless Microsoft's Internet efforts. When it came to cooperation in the industry, he said, Netscape was acting the way people expected Microsoft to behave, arrogantly and unilaterally imposing its own new standards. Microsoft was playing the role that seemed more suited to Netscape, cooperating with industry standards efforts and reaching out to outside developers.

The biggest coup was the announcement from AOL. A day earlier, Netscape had announced its own deal with the largest online service. But that was dramatically trumped by AOL's pact with Microsoft to make Internet Explorer the default browser in AOL's service.

Microsoft provided a major incentive for AOL to jump ship from Netscape by offering to include AOL's software in every copy of Windows. But it was Netscape's arrogance that helped drive AOL into Microsoft's arms. During the round-robin negotiations, Steve Case, AOL's chief executive, had told Netscape's executives in Mountain View, California, that he needed access to their source programming code and a joint team to make sure AOL users wouldn't have to leave the AOL "experience" to surf the Web with Netscape's browser. In Redmond the next day, Case complained to Silverberg that the Netscape executives had told him, "We'll give you what the fuck we want to give you, when the fuck we want to give it."

Microsoft showed off an early version of the next release of its browser, Internet Explorer 3.0. The team had pulled the browser apart and rebuilt it in discrete components. The architectural advance gave IE added appeal to makers of software applications, like AOL or Intuit, who could use the underlying technology to add Internet features to their own offerings and let users go directly to the Web from their programs. "Componentization" turned Internet Explorer into a platform. To use Netscape's browser, a user of Intuit's Quicken financial-planning software would have to leave the financial-planning software and call up a separate browser screen.

The developers' conference sent a signal that Microsoft intended to be at the center of the Internet revolution. "I remember feeling the two barrels of the shotgun being lowered to my forehead," remembers Mike McCue, who had just joined Netscape at the time. In many ways, McCue says, Microsoft understood the potential of Netscape's browser better than Netscape did. "Everywhere where Netscape should have been getting it, Microsoft was getting it, and Netscape wasn't."

Indeed, Microsoft's Internet doves believed they were doing more than just "winning the browser war" or "leading the Internet turn-around." As they were carried further by the Internet wave, they fan-cied they were reinventing the company, crafting a new positive image, and establishing a new set of working relationships with the rest of the industry. They were helping Microsoft make the transition from defensive adolescent to confident, respected adult. Silverberg was advocating a new way of gaining a competitive advantage.

Brad Chase, Silverberg's marketing vice president, defined the mission of the new Internet Platform and Tool Division in an internal memo: "Embrace and extend Internet standards and work in an open, cross platform way." The code words carried deep meanings inside Microsoft.

"Open" is perhaps the most abused word in the industry. Stripped of its moral attributes, it is simply a tactic. Attackers with low market share are apt to support "open" industry standards as a way to enlist allies to undermine an entrenched incumbent. Incumbents prefer to rely on proprietary, or "closed," interfaces to lock customers to their product line for as long as possible. "Open" is useful when you are coming from behind. "Closed" is what you can get away with when you gain market power. Because Microsoft was once again the chal-lenger, not the incumbent, Silverberg's group pledged to support the Internet's open standards and to submit specifications for its new fea-tures to industry standards bodies.

The idea was to turn the competitors' tricks back on them. Sun de-clared its Java software "open" in contrast to Microsoft's "closed" ap-proach and repeated the phrase so often that it was years before most of the industry figured out that Java was as proprietary as any soft-ware had ever been. Sun fiercely kept Java under its sole control.

Netscape similarly had been identified with an open, standards-based approach, maintaining the rhetoric even when it turned to uni-lateral extensions to defend its early market share lead. The press generally gave Netscape a pass, declaring them "open" even when they weren't. Netscape, as the incumbent on the defensive, was the one using its market share to lock in customers, while Microsoft, as the challenger, was starting to regain a measure of industry trust.

"Cross-platform" is another age-old debate. It's a classic trade-off: Software that works on multiple platforms can reach the largest possible market, but sacrifices the optimal performance and rich features made possible by taking advantage of each platform's unique features. Cross-platform software reduces performance and functionality to the lowest common denominator. Microsoft had long placed all its bets on the Windows platform. Silverberg's group was challenging that proposition.

What was emerging in the industry was a new mode of competition for the networked age. The way to gain an edge was by framing the debate and then executing fast enough to stay a step ahead of the competition. Delivering the first and best implementation of new technology won customers and market share, making it easier to frame the next debate for the next round of competition. It was possible to get the best of both worlds, a competitive advantage and the halo effect of being a good corporate citizen. In the early days of the browser war, Netscape had Microsoft "on a treadmill," scurrying to catch up by cloning its features. With the release of Internet Explorer 3.0 in August 1996, it was Netscape that was increasingly on the treadmill. The Microsoft Internet team fulfilled nearly every objective in the "How to Get to 30% in 12 Months" strategy paper.

Gates was eager to sing the praises of his Internet team. "Netscape said they were moving on Internet time, and they were quite a bit ahead of us," he said later. "So we must have been moving on two-times Internet time. Otherwise, how do you catch somebody moving on Internet time?"

COUNTERREFORMATION

As Silverberg's doves were riding high at the Professional Developers Conference, Allchin's hawks were fuming. The so-called Active Platform, Allchin said, was nothing but "marketecture," a coinage that merged "market" and "architecture" to imply the technology was little more than a set of PowerPoint slides to hoodwink the trade press.

"It was such a disaster, such a disaster," he told me later. "It was incomprehensible to me. Not from the presentation, because it sure looked good. But what was it? What pieces of code were included? Can you get a programming manual for this? Just ship me over a programming manual. I want to check out what kind of code I can write here. Where was the code? Do you have a manual? It was hugely confusing about what was in it."

Allchin's complaints were not merely technical. Now that he had been put in charge of the Windows groups, he was increasingly concerned that the new Internet platform effort was undermining his business.

After the release of Windows 95 in the summer of 1995, Allchin had gained responsibility for the entire Windows product line. The goal, as always, remained the unification of both strains of Windows on the NT code base. But with NT still not ready for the broad consumer market, Gates reluctantly decided that Microsoft needed to do yet one more release of classic Windows for consumers. The software, code-named Memphis and later called Windows 98, was to be a minor, perfunctory project that even Gates acknowledged lacked a clear "value proposition."

Allchin felt he had been sold a bill of goods. Silverberg had handed off responsibility for Windows 98 to Allchin but managed to keep most of the best programmers and managers from the Windows 95 effort by absorbing them into his new Internet division. To Allchin went the rump of the development team. "There wasn't much of a team left after Windows 95," Allchin says. "Most all of the higher IQ people were moved under Brad. There were basically no seasoned managers. Few to none of the senior developers stayed."

At least, he had hoped, with Windows united for the first time under a single executive there would be an end to the grueling parallel development efforts.

Instead, the old rivalry between Silverberg's Windows 95 team and Allchin's NT team morphed seamlessly into the new rivalry between Silverberg's Internet division and Allchin's Windows group.

As Allchin saw it, the Internet platform group was killing the incentives for users to upgrade to the next version of Windows, or for PC makers to install it on their machines. Some of the best features of the next release of Windows were being given away for free. In addition to the basic browser, Internet Explorer had grown to include other nominally separate Microsoft programs, including Outlook Express for e-mail, NetShow (later renamed Windows Media) for streaming audio and video, NetMeeting for group collaboration, and FrontPage Express for Web site creation—all for free.

"Grabbing more and more of Windows and shipping that everywhere for free—that's a way to destroy the business," Allchin said. "The team was just grabbing the source code out and then shipping, using it any way they could to serve their mission. That means the next version of Windows doesn't have any of those features, because they were already given away for free. . . . This was especially painful because of the user interface—which is a key upgrade generator. Absolutely, Windows 98 was hurt."

Silverberg's group was following through and delivering on the mission to which it was assigned—gain browser market share. As Chase had written, "The amount of revenue or income generated alone is not the right metric for our success moving forward." In contrast, Allchin was hard-core in defense of Windows' revenues. He mocked the mission of the Internet division: "Usage, usage, usage. Give away anything, it doesn't matter."

To rescue Windows, Allchin felt he needed to reclaim control of the crucial user interface. The shell was critical to how users experienced Windows. To have to depend on Silverberg's group to deliver it grated on Allchin. How could he accomplish the goal of Windows unification when he had no control over the very part that users would see, the technology that would define the products' look and feel? Once again, Silverberg had control of the center of innovation.

The executive nominally responsible for reconciling the conflict was Paul Maritz, effectively the third-ranking executive at Microsoft and the one responsible for almost all software development. Both Silverberg and Allchin reported to him. Born in Zimbabwe (then Rhodesia), raised in South Africa, and educated in Scotland, Maritz had a calm demeanor and sardonic wit. His low-key style helped moderate the strong opinions and raging egos that characterized many of Microsoft's best people. He prided himself on being a consensus-builder, but when it came to Microsoft's response to the Internet, consensus was hard to find.

As Ballmer once told a colleague, Allchin had an aggressive personality. Silverberg was passive-aggressive. Maritz, he said, was simply passive.

Maritz was torn. No one set of goals would remove the conflict. The only alternative was to pursue both strategies and tolerate the animosity. His instincts took him in the direction of the broader, more expansive view advocated by Silverberg. But his political instincts and the reality of protecting Microsoft's revenues in the short term led him toward Allchin's insistence on protecting the Windows franchise.

It was more than a popularity contest. Maritz controlled the flow of the most precious of Microsoft's resources—the ability to hire more engineers. At Microsoft, even senior vice presidents like Silverberg and Allchin don't have the authority to approve additional hires on their own. For a business like Microsoft, with no capital investment to speak of, humans are the capital. Control of "head count" is the ultimate lever to control the direction of the company.

Silverberg wanted more talent dedicated to pressing Internet challenges. "I don't see the top people mapped to the top challenges," he wrote to Maritz.

Concomitantly, Allchin feared he was losing influence with Maritz. As he saw it, the Internet team, with a head count of more than twenty-five hundred and growing, was sucking up all available resources and drawing the company's most talented people from Windows.

In a June 1996 memo detailing priorities for the coming year, Maritz declared, "Without browser share, everything is hard. So job #1 is browser share." The depth of the hole Windows was in was clear. Under "Windows and Overall Vision," he acknowledged, "Of necessity, we have focused most of our energy on the 'Internet' over [the] last 12 months. As a result of this, and other factors, we have lost our 'Windows' vision. . . . We need to re-create a positive vision of why Windows will be a rewarding environment over the next three years."

For most of 1996, Allchin fought a rearguard battle. Allchin didn't agree with Maritz's emphasis on browser share. If everything was free, all the market share in the world wouldn't generate any revenues. To Allchin, the issue was how to drive upgrades to Windows. That's what Microsoft got paid for.

Allchin had to turn Maritz around. "He controlled this. He wasn't operating the way I wanted him to operate," Allchin told me. "He and I had a difference of opinion about the impact that some of the decisions might have."

Indeed, by the fall of 1996, Allchin was making headway. He convinced Maritz to drop the marketing buzzwords if not the strategy effort around the Internet platform and to make clear that Microsoft's platform remained Windows.

As for Gates, "Some of this was happening underneath his radar. That's why I was trying to get it up. I don't know if he really knew what was happening." Eventually, Allchin told me, "Bill did weigh in to help this."

In a reorganization in October, Silverberg was reluctantly persuaded to take over supervision of the group in charge of Office, Microsoft's other blockbuster product. Silverberg still had control of the

Internet Explorer browser, but the word "platform" had been dropped from the name of his division. The golden era of the Internet Platform and Tools Division had lasted barely six months.

For Allchin, the changes didn't go far enough. "The marketing had pulled back some, but not all the way to where things were clearly unified," he says.

During the 1996 holiday season, he hammered home his point in a series of e-mails to Maritz and Gates. On the Friday before Christmas, Allchin worked at home because he had a dentist's appointment later. He pounded out an impassioned note to Maritz, "Concerns for Our Future."

"I said I would drop you a note with some of my concerns," he began. Under the heading, "Ensuring that we leverage Windows," Allchin wrote, "I don't understand how IE is going to win. The current path is simply to copy everything that Netscape does packaging and product wise." Because Netscape commanded 80 percent market share, users wouldn't switch if Internet Explorer merely matched Navigator feature-for-feature. "Maybe being free helps us, but once people are used to a product, it is hard to change them," he said.

He drove his point home: "My conclusion is we must leverage Windows more." Treating IE as just an add-on to Windows loses Microsoft's biggest advantage, he said: "Windows market share."

In the next line, he suggested finding ways "to leverage Windows technically more. . . . We need to advantage Windows," Allchin said. "We should think first about an integrated solution—that is our strength."

Allchin's primary concern came in the second section, headed "Making Money on Windows." He was trying to block retail distribution of Internet Explorer, which he believed would undermine the appeal of Windows. "I'm being simplistic, but I think our money should come from Office and Windows," he wrote. "Our strength is Windows, let's not get confused."

Allchin signed off at ten minutes to nine. "I have to go to the dentist. . . ."

Allchin's next long e-mail exchange with Maritz, just after New Year's 1997, pressed the integration argument again.

"You see browser share as job 1," Allchin began, making clear he didn't agree with the formulation. The real platform battle, he said, was not Microsoft's browser versus Netscape's browser, but rather

Windows versus browsers generally. Allchin wasn't worried about Internet Explorer. He was worried about Windows.

"I do not feel we are going to win on our current path. We are not leveraging Windows from a marketing perspective and we are trying to copy Netscape and make IE into a platform. We do not use our strength—which is that we have an installed base of Windows and we have a strong (PC) shipment channel for Windows. . . . I am convinced we have to use Windows, this is the one thing they don't have. . . . For some reason, we are in heavy copy mode against Netscape. . . . It is not a long term winning strategy. We have to be competitive with features, but we need something more—Windows integration."

Allchin continued: "If you agree that Windows is a huge asset, then it follows quickly that we are not investing sufficiently in finding ways to tie IE and Windows together. This must come from you. . . ."

The two executives appeared to agree to delay the release of the next version of Windows in order to more tightly integrate the browser into Windows, even if PC makers "suffered." The government used this e-mail later to bolster its argument that Microsoft harmed PC makers, and thus consumers, by delaying improvements in Windows for the sake of advancing the browser war against Netscape.

Allchin argued for marketing new features as Windows, not IE. "The platform is Windows. Our upgrade is Memphis [Windows 98]. And included in the upgrade should be everything we can possibly think of to make it compelling—every drop of new IE features we can get."

Maritz seemed to agree. "I agree that we have to make Windows integration our basic strategy." Windows would be delayed to enable Microsoft to "synch" it with the next release of Internet Explorer, "even if it means missing" the June deadline for delivering the new version of Windows to PC makers in time for Christmas sales.

Allchin was only partially mollified. "The 'platform' issue and how we are going to win with IE is very confusing. We are risking Windows' future here in a serious way."

A month later, Allchin took his case directly to Gates in a long e-mail dramatically titled "Losing a Franchise—The Microsoft Windows Story (a new Harvard case study)."

"I'm sure this subject got your attention," Allchin wrote. "It's what I worry about every day when I shower, run, eat, etc."

Most frustrating to Allchin was the Internet Explorer team's plan to release versions not only for Windows but for other operating systems as well. That would make other platforms as attractive as Windows and confer no advantages on Microsoft. "I consider this cross-platform issue a disease within Microsoft," he wrote. "We are determined to put a gun to our head and pull the trigger."

Allchin pursued his agenda of reclaiming control over Microsoft's primary user interface, the key to the evolution of the platform. "On our current path, Internet Explorer 4 will not be very integrated into Windows," he wrote. "The IE team is not focused on this problem and I was requested to shut down my user interface/shell team. On our current path, I just don't feel that Windows can win."

The next morning, Gates responded to Allchin's pleas. The company had lost its way, he agreed. Like Allchin, Gates was less afraid of losing the Internet than he was of losing the Windows franchise. As Microsoft's "single point of integration," Gates was the one person with ultimate responsibility for all parts of the company. It was his duty to enforce decisions for the overall good of Microsoft as he saw it, even if that might put individual products at a disadvantage in a particular market. Many of Microsoft's best innovations were killed before they ever came to market. Inside Microsoft, such sacrifices were known as paying the "strategy tax."

"I agree that making sure applications are primarily on Windows is something we have lost site [sic] of," Gates wrote to Allchin. The notion that Microsoft should provide advanced features for other platforms besides Windows is a result of the "free lunch syndrome we have allowed to develop."

Allchin's e-mail messages later became central to the government's antitrust case. Allchin's suggestion that Microsoft use technical integration to "tie" the Internet Explorer browser to Windows, and use Windows' market share and clout with PC makers to drive browser adoption were red flags for prosecutors looking for violations of the antitying provisions of antitrust law.

The government's interpretation of the e-mails largely ignores the context in which Allchin argued his position. The e-mails primarily illustrate corporate infighting, Microsoft-style. Allchin's real agenda was to unify Microsoft's marketing and technical approach around Windows and reestablish his NT effort as the center of Microsoft's strategy. In particular, he wanted to eliminate the annoying dependencies he still had on Silverberg for technology pieces like the user interface shell.

"We were scattering our powerful momentum," Allchin told me

later. "Let me make it more blunt: We were scattering both strong teams."

Allchin is convincing when he argues that browser market share was not his primary concern; his priority was Windows revenues. "This is at the core of most everything I was doing," he said. "I was trying to make money for Windows."

More damaging to the government's interpretation is the sequence of events. Whatever his motivations, Allchin's suggestions for deeper integration between Windows and Internet Explorer were not responsible for IE's success. Allchin was simply wrong about the prospects for Internet Explorer. Internet Explorer 3.0, released in August 1996, was already generating huge momentum in the war for browser market share. Microsoft succeeded in blunting the platform challenge from Netscape and Sun even before the company adopted the strategy of deeper technical integration that Allchin advocated. Microsoft's browser market share was only 20 percent when Allchin sent his messages. But it was already on an inexorable march to market share dominance. Internet Explorer usage passed the magic 30 percent mark in April 1997, only a few months after Allchin's e-mail. According to Microsoft's internal surveys, it hit 36 percent by September and 40 percent by November, long before Microsoft implemented his suggestions. Internet Explorer's browser market share eventually surpassed Netscape's in June 1998, at the very time the more extensive integration of Internet Explorer and Windows was finally implemented.

As Internet Explorer gained momentum, it was becoming clear to Gates and others that the biggest threats to the Windows platform came not from outside competitors but from Microsoft's own Internet team. Netscape and Sun had been largely contained. Now it was Microsoft's own Internet team that was encouraging developers to build Web-based application programs that worked on multiple operating systems, not only Windows. As Allchin had argued, Microsoft's own architects were laying the foundation for a cross-platform Internet strategy that would let customers switch from Windows with no real penalty. Without the hooks to Windows, developers and users would be free to switch to rival offerings, effectively commoditizing Windows. The most formidable competitor to Allchin's Windows group was not Netscape but Silverberg's Internet team.

If Microsoft had "turned on a dime" to join the Internet revolution in 1995, now it was turning partway back. The counterreformation had begun.

Gates saw an opportunity to correct the situation in January 1997. Microsoft's other mainstay, Office, was finally getting overhauled for the Internet. Many members of the Office team naively believed that simply building a better product would be enough. But Gates was insecure, nervous about the fleeting nature of popularity. If something better came along, people could simply switch. He wanted Office to raise the switching costs. He directed them to build in hooks to lock in customers. Gates pummeled the Office team in regular product review sessions for not being "strategic" enough.

The Office team faced an increasingly common paradox at Microsoft—whether to continue to use Microsoft's proprietary formats or adopt the open standards of the Web. For developers planning the new version of Office, the issue was whether to use only the Web's industry-standard presentation method, known as hypertext markup language, or HTML. By sticking to the plain-vanilla version of HTML, documents and spreadsheets created in Office would look equally good with any browser. Alternatively, Microsoft could improve the presentation of documents by adopting its own "tags" or extensions and offer specialized features that worked only with Internet Explorer. The second approach would require anybody who wanted to take advantage of those features in Office to use Internet Explorer, even if they otherwise preferred Netscape's browser.

The question was emblematic of the strategic crosscurrents that Microsoft faced in trying to move toward the Internet while protecting its own entrenched products. Left purely on its own, the Office team might well have opted to satisfy all of its customers, Netscape and IE users alike. Since Netscape held by far the larger share of the market, the customer-centric approach would have been to make Netscape support the highest priority. Moreover, the team knew that customers resent artificial complications that make it harder for them to do their jobs.

In an e-mail titled "HTML 'Openness,' " Gates bluntly signaled to his key lieutenants that he placed Microsoft's strategic advantage above concern for customers. Customer needs were nowhere mentioned in the message.

"People were suggesting that Office had to work equally well with all browsers and that we shouldn't force Office users to use our browser," Gates wrote. "This is wrong and I wanted to correct this." Gates decreed Microsoft needed to lock users to the browsers through tags "that we view as Office/Windows/Microsoft specific."

If Microsoft doesn't get to do anything "proprietary" with HTML in the browser, Gates wrote, then "we have to stop viewing HTML as central to our strategy and get on another strategy."

To Silverberg's Internet team, Gates's e-mail was confirmation that the counterreformation was in full swing. Gates's e-mail was a signal to the top executives on the product teams to take a sharp turn away from Internet standards and away from HTML. Now that the immediate Netscape threat had been turned back, Microsoft was retrenching around Windows.

Similar debates were playing out across Microsoft. In the same way that Gates began to view Microsoft's Internet team as the internal representation of Netscape, he came to see Microsoft's Java team as the internal agents of Sun Microsystems.

It wasn't that Silverberg's Internet doves were soft on Sun. Indeed, Slivka and Ludwig urged, let's sue them before they sue us. Almost as soon as Microsoft agreed to license Java from Sun, it became clear that any cooperation between the two companies was unlikely. Sun complained that Microsoft was pushing proprietary extensions to splinter the Java community; Microsoft complained that Sun was excluding it from information about its plans that was called for under the licensing contract. But caution prevailed at higher levels. Maritz and Bob Muglia, the senior vice president who negotiated the original deal, advocated détente with Sun. (In October 1997, Sun sued Microsoft in U.S. District Court in San Jose, California. The dispute was settled in January 2001.)

It was that a new Java platform, whether it came from Sun or Microsoft, threatened Windows. Sun's missteps and the performance limitations in the technology had blunted the immediate threat from Java. Now, Microsoft's team was effectively overcoming those limitations with some of the best Java technology in the industry. "We are racing to improve a technology that competes with our core franchise," Charles Fitzgerald, one of Microsoft's sharpest strategists, wrote in a November 1996 e-mail.

Gates began to redirect Microsoft's own Java efforts. At a crucial meeting in March 1997, he jumped on Slivka, who was assigned to work on Java after leading the IE 3.0 effort.

Slivka advocated an embrace-and-extend strategy to beat Sun with better features, performance, and execution in Java. If Microsoft could do a better job than Sun in appealing to Java programmers, it could effectively wrest control of the platform.

Now, as he started his presentation, Slivka showed a PowerPoint slide on Microsoft's Java strategy that made no mention of Windows.

"Why don't you just give up your stock options and join the Peace Corps?" Gates is said to have thundered. "Hasn't anybody here ever heard of Windows? Windows is what this company is about!"

It wasn't the first time Gates had lit into Slivka. Gates had called him a communist and worse. "What are you on, the 'Fuck Windows' strategy?" Gates once asked him.

This time, Slivka was devastated. "Bill is really pissed about this Java stuff, doesn't respond to my email and that one review meeting we had he just jumped all over me, accusing me of trying to destroy Windows," Slivka complained in an April 1997 e-mail to a colleague. "Bill was amazingly, unnecessarily rude to me."

Later, Slivka was philosophical about the drubbing he took. "Bill has to be a pillar and a rock in what Microsoft is doing, and that's Windows and Office. Whenever anybody attacks that, he has to defend Microsoft. That defensiveness overshadowed everything else."

After Gates's outbursts, the demoralization spread beyond the small Java group to the rest of Silverberg's Internet team. Their high-brow pretensions about pioneering a new way of doing business at Microsoft appeared to be hopelessly naive. The Internet team was enjoying growing market share and the attention of a new generation of software developers eager to exploit the new Internet opportunity. But rather than reinvent the company, it seemed the team had simply won a defensive battle that allowed the company to retrench.

Allchin wanted his Windows team to be given responsibility for combating Java. "I do have a major problem about ANY of this work reporting to Bens," he said, using Slivka's e-mail handle. "I do not support this. If you want some other team to do this work, then you should move it to the tools group away from Ben."

Silverberg had already started to count the days until he could take off on a long-planned sabbatical. By April and May 1997, he was taking long training bike rides during lunch and spending hours planning the itinerary and logistics of a major bike trip. The rides helped him burn off his pent-up frustration. The rest of the Internet team seemed to retreat into their offices, no longer able to summon the energy needed to try to convince Gates that they were trying to save Microsoft, not kill Windows.

By the time of Microsoft's next Professional Developers Conference, in August 1997, the Internet platform initiative was dead and Windows was back at the center of Microsoft's plans. "The right things happened," Allchin says. "A whole bunch of confluences happened that made people reevaluate. Confusion from developers was certainly one. Confusion internally was another one."

Allchin makes no apologies for defending the Windows franchise. In our interview, his voice rose, taking on a steely intensity when he talked about the responsibility he feels.

"Do you know how hard it is to make the kind of money we make here?" he asked. "It's not like that's so easy. It's so hard. It consumes my thinking, totally, my life. I've become consumed, like so many of us are here. Bill has had many sleepless nights and so have I, where we are trying to figure out, how could we be run over? What's the next thing we could possibly do to grow revenues?

"I don't want to be remembered as the guy who destroyed one of the most amazing businesses in history. We could have done it with engineers who didn't understand and didn't have any responsibility for financial aspects of the company at all. Who live in this paradise where the stock goes up, revenues keep going up, earnings keep going up. And all they have to do is crank software. Somehow it gets into packages and makes us money. Well, it doesn't work that way. I've written a lot of software and you have to think about how to make money with that software. We're running a very fast race car here. You can take it off the road pretty fast.

"I know that when the day is over, I will be judged as 'Am I the guy that kept the company funded?' There is tremendous responsibility on me to not screw up.

"I'm on shift now. I'm on duty. I'm on watch."

The Path Not Taken

STALL

Bill Gates's public persona as technology visionary masked his private agenda as he greeted VIPs in the back of the cavernous warehouse on San Francisco's waterfront. In the front of the hall, Internet arrivistes, Microsoft employees, and media camp followers like me sipped the company's wine and traded gossip and business cards. It was September 1997, and Wall Street was in love with all things Internet. Venture capitalists were ladling out money to nearly any start-up with a business plan laying claim to a corner of the Web. The warehouse at Fort Mason, the closed army base turned trendy conference and arts center in the city's Marina district, was filled with demo booths. At each one, fresh-faced marketers from the fourteen Internet service providers, fifty PC makers, and two-hundred corporations Microsoft lined up for the launch were touting their support for Internet Explorer 4.0.

Raffle prizes included a $25,000 travel spree, thousands of music CDs, and walk-on roles on television's *Friends* and *er*, courtesy of Warner Brothers, which had secured one of the TV-style channels featured on the revamped Windows desktop screen that came with the new browser. With the launch of its newest Web browser, Microsoft was going all out to proclaim its leadership of the Internet revolution.

Gates was to deliver the keynote speech. An undistinguished orator, he could nonetheless usually be counted on to paint a picture of the bright digital future. But tonight, rather than pumping up the pace at which the Internet was transforming the software industry, his intent was to slow it down. Like a college basketball coach calling for his players to go into a stall, he was trying to shift the browser war to a slower tempo with which Microsoft was more comfortable. Gates had reason to think he held the deciding vote in determining how fast the Internet changed the software business. And he was voting to slow it down.

One phase was over, another was beginning. Microsoft had completed the Internet Day strategy Gates had announced twenty months earlier. Microsoft's projections showed that the new version of IE would push the company's market share versus Netscape's Navigator above 50 percent. All that remained on the browser front was the mop-up operation.

As a result, Gates had decided to dismantle Silverberg's Internet team that had brought the company to the brink of victory. The team, which since 1995 had operated on the frenetic pace "Internet time" with its own goals, marketing, and breakneck release schedule, would be merged into Allchin's more deliberate Windows organization, which released new versions only every two years, if then.

Allchin would get control of browser development and, with it, the all-important Windows shell. Internet Explorer is the shell for Windows. The browser is part of the operating system. Ergo, the team goes to Allchin. Silverberg would just have to get with the program.

Persuading him was not going to be easy. "Something happens to a guy when his net worth passes $100 million," Gates mused to associates. Gates shouldn't have had to deal with Silverberg at all; Maritz was nominally in charge of such things.

Silverberg hadn't displayed any particular urgency about getting back to work. His meeting with Maritz to discuss his new responsibilities was postponed several times. Maritz says he wanted Silverberg back, and so did Gates, but it was time for him to fall into line. The split, both strategic and personal, between Silverberg and Allchin had gone on too long.

The previous October, Maritz had shut down Silverberg's Internet Platform and Tools Division but let him keep control of the browser as long as he also took over responsibility for Office. Now that IE 4.0 was finished, the other shoe was dropping. Microsoft no longer wanted an Internet team separate from Windows evangelizing developers with a message different from the Windows message.

When they did meet, Maritz got right to the point. The browser is going to Allchin, Maritz told him. Your job is Office.

"I guess there's no place for me at the company," Silverberg said.

Silverberg considered his efforts from 1995 to 1997 to lead Microsoft's Internet turnaround to be the high point of his career. "It was a magical experience," he says. "The team and I were completely tapped into the positive energy of the Internet."

In contrast, Office was the big, lumbering desktop software suite that was nearly as dominant as, and even more profitable than, Windows. Office's run as the company's cash cow lasted far longer than anybody at Microsoft had predicted. But now it needed a major overhaul. Silverberg never clicked with the Office team; his year overseeing the group was one of the worst of his life. He didn't have any interest in arm-wrestling again with the Office veterans. Office projected no larger vision, in Silverberg's view; the team was doing little more than adding feature after feature to Word, Excel, PowerPoint, and Outlook.

No move at Microsoft was really final until all appeals were exhausted. That laid nearly all important decisions at Gates's feet. But the unpleasantness could wait until after the festivities. Gates invited Silverberg to fly back to Seattle with him on his chartered jet. Gates and Silverberg would have a chance to talk.

Rather than delivering a rousing pep talk for the browser launch, Gates delivered a sobering reality check. His predictions for the growth of the Internet were hardly bold. "It's my belief, or my prediction, that a decade from now, the majority of Americans will be living a Web lifestyle," he said. "They will all turn to the Web several times a day for information, entertainment and communication."

But, he said, "This is going to take a long time to catch on in a big way." As for dramatic predictions about the growth of the Web in 1998 or 1999, he said, "we always fall short." It would take until about 2007, Gates believed, for the Web to reach "critical mass," which he believed required widespread availability of high-speed connections, large-screen flat-panel displays, voice recognition, and PCs that cost less than a reasonably priced television. Lots of people were trying to figure out "what business will be valuable, what businesses will be less valuable than they are today." But he warned, "Critical mass takes time."

To many in the crowd, Gates's forecasts seemed tepid in light of the near-vertical growth curves over the previous two years for anything connected to the Internet. Broadband connections and flat-panel displays might indeed be slow in coming to homes, but many people were surfing the Web and using e-mail over the high-speed lines in their offices. Pent-up demand, inventive hacks, and the flood of new Web-based shopping and services meant that the Internet was already growing much faster than Gates's projections.

"In some ways I feel like taking a 10-year time frame for my prediction is being very conservative," Gates acknowledged. "One thing that forces me to be conservative is, I know I'll be here in ten years and so people will be able to tell me whether I was right or wrong about that."

Silverberg listened to Gates from the shadows at the edge of the hall. He was in West Coast outdoor-casual, blue jeans, and fleece pullover, and his tanned face and lean body projected fitness. His receding hairline was offset by his thick, full beard. By rights, he could have been on center stage for the launch festivities. Officially, it was still his team that had delivered the new browser. But he had no desire to be part of the carefully scripted event. He was as good as gone. He knew he was a ghost. A calm, relaxed ghost, but a ghost nonetheless.

Silverberg recognized Gates's tone as more than simple caution. Gates liked to say that if Microsoft went out of business it wouldn't be because it was not focused on the Internet; it would be because it was *too* focused on the Internet. Now, however, he was laying down a rationale for his decision to subordinate the development of a new Internet platform to the defense of Windows. Gates thought that the Web was going to take ten years to reach critical mass; that gave the company a decade to make the transition from its current PC-based business.

This was far too slow for Silverberg. The company, he thought, had always been slow to grasp the Internet. They preferred to believe the PC wave would continue to dominate the computer industry.

"The company made some of the wrong choices by taking the go-slow route," he said later. "Change, especially change that so directly affects a company's foundations, is hard. Life would have been easier for Microsoft if the world wasn't changing so fast. But it was. There was no turning it back. My view was to either get out in front fast or fall behind."

In Silverberg's seven years at Microsoft, he and Gates had established a workable entente but had never become particularly close.

Now the two men were more distant than ever. Intuitive and intense, Silverberg lacked the glib, rapid-fire style of Gates's favorite play-mates. He was certainly "hard-core," delivering a string of block-busters, from MS-DOS 5 and 6, through Windows 3.1 and 95, to Internet Explorer. But he insisted on complete mastery of his own domain and tightly controlled communication into and out of his groups. He spent more time trying to keep Gates from meddling in his projects than he did in cultivating a close relationship.

"To be honest, I worry that sometimes you get a distorted pic-ture/account of things," Silverberg wrote to Gates in a June 1995 e-mail. "For the guy at the top, that can be dangerous, as you need the best info possible so you can make the best decisions."

Silverberg had been 90 percent sure that he wasn't returning to Microsoft when he left on his bicycle trip. He rode seventeen hun-dred miles through British Columbia during his sabbatical in the summer of 1997. It had taken too much pain to get the company turned around on the Internet only to have them then treat it as an opportunity to retrench rather than change. Silverberg rejected the suggestion that his efforts were killing Windows. As he saw it he was trying to save Windows and to reclaim the mantle of leadership for Microsoft, and was doing a decent job at it.

The bike trip had changed him. Before he set out, he had become friends with Lance Armstrong, the world-class bicycle racer who right then was going through aggressive chemotherapy for a cancer that had spread from one of his testicles to his lungs and brain. Sil-verberg had read about Armstrong in a cycling magazine, and the two communicated frequently by e-mail and phone. Armstrong's story helped Silverberg keep the disputes at Microsoft in perspective.

"My illness was humbling and starkly revealing, and it forced me to survey my life with an unforgiving eye," Armstrong later wrote in his memoir. "I had to ask myself, 'If I live, who is it that I intend to be?' I found that I had a lot of growing to do as a man."

Silverberg helped support Armstrong's cancer foundation, and Armstrong sent Silverberg a couple of racing jerseys, which he wore for inspiration through the long, tough mountain passes.

In June, Silverberg had set out from Arlington, outside Seattle. He rode east along Washington State Route 20, one of the most beauti-ful roads in the world, bisecting North Cascades National Park. He traversed the Idaho panhandle and a corner of Montana and crossed into Canada through Glacier National Park. He eased into the rhythms of cycling, far more peaceful than Microsoft's frenetic pace. Two weeks into the trip, he climbed the 4,580-foot Crowsnest Pass from east to west, dropped into the town of Fernie, and phoned home. The answering machine message alerted him that his wife had gone to Germany to be with their eleven-year-old son, Danny, whose summer in Europe was cut short by a stay in the hospital for an emergency appendectomy. Silverberg joined them there as quickly as he could.

Near the end of August, Silverberg resumed his trip, this time riding in the opposite direction. Heading west from Lake Louise, he crossed back into British Columbia. The frustrations of the previous year at Microsoft receded. He resolved to change the balance in his life, to be a better father and husband. He turned south at Golden and rode through Rogers, Revelstoke, Nakusp, Ainsworth, Cranbrook, back to Fernie, and finally to Glacier National Park again, where his family met him for the drive home.

Now, a month after the end of the bike trip, he was even more sure he would not return to Microsoft. At forty-three, wealthier than he had ever imagined, he had to be true to himself. He would go back only for something he believed in and felt passionate about. It had to be something he enjoyed at least as much as he enjoyed his freedom, which was a lot. Otherwise, he thought, why do it?

The Internet Explorer launch was his first public appearance since he had come back. Silverberg spotted Greg Maffei and handed him a twenty-dollar bill. Maffei knew exactly which bet he had won. Before he left, Silverberg had wagered that Maffei couldn't strike a deal with Apple before he returned. All through the spring of 1997, Silverberg had been working on Apple as well, trying to get them committed to Internet Explorer while at the same time defusing a threatened patent infringement lawsuit, for which Apple was demanding a staggering $1.2 billion to settle. Silverberg tried to interest Gil Amelio, Apple's chief executive, in the vision of standing on stage with Bill Gates, arm in arm, announcing a strategic partnership between the two old enemies. Striking an Apple-Microsoft alliance required a Nixon-going-to-China stroke of boldness; Amelio wavered. When Amelio resigned and Steve Jobs took over as acting CEO, Maffei closed the deal. Silverberg read about it in the newspaper during a rest stop on his trip.

It wasn't hard to understand Gates's affection for the PC era. It had been the company's finest hour. Brad Chase, Silverberg's marketing vice president, laid out the appeal in an April 1997 planning memo titled "Preserving the Desktop Paradise." Chase wrote: "We have the opportunity to regain total leadership within a year and pass the 51% share mark with IE 4.0. If we do that, we will enjoy the comfortable position of the leader that we have achieved in most of our businesses."

Jeff Raikes caught perfectly the company's mood in a slick music video he produced for the annual sales meeting. Raikes's takeoff on Coolio's "Gangsta's Paradise" began *"Been working most our lives getting to a Windows paradise."* Microsoft executives, dressed like Guardian Angels, strutted through an inner-city concrete jungle.

> *Clark and Andreessen*
>   *There's no Net-escaping*
> *It was fun while it lasted,*
>   *enjoy the ride*
> *Now we're back,*
>   *better run and hide*
> *. . . We're going to win this fight to keep our Windows paradise.*

Silverberg's sense of separation deepened when Gates turned the podium over to Chase, Microsoft's top product marketer. He had been at Silverberg's side for the spectacular success of Windows 95, and they were comrades-in-arms all through the early days of the browser war. Chase was one of the people at Microsoft with whom Silverberg felt the most kinship. The two were so closely identified they were known to the PR people, and thus to reporters, as "The Brads," or sometimes, Big Brad and Little Brad.

The early plans for IE 4 had been so impressive that in 1996 the *New York Times* had trumpeted on its front page that Microsoft was "preparing to release new software that would bring the most fundamental change to personal computers since the machines were invented in the 1970s."

Now that it was done, IE 4 hardly seemed to merit such claims. Instead of replacing the decade-old Windows screen, with its clunky icons and folders and drop-down menus, with the more intuitive, fluid feel of a Web browser, Microsoft had done the opposite: preserved the classic Windows desktop and cluttered it even further with the "channels" for specially created Web sites from major media companies.

"This year, we are betting the farm on channels," Chase had written in an April 1997 global marketing plan. "We strongly feel that channels is the single most compelling hook for users and this is the killer feature we will promote the most."

Microsoft's goal was to convince Web producers to create sites that worked best, or only, with its browser. In a 1996 strategy memo, Chase wrote, "The best way to make people switch browsers is to make sure they have to, in order to get the best content."

Winning any kind of preferential treatment for Microsoft was a tough proposition when Internet Explorer's market share was negligible compared to Navigator. Now, with "Active Desktop," Chase could lure major media companies to produce Web sites specially tailored for Internet Explorer by using the power of Windows. Instead of merely a spot on the browser, Chase offered a button, or channel, right on the familiar Windows desktop of nearly 100 million new PCs a year.

Chase gamely soldiered through his presentation. Blah, blah, blah: "Take my entire desktop and create an HTML page." Blah blah blah: "Customize my desktop with the information I need." Blah blah blah: "Latest news or sports scores."

As he watched the demonstrations and listened to the speeches, Silverberg couldn't shake the feeling that Internet Explorer 4.0 had gone badly awry. "I just didn't like it," he later told government lawyers. Pressed to explain, he hedged. "I'm just not happy with the way it turned out. And I wasn't happy during the development of IE 4. My team knows it."

INTEGRATION

Microsoft's organizational and technical problems mirrored the legal challenge they were about to face. They all had roots in the same core question: how tightly to tie together the Internet Explorer browser and the Windows operating system.

Microsoft, as usual, wanted it both ways: the Web and Windows, the new thing and the old thing, offense and defense. The company wanted to create a next-generation Internet platform while at the same time defending Windows' dominance.

Either strategy separately had merits. Straddling the line is what mucked things up.

The browser team under Silverberg had paid homage to the company line that Internet Explorer was always "a part of Windows." But for two-and-a-half years, since the summer of 1995, the company had kept Internet and Windows development separate, with separate teams, separate release schedules, separate technology initiatives that in some cases were directly competitive and separate measurements for success.

To be competitive with Netscape, Silverberg had successfully fought to uncouple the browser team's timetable from the Windows release schedule, which he thought was too slow and encumbered by the requirements of testing a massive operating system against thousands of combinations of hardware and software. Because the browser was "lighter," and didn't have to do everything, it was possible to "rev" it much faster than Windows.

That didn't stop them, of course, from using Windows' marketing clout to boost distribution of the browser. Internet service providers that adopted Internet Explorer, for example, got a spot in the ISP folder on the Windows desktop; content providers that promoted IE got a spot on the new "channel bar" on the Windows desktop; and PC makers that bundled Microsoft's browser got a lower price for Windows.

But now, Microsoft's Internet technology and market momentum had advanced far enough so that many members of the team felt ready to let go of the Windows crutch. They began to resent the implication that they needed Windows' coattails to prevail over Netscape.

From the other side, Allchin argued the company should never have given Internet Explorer a life of its own. Browsing was simply a function of Windows. IE 4 should simply be the next release of Windows, at the time code-named Memphis and later released as Windows 98.

The strategic split had hobbled the development effort from the start. In February 1997, Allchin had written to Gates, "On our current path, IE 4 will not be very integrated into Windows. The IE team is not focused on this problem." Allchin complained to Maritz that the poor quality and bloated size of the IE 4 software was hampering his efforts on Windows. "Both the Memphis and NT teams are totally frustrated with the IE 4 situation," he wrote. "They say, 'You committed they would do the right thing and they aren't. Either make them or give us control of the pieces we need.' " The Windows group was blocked from even checking out the latest code from the

IE 4 team's central server. "They are told they cannot because IE is trying to get a beta, etc. So progress here stops. The objectives are just different."

Gates took notice. In his March 1997 review of the Memphis efforts, Gates declared "IE 4 and Memphis are joined at the hip."

But cooperation between the teams was at a new low. Jonathan Roberts, in charge of Windows marketing, lobbied Silverberg's team to pay more attention to Windows. "I believe our current path where it is the third or fourth priority is off strategy," he wrote.

"IE 4 is not being developed as joined to Memphis at the hip—at present Memphis is an afterthought," Carl Stork, who headed the Windows 98 effort at the time, reported to Allchin a few days later. The browser team wasn't even using Memphis to test its code and was advising the Windows team to release its early "beta" version—when most of the final features are supposed to be in place—with the old shell.

The Windows 98 team decided to use the old shell but to keep the change secret. "We cannot disclose the possibility of shipping Memphis without IE 4," wrote Moshe Dunie, Allchin's deputy. "Plan of record is still to have IE 4."

The challenges facing Internet Explorer 4 had become clear months earlier at the Comdex computer show in Las Vegas in November 1996. In Netscape's suite at the Las Vegas Hilton, Mike McCue, one of Netscape's top developers, showed me how Netscape's "Constellation" software could wrap around Windows and provide users with access to both the Internet and the contents of their own hard disk drive. McCue was on the verge of closing deals with major PC makers to package Constellation with their machines. It had all but signed up content providers who were eager to "push" information straight to the Constellation desktop. McCue assured me Netscape had a deal with PointCast, at the time the leader in desktop delivery of news and business information. Netscape was gaining traction in its efforts to push Windows off the PC desktop altogether.

A competing shell around Windows was exactly what Microsoft long feared. If it became popular, other software makers would begin to tailor their applications to the new shell rather than to Windows. The balance of power would shift. The leader would become the follower. Microsoft knew how that game worked: It had done the same thing in making the switch from DOS to Windows.

Even before McCue went to Las Vegas, he knew Microsoft had already taken steps to defend its desktop franchise. In September, an IBM executive told McCue Microsoft had created new restrictions in its Windows 95 license to protect the "Windows Experience" by preventing PC makers from modifying the Windows shell. "This effectively locks" PC makers into Internet Explorer, McCue wrote to colleagues at Netscape, and "shuts out" alternative shells, such as Constellation.

The new licensing restrictions put a strain on Microsoft's relations with PC makers. Some of the manufacturers developed shells of their own to help new users. Others had hoped to auction off their valuable desktop real estate to the highest bidders. The new restrictions effectively prevented PC makers from installing any software that interrupted a PC from displaying the Windows screen when a new computer was first turned on.

Gateway executives, in an internal memo in preparation for a meeting with Ballmer, chafed at being treated like a mere distributor, rather than a partner, by Microsoft. Microsoft's position, according to a Gateway executive, was "No Flexibility" in regard to Gateway's efforts to greet its own customers and "define a Gateway appearance/experience." John Romano of Hewlett-Packard's PC division wrote a scathing letter to Microsoft objecting to the new terms, which forced H-P to remove the welcoming software H-P designed for first-time computer buyers. "If we had a choice of another supplier," he wrote, "I assure you you would not be our supplier of choice."

Contract restrictions could stall the defections for only so long. Microsoft had to offer something truly compelling. If Netscape's browser could become a new shell for Windows, Microsoft would step up efforts to use its own browser to wrap a new shell around Windows. With Active Desktop, Microsoft could trump Netscape's offer to promote media partners on its browser. Microsoft could offer to showcase them on Windows itself. PointCast, for example, quickly dumped Netscape and signed on as Microsoft's first premier partner. Microsoft offered to give each PC maker a channel of its own.

Internet Explorer 4 had initially been conceptualized as a simple browser upgrade. After Netscape's demonstrations at Comdex, the browser team was given the additional job of creating a shell for all of Windows. Active Desktop was to be the vehicle for delivering Chase's cherished channels.

"That was a surprise to me," said Adam Bosworth, who in early 1997 found himself in co-command of development for Internet Explorer 4. "People were starting to think, 'Gee this is no longer just a browser, it's a complete shell. It does everything.' "

Bosworth was skeptical of Active Desktop. He had joined the Internet Explorer effort when Trident, an engine to speed up Web pages and editing, was adopted as the guts of the next version of the browser. Trident was the engine for everything inside the frame—the rendering on the screen, the animations, the forms, and the applications. Active Desktop was to supply the browser frame—the front and back buttons, the favorites list, the drop-down menus, and all the other features of a browser other than the Web pages themselves.

The Trident and Active Desktop teams didn't mesh well. Active Desktop fell behind schedule, holding up the rest of the browser effort. That in turn dragged down morale for the rest of the team. There was a more serious problem. The code was slow and unstable. Any Windows "shell" needed to be extremely reliable because it is the way users get to the underlying resources of a computer. If the shell itself crashes, a user has to reboot. To have the shaky Active Desktop run the equally untried Trident engine underneath was too risky for a mainstream software product.

Bosworth wanted to cancel Active Desktop and strip it from the browser. The browser team shouldn't be doing a Windows shell at all, he said. He believed the Active Desktop—the very feature that Gates was touting as the fulfillment of Microsoft's pledge to integrate Windows and the Web—simply did not meet users' needs.

He wasn't alone. A survey of users found that people had little interest in the feature. They were even confused about how to use their mouse. Single-click, like a Web page? Or double-click, like in Windows? It's a more complicated question than it seems—how does a PC user drag an icon across the screen if it activates with a single click?

"The concept of unifying the user's desktop and Web experience sounds good and reasonable, but it's not clear that this is what users want and certainly is not what they expect," concluded one planning memo.

Finally, Bosworth moved to kill the Active Desktop project.

In revolt, several members of the shell team went straight to Ludwig. Either Bosworth goes, or we go, they said. Ludwig told them to continue working on Active Desktop.

When he heard, Bosworth charged into Silverberg's office. "You put me in charge," he said. "You either get the hell out of the way or take me off the project. This kind of micromanaging that John Ludwig is doing is intolerable."

Silverberg called a meeting with Chase, Ludwig, and Bosworth. The meeting ended without any resolution. But within a week, Bosworth received an e-mail from Ludwig telling him he was no longer working on Internet Explorer. Bosworth was furious and came within a hairsbreadth of quitting the company. That he didn't turned out to be of crucial importance to Microsoft two years later.

In the end, Silverberg split the difference on Active Desktop. By the time the new browser was released, the feature was still in the product, but it had been switched off unless specifically turned on by the user. It was a have-your-cake-and-eat-it-too decision. Microsoft could still claim progress on Windows-Web integration, which it had promised back in 1995, but with Active Desktop off, the browser could achieve reasonable performance.

Chase signed up his media partners, including Time Warner, the Walt Disney Company, and Dow Jones & Company, publisher of the *Wall Street Journal*. In negotiations, he and his team offered to provide heavy promotion, but insisted not only that the new channels exploit Microsoft's new technology features but that the media companies refrain from paying the fees Netscape was seeking for inclusion on its similar offering. The contract provisions would later cause legal and political trouble for Microsoft.

The more immediate problem was the utter lack of popular interest in the "channel" feature at all. With Active Desktop off, the channels generated almost no traffic for the media partners. The only consolation was that Netscape, which had also tried to make a splash with major media channels and other "push" offerings, executed even more poorly. The notion of desktop channels was an utter nonstarter.

Nonetheless, Gates continued to tout Web-Windows integration as a boon to customers. It became a mainstay of Microsoft's legal defense—the company's actions were justified because it was simply responding to overwhelming customer demand and expectations. From the beginning of the court case, Gates argued that customers were the ones who decided what features should be in Windows.

As late as January 1998, he cited Active Desktop as Microsoft's key innovation in Internet Explorer 4. "Taking the best of the shell, which is hierarchical navigation and the best of the browser, with the history list, backwards and forwards, bringing those together and letting you seamlessly move between links into the file system and operating system and into the Internet—that to me is innovation. Certainly, users love it."

Later, Gates glibly reversed himself without looking back. Active Desktop was overreaching by the Internet zealots, he told me. Performance was terrible, he said, though it improved in later versions.

"That's a case where the browser guys, they had the Internet religion, but they pushed it too far in terms of what was a practical user experience," he told me. "Thank God we turned it off."

The legal problems were more difficult to turn off. As the September 1997 launch date for Internet Explorer 4 neared, the Internet team crossed its fingers, hoping that Microsoft's lawyers would find a way to head off action by the Justice Department. Perhaps Microsoft could simply offer to allow PC makers to remove the Internet Explorer icon from the Windows desktop. That was the issue that had caused the problems with Compaq, the largest PC maker, and that had played a big role in spurring the government to act. Microsoft, in writing, threatened to cancel Compaq's Windows license if it removed the Internet Explorer and Microsoft Network icons from the desktop screens of one of its lines of computers.

At one meeting, the Internet team observed a moment of silence in support of Microsoft's legal team, praying for a settlement. Joel Klein, the antitrust chief, summoned Microsoft's lawyers to Washington, D.C., for a ritual meeting known as the "last rites." It was a final chance to offer concessions before the feds asked a district court judge to hold Microsoft in contempt for violating a 1995 consent decree that Microsoft had signed in order to avoid a full-blown antitrust trial.

Microsoft's lawyers repeated their standard refrain: Windows was an integrated product. The inclusion of the browser was an incremental step, a logical step, no different from including dozens of other features through the years. At the meeting, Klein held up two compact disks, one containing Windows and the other Internet Explorer, and told them, Simply untie these two physically separate products. According to Microsoft, showing flexibility on the icon alone would not have been enough to avoid legal action.

Gates dismissed the legal skirmish as a minor annoyance. The company had faced legal scrutiny for years and nothing had ever come of it. On October 11, 1997, two weeks after the San Francisco launch event, the Justice Department finally dropped the dime on Microsoft. The government's first action was narrow, a request that the Washington, D.C., district court move to hold Microsoft in contempt for violations of the 1995 consent decree. Joel Klein asked the court to fine Microsoft $1 million for every day that the company continued to "tie" its Web browser to Windows.

MANY of Microsoft's most respected thinkers were also trying to untie the company's Internet efforts from Windows. The oath every Microsoft employee still recites is that the browser has always been, and will always be, a part of Windows. But there were plenty of reasons to separate the two efforts that had nothing to do with antitrust concerns. Letting browser development proceed separately would liberate innovation from the burden of pulling the Windows strategy along. Windows had become—in a phrase that would make Gates wince—"legacy."

Outside developers were clamoring for something new. As early as 1995, it had been clear that Windows' run as the preeminent platform was fading. Venture capitalists and bleeding edge start-ups were no longer targeting Windows. Its community of developers was starting to decay, and there was little Microsoft could do with Windows to stop it. It couldn't in the long run bribe or coerce developers to abandon the new opportunities that they saw.

The Internet opportunity was bigger—a whole new business model, a whole new way of developing applications, and a whole new market free of Microsoft's domination. It was hard to imagine a big new company developing on the Windows platform; it was easy to imagine one on the Internet platform.

The Internet doves argued that if Microsoft wanted to continue to be the preeminent platform vendor, it had to wade in and lead the industry in a new direction, even if the company's new platform in many ways was at cross-purposes with the old one. If Microsoft was to truly deliver the higher-level network services for the Internet, classic Windows would be reduced to underlying plumbing—commoditized. But so be it: Microsoft had to think harder than its customers about the new opportunities and create the kind of platform that they needed, not the one Microsoft might have wanted them to have. "Bill thinks he can increment his way from Windows to get to the Internet," Slivka said. "I don't think he could do that any more than IBM could do that to get to the PC business from mainframes."

The Windows hawks countered that if Microsoft could continue to drive forward and make Windows compelling, no one would drift away. That turned out not to be true. "We found that no matter how compelling we made Windows, there is a bigger opportunity," said Tod Nielsen. "Connectivity. People are willing to sacrifice features for connectivity. You can only run so far, and nobody cares about the features above and beyond a certain point. That realization took us a long time to get to."

Furthermore, there was certainly plenty of Internet work to do in Windows. Windows wasn't by nature Internet aware. It had been nursed in that direction, step-by-step for years. But inside Microsoft, people knew there was a lot more to be done to fully adapt Windows to the Internet. This was abundantly clear to anybody who had ever set up a high-speed Internet connection at home. Or tried to secure a Windows machine from hacker attacks. Or tried to protect data from viruses that propagate through Microsoft's own programs. Or tried to transfer Windows settings and software from one machine to another. Or tried to obtain product support over the Internet to find out why running a new software program mysteriously freezes the computer. Or tried to find and install the latest software drivers for printers or modems. None of these necessary improvements required a browser to be part of Windows.

Windows was increasingly seen as old and fragile. The Windows group could have put a lot of people to work for a very long time doing everything possible to take advantage of the Internet to make Windows better, making customers happy and selling lots of software, without touching the browser.

As a matter of code design, Microsoft could produce flexible, more modular code by making the Internet, not Windows, the centerpoint of its design. Microsoft had won with interoperability before—the company's pitch had always been that Windows worked with IBM's mainframes, with Novell's file servers, and with thousands of other programs. Now the Internet team was just extending that—Internet Explorer worked with other platforms, even if that in some cases undermined Windows' advantage.

Microsoft would have to learn to play by the new rules. The open-standards world of the Internet required that Microsoft stake out the position of missionary, vanguard, and leader and always stay a step

ahead in implementing the same standards that were available to anybody. By integrating enough standards, even open ones, it was still
possible to create a sustainable competitive advantage, but without
leaving developers and other stakeholders worried they're about to
get screwed. Microsoft's old strategy was no longer optimal for creating value in the new stage. Open standards were a reality. Microsoft
would just have to be better.

As Thomas Reardon put it, "You've got to give up a little to get a
lot."

It was a warm late-summer night when the San Francisco browser
launch event finally wrapped up and Silverberg was dragged out to a
nearby bar in San Francisco's Marina district. Everybody sensed that
it might be the last time the Internet team would get together like
this. So the team that outmaneuvered Netscape was running one
more covert mission. A nervous Brad Chase tried to veto the operation, but Silverberg gave the go-ahead. They found a truck driver to
load the fourteen-foot-high "e" logo from the stage. The "e" was de-
posited in front of Netscape's headquarters down the peninsula in
Mountain View. Netscape took the prank with good humor. By the
time news crews showed up for the photo opportunity the next
morning, Netscape's mascot, Mozilla, stood atop the "e."

At the bar, Silverberg got drunk and emotional. In his eyes, the Internet team had turned around the company, persuaded the world to
see Microsoft as a leader again, and was finally gaining the industry's
trust. "To tear it apart, that's a killer," Silverberg thought.

"I think he was really out of the company at that point," Reardon
recalled. "But he got really jazzed seeing everyone. He thought he
might want back in."

Silverberg had hand-picked his team over the course of years. His
best memories of Microsoft were of the "smart, committed, hard-
working and passionate people," driven to make the visions of Windows, and then of the Internet, come true, he said. "It's really
intoxicating to be part of that kind of environment."

The three who stood out were his longtime lieutenants: Brad
Chase, David Cole, and John Ludwig. The troika had been in limbo
since Silverberg had gone on leave. Now, Silverberg's pirates were
wary of working for Allchin. Allchin's more buttoned-down enterprise group considered Windows 95 and Internet Explorer to be am-
ateurish, buggy code.

Chase was especially eager for Silverberg to return. Otherwise, he

was off to Allchin's group to pull together the marketing plan for
Windows 2000. Getting the spectacularly complicated and chroni-
cally late product out the door was going to be tough sledding. Microsoft was touting Windows 2000 as its most important product of
the decade, but after the spectacular launch of Windows 95, it was
hard to avoid the feeling of been there, done that. "Even if we
couldn't be together, it would have been better if Brad was back in a
major role," Chase told me later. "I was trying to help facilitate the
right thing done for the company."

Cole was one of Microsoft's best "ship-it" guys. His first job at Microsoft, straight out of college, was in product support, answering
questions from befuddled customers. Cole missed the Internet Explorer 3.0 effort, the team's Golden Age. After getting Windows 95
out the door, he had been assigned to salvage Microsoft's long-
troubled consumer devices projects, unwinding much of the company's work in interactive TV. When the IE 4 project became mired
in the internal battles between Bosworth and Ludwig, he had come
back to push it out the door.

Ludwig supplied the intellectual horsepower on the Internet
team. Silverberg "worshiped" him. His ability to simplify complex
technology and business considerations into crystal clear goals dated
from his graduate-school days at Carnegie Mellon University, where
he received a joint master's degree in business and electrical engineering. At business school, he hung around with guys in suits
reading the *Wall Street Journal*, talking about things like the Black-
Scholes value of options, and dreaming of working at Chase Manhattan. Late in the day, he went to engineering school and worked
through the night, writing code, surrounded by ghoulish hackers obsessed with killing twelfth-level necromancers in the multiuser game
Rogue.

Ludwig honed his strategic thinking in four years with Booz Allen
& Hamilton. As a management consultant he worked with managers
in everything from auto parts and steel tubing to telecommunications
and hospitals. He applied the lesson he learned after joining Microsoft in 1988: Strategic planning is not something you do every
three years. It's something you do every day, in making every business
decision. You have to ask yourself, What's our business goal? Why
are we doing what we're doing? How does it differentiate us compet-
itively?

Ludwig provided the most lucid description of the choice facing

Microsoft. "When you enter a new phase of business, what do you prioritize—getting the right team with the right culture on the job, or controlling some proprietary intellectual property?" he asked. "When the Internet pops up as a challenge, do you spin up a great team with a great culture to go address the opportunity and not worry about controlling the proprietary intellectual property right away, assuming that over time the team will develop a great business and that proprietary intellectual property will result? Or do you focus first on controlling the intellectual property and making sure that you have something proprietary to control, and then building around that intellectual property? If a team is engaging with customers, growing share from 0 percent to 30 percent, making developers happy—do you shut down the effort because of the lack of a proprietary position? Or do you congratulate them on their success, and encourage them to continue, and know that over time as they make customers happy, that a strong position will result? These are quite different approaches to a business."

It wasn't that Microsoft's top executives couldn't see that change was coming. It was clear to everybody: Support among developers was eroding. But Microsoft could no sooner create its own Internet platform than it could allow Netscape's and Sun's to succeed. Both would have the same effect, breaking the Windows lock by attracting developers to a fundamentally different proposition—open standards, cross-platform, and largely server-based software.

Silverberg didn't have a credible business plan for replacing the revenues that Microsoft would lose. In Microsoft's early days, nobody would ever have mentioned revenues in a technology discussion. But now there was a big beast to feed to keep earnings up and shareholders happy.

Nonetheless, he began to warm to the idea of resurrecting his "A" team to finally build his long-sought Internet platform.

On the plane the next day, Gates confirmed that the browser team was going to Allchin. He tried to put the best spin on the new world order. We need you, he told Silverberg. The Office group needs to do the Internet stuff, too. You're the right guy.

No, Silverberg told Gates. But seeing the team again had persuaded him to at least leave the door open. Rather than quit, he suggested extending his leave for another three months. The pendulum always swings back. In the meantime, he could vest some more stock options.

THE DANCE OF BLIND REFLEX

Morale problems weren't unique to the browser team. Microsoft was at the peak of success. The stock price had skyrocketed. Why was everybody so unhappy?

Even some of Microsoft's most loyal lieutenants were frustrated. Jon De Vaan, earnest and painfully shy, rose through the Office group to vice president and later senior vice president. He was a die-hard loyalist, but at one executive retreat, according to another participant, he told Ballmer, "I'm a senior vice president. I've been with the company sixteen years. I've built a multibillion-dollar business. I just wonder, what level do I have to be promoted to in order to be able to approve a single additional head count on my own?"

The wide perception inside Microsoft was that the company sacrificed innovation for "strategy," the complex set of hooks and lock-in techniques that Gates invariably insisted on to steer customers toward Microsoft's end-to-end product line and keep them from being able to easily switch to competitive products—and which customers hated for the very same reason.

To developers convinced their product was good enough to win on its own, Microsoft's culture seemed increasingly defensive and moribund. "A lot of us resented that," Bosworth told me.

"Before 1996, the entrepreneurs ruled at Microsoft," Bosworth said. "It was paradise. It was a blast. All of us were very happy there." His product, Access, had been a scrappy underdog taking on Borland and Ashton-Tate, at that time the leaders in the desktop database market. "Microsoft was filled with people who had had to compete against entrenched winners and win. Many, many people were very happy to go out and compete. The organization was built for that."

Now, Microsoft was choking on its own interdependencies while strategic challenges were being ignored. Decision making became laborious and slow. Like its code, Microsoft was too tightly coupled.

The "strategy tax" could often be deeply demoralizing. Anthony Bay, a veteran of Apple Computer, watched his project crash and burn in spectacular Microsoft fashion. His Normandy e-mail and Web-publishing server passed its beta tests. But the low-cost Internet server competed with Microsoft's higher-priced Exchange server. Microsoft effectively killed Normandy.

Management methods were sometimes simply ham-handed and

insensitive. Ben Slivka was still smarting from the indignity of having his Java team reorganized out from under him without even a heads-up from the company. He had been assigned the thankless task of running point on Microsoft's strategy for competing with Sun's Java typhoon. He could take the rough treatment he had received from Gates in the spring of 1997. But a week before he returned from his summer sabbatical, a colleague phoned him and unofficially advised him to come to campus: Maritz had called a big meeting. Only when he showed up did he learn that his 116-person team had been transferred to Allchin's group. The team was moving, but not Slivka.

These were the key middle managers upon whom Microsoft had counted to lead the troops into battle against its competitors. Now their rumblings of discontent were growing too loud to ignore. Natalie Yount, a director in Microsoft's Human Resources department, had heard good things about Barry Oshry, a quirky Boston consultant who for twenty-five years had run a "power laboratory" on Cape Cod to better understand the tricky dynamics of organizational life. Yount selected a sampling of fourteen of Microsoft's next-generation leaders, vice presidents, and soon-to-bes, all with ten years or more at the company, leading teams of from sixty to four hundred people. They were all deemed to be Microsoft success stories.

In addition to DeVaan, the Office vice president, and Bay, the leader of the Normandy effort, the group included Chris Peters, who led the acquisition of the FrontPage software to jump-start the Office group's Web efforts; Harel Kodesh, in charge of squeezing Windows into palm-sized computers and cell phones; Cameron Myhrvold, Nathan's brother, who fought a grueling battle to get Internet service providers to adopt Microsoft's technology; Rick Thompson, who was creating a hardware division inside the software company to sell keyboards and computer mouses; Robbie Bach, who was later to be put in charge of Xbox, Microsoft's new video game console; and Slivka, who delivered Microsoft's early Internet browsers and then tried to blunt the threat from Java.

Before they went east, the fourteen managers were divided into three "classes," corresponding to the three-tier structure common to most societies or, indeed, most corporations. At the Power Lab, Elites, or Tops, would control the wealth and institutions. The Managers, or Middles, would run the institutions on behalf of the Elites. Immigrants, or Bottoms, would enter the society with no funds, no resources, and no power.

For a week, the Managers became the members of a temporary society in a small 130-year-old village on a bluff above Nantucket Sound near Hyannis. A tabernacle at the center of rustic cottages and dormitories housed the society's courtroom, newspaper, company store, employment center, pub, and theater. Oshry and his team would set the scenario in motion, then assume roles as notebook-toting anthropologists to watch the drama unfold.

The three Elites arrived first, followed by the three Managers and the eight Immigrants. Early on Monday morning, the Immigrants were driven to the conference center, where they were told to turn over everything—wallets, cell phones, computers, keys, coats. They were each given a brown paper bag to carry a single change of underwear.

Oshry provides little structure or direction in his Power Lab workshops. Yet the dynamics of the social structures and organizational systems play out in ways large and small. Elites, or Tops, enjoy having lobster and wine delivered to their comfortable homes, but often grow territorial. Immigrants, or Bottoms, grumble about the dormitories and their dinners of franks and beans, but in considering alternatives often succumb to groupthink. Managers, or Middles, share a common house and eat at the same table, but largely identify with their respective Tops and find it hard to collaborate as a cohesive group. Teams that at the outset seem full of promise deteriorate into noncommunication and dissolution.

Like most groups, the mini-Microsoft quickly fell into a familiar Power Lab pattern—what Oshry calls the Dance of Blind Reflex. Tops, accountable for success in an ambiguous and unpredictable environment, feel burdened by unmanageable complexity. Bottoms feel invisible and oppressed by the insensitivity of their superiors, and see themselves as the victims of reorganizations, wage cuts, mergers, and constantly changing plans. Middles feel torn, weak, and confused, and resent being forced to go to others to get what they need to do what they're told. Rarely can the players see their full part in creating the situation.

On the plane home, Slivka hunched over his laptop, composing an e-mail to Maritz, the executive perhaps most aware of the brewing crisis in the product teams. As Microsoft grew, the problems had gotten worse. Half the employees had been with the company for less than five years. The early culture was fading. Just like the Middles in the simulation, Microsoft's Middles were disintegrated, alienated from each other, unable to effectively work across product lines. Between the engineer who wrote the code and Gates and Ballmer, who charted macro strategy, most of the company's most creative ideas never saw the light of day.

When he got back to Redmond, Slivka went directly to Gates. In their meeting, Gates expressed his frustration that Microsoft didn't very often stake out leadership on industry trends. "Innovation versus strategy" was one of Microsoft's longest-running debates. Slivka lived up to his reputation for practically inviting Gates's abuse. Following up on their meeting, Slivka sent Gates an e-mail titled "Getting out in front on more issues vs. sharing code and reducing redundancy." Slivka offered Gates a few examples of how Microsoft's prevailing culture stamped out creative initiatives—"dynamics that exist, that you may not be aware of, that are unhealthy."

What made sense from Gates's Top perspective had the effect of murdering a Bottom's good idea in the crib, Slivka argued. Slivka recounted the experience of one Windows developer who presented Allchin with his ideas for a simple, reliable operating system suitable for home users. Instead of saying "Great idea, go do it," Allchin had insisted that the new operating system be based on Windows NT. The developer objected that the huge NT operating system wasn't suitable for the drop-dead simple appliance he had envisioned. Allchin challenged him to list the parts of Windows NT he would strip out.

"So, almost immediately, we've gone from entrepreneurial 'getting out in front' to constraining and justifying how this innovation might occur," Slivka told Gates.

In Slivka's view, this was why Microsoft never seemed able to create a home PC simple enough for the 60 percent of households that did not yet have computers. He urged Gates to "take a step back and rethink our (operating system) architecture. . . . I think we can (and should!) afford to take a different, unconstrained run at it."

The solution, Slivka said, lay in "unfettered innovation" from the product teams, the part of Microsoft with the greatest practical experience and knowledge of customers. Any eventual vanquisher of Windows, he said, won't be constrained by Microsoft's existing code base. Microsoft's teams should similarly be cut free from the constraints of the company's historical franchises.

He was blunt: "I think your focus on 'common code' as a goal in itself has served to stifle innovation."

Just like a Top at the Power Lab, Gates walked right into the Dance of Blind Reflex. He knew very well what problems Microsoft faced. And he knew equally well that there was no easy way to solve them. He blew up. Did Slivka know how impossible his proposal would make Allchin's job? he virtually screamed in his e-mail response. Coordination was what was important! Sanity was what was important!

Gates was so harsh in his response that even he knew it wasn't productive. He woke up in the middle of the night and realized how damaging his response had been. The next day, a rainy Sunday afternoon, he did something rare.

"I want to apologize for my last email," Gates wrote. "It was extreme and rude (and not very empowering)," he wrote. He stood by the points he made but said, "I really said this in a bad way that I feel bad about. I don't make this mistake often—maybe three times a year."

Unfazed, Slivka blundered on, reinforcing his message in a second e-mail to Gates. "When I see managers telling people to put on blinders about exploring the future, I am very afraid that we're going to cut ourselves off from the best possible future."

If Gates was indeed deftly navigating the company through the treacherous waters, the direction was no longer clear to his deckhands. Slivka suggested that Gates lay out his view of Microsoft's primary challenges for the top fifty or one hundred technical people at the company—maybe they could solve some of the problems. "I also bet you'll get feedback on why you are on drugs in some areas," Slivka said, "and there are other problems you are missing altogether. This communication would be great . . . it seems to be totally missing at present," Slivka wrote. "I haven't seen a strategy memo from you since the fall of 1995 when we did Internet Strategy day."

A signal from the top that Microsoft was making a decisive bet on the Internet might resolve many of the endless, debilitating internal debates. Maybe the company would be able to move forward.

Slivka enlisted some veterans of the Power Lab experience to cosponsor a Middle Managers Retreat for two days just before Thanksgiving 1997. Some of the participants winced at the name— "middle managers" sounded so corporate, so IBM. But they had reluctantly come to the conclusion that Microsoft *was* corporate and they'd better learn to deal with it. In corporations, people manage up, to their bosses, and down, to their employees, but rarely talk to each other across organizational lines. Microsoft, which had previously thrived precisely because that wasn't true, had finally succumbed.

At the end of the first day of the retreat, the forty-five Microsoft participants lingered after dinner in the banquet room of the Salish Lodge, where wide windows opened onto the 268-foot Snoqualmie Falls. They were feeling ambitious. They were sure they could "fix" Microsoft. The next day, they broke into four groups and brainstormed. The Middles wanted to move! Once they started talking, they found that the notions they were afraid to raise at Microsoft were in fact exactly what the company needed. Someone threw out the idea of an "Open Internet Standards Pledge." How about a "Users' Bill of Rights," one manager suggested, to let customers know what they could expect from the company's software? Simply issuing a "Business Goals White Paper," describing where and how Microsoft intended to compete, would go a long way toward countering the FUD—industry slang for Fear, Uncertainty, and Doubt— spread by competitors that Microsoft wanted to own everything. As with DOS, Windows, Internet Explorer, and many other projects in which Microsoft was successful on its third try, maybe the company as a whole could get it right in the third generation. Microsoft version 3.0!

The next day they broke into groups and then reconvened to vote on the top priorities. It felt like an insurrection, but the group was careful to mute appearances. The presentation was pitched as Ideas to Move the Company Forward, rather than a re-invention or a repudiation. The broad categories were stated as flatly and positively as possible. A new mission statement! Customers at the center! The Middles are here to help! Push down responsibility and authority! All these fresh ideas and Gates and Ballmer never get to hear them, somebody pointed out. By the end of the day, the group had decided to present their ideas to Gates, Ballmer, and the rest of the executive staff.

Three weeks later, more than a hundred of Microsoft's top technical people—so-called Level 15s—crowded into a conference room. In addition to Gates and Maritz, Silverberg, who was still on leave, and Mike Maples, a popular executive from Microsoft's early years who had officially retired, came in for the two-hour meeting. Ballmer was absent.

Slivka served as the master of ceremonies. In an e-mail before the meeting, Andrew Kwatinetz, a popular team leader in the Office group, offered "customer at the center" as one way to break through the innovation vs. strategy deadlock. Kwatinetz presented the group's suggestion that the company slice through the product groups and organize itself around the needs of customers. That way, products and features could be brought to bear on the very different scenarios faced by different kinds of customers. A corporate information technology manager might face the nightmare of deploying new software to thousands of users, whereas a lawyer or consultant might need to collaborate with colleagues on a complex document. The best approach for those customers invariably cuts across Microsoft's existing product lines, Kwatinetz said. The way Microsoft was currently organized, it was in no one's interest to tackle the problem.

"This is somewhat controversial and people will get upset," Kwatinetz wrote on the eve of the presentation.

Even more controversial was the change in the mission statement. The company's motto had been "A computer on every desktop and in every home" ever since Bill Gates coined it in 1975. In late 1997, it was still a radical concept inside Microsoft to say the Internet had displaced the PC at the center of the computing universe. Yusuf Mehdi, a rising young marketer on Windows and Internet Explorer, agreed to make that part of the presentation. "Bill and Steve could have thought, what is this meeting? Is it almost mutinous?" said Mehdi. "It was definitely a nervous presentation for me."

According to the slides Mehdi presented, the old mission statement left employees confused and failed to resolve conflicting charters between different groups, such as the Internet Explorer and Windows team. It left out the new investments the company was making in non-PC technologies, such as WebTV.

Externally, it was even worse: "Not future-focused or industry leading," Mehdi wrote. "Press struggling to understand Microsoft's customer value proposition." A new mission statement, he wrote in another e-mail, "can help address today's company image of a ruthless competitor that is focused primarily on the competition."

It wasn't yet possible for a junior marketing guy to completely overthrow Gates's loyalty to the PC, so Mehdi straddled the divide, proposing cumbersome mottos such as "We are about connecting every person and business together via the personal computer to access the new world of thinking and communicating," or "Providing PC capabilities and global connectivity for every individual."

Gates sat in front, taking notes and asking occasional clarifying questions. Gates seemed reflective, Mehdi said. "I thought he took it all in."

Slivka was less sure. "Bill was clearly uncomfortable with the whole thing. He didn't seem to really understand what we were saying then, and he certainly failed to act on it."

Chris Williams, the vice president for human resources, regretted that he had encouraged Microsoft's "middles" to join together to re-form the company. The middle managers' retreat, he told me, "stirred up a lot of pent-up desire to fix a lot of things that were very difficult to fix. It probably caused more strife than repair."

COMEBACK

The pitch that works best with Bill Gates is you *can* have it all. He was the most steadfast defender of the profit model Microsoft had so as-siduously created. That tilted him toward Allchin's argument that browser development should be subsumed in Windows. But he knew the browser could be the foundation for something new. He hated the suggestion that he had to choose between the two; he was open to proposals that promised to give him everything.

Gradually, a loose-knit plan took shape to get Microsoft unstuck and move the company forward.

Mehdi sketched the basics of the market strategy. As he saw it, the browser had drawn people onto the Internet. In turn, the growing number of Web users had spawned an explosion of Web sites. It was clear that the center of gravity for the software industry had shifted away from the desktop and toward the Internet. But desktop comput-ers, now with their superfast chips and huge hard drives, still had a role to play. Microsoft's clear advantage was its ability to bring the power of client software to the Internet. Microsoft didn't simply need a better Windows; it needed to provide a complete "experience" for both Web users and developers. The situation was ripe for somebody to make everything work together simply and easily. The combina-tion of Internet Explorer and MSN, Microsoft's online service, was simply the next logical extension of the browser.

Silverberg was the obvious choice to lead the effort. Mehdi and others, including Charles Fitzgerald, a trained marketing assassin who often took on the company's most challenging sell jobs, made the case both ways. They lobbied inside Microsoft for Silverberg's re-turn and pressed the case with Silverberg himself.

Microsoft was at its best when it targeted a single competitor, par-ticularly one that was way ahead. That had worked in the browser war. Many at Microsoft watched happily as Netscape missed the op-portunity of a lifetime when it failed to effectively capitalize on the traffic its browser generated. In March 1997, Netscape's Web site was still the most heavily trafficked site in the world. But Netscape handed off responsibility for programming its search button and other popular services to Yahoo! and other newcomers—who quickly grew to be more valuable than Netscape itself. Yahoo! was only the leading example of Web sites that were starting to provide services, such as e-mail and home finance, that felt like traditional software applications but ran on big Web servers and were accessible via any browser.

But Yahoo! and the other new Web-based competitors were less interesting to Microsoft than a company long dismissed as a technology lightweight. America Online, which had defied repeated predictions of its imminent demise, had grown to command more than half of all Internet traffic and was clearly a marketing powerhouse. By the fall of 1997, it was clear AOL had become Microsoft's biggest competitor for the attention of customers.

Silverberg peppered Gates with e-mail sketching the outlines of the new thing. As Silverberg saw it, AOL's strategy was to displace Microsoft by commanding more and more of the attention of computer users, providing all the stuff that users saw and interacted with while at their PCs, the services that tens of millions of people relied on every day. In Microsoft-speak, AOL was defining the end-user Internet experience. If they could insert themselves between the underlying operating system and the user, and win loyalty, Windows would become plumbing, a commodity. It was AOL, not Netscape, that was most likely to fulfill Andreessen's pledge to turn Windows into a "partially debugged set of device drivers."

By 1997, the rules of the game had changed. As the Internet became a mass medium, the technical battles of the mid-90s had given way to a race to create the most compelling end-user experience. The metrics for success in this new era would be far different than in the earlier PC era. The high-order bit, as programmers like to say, was not to get thousands of developers to adopt your arcane PC programming interfaces but rather to get tens of millions of users to use your services every day. It was about developing an ongoing relationship with the mass market of consumers. The company that successfully defined the Internet user experience was going to be technology's next big winner. AOL, on its way to signing up nearly 30 million subscribers, had laid the foundation for enormous influence.

Silverberg had a simple way to define the new challenge: We beat Apple. We beat Netscape. Now it's time to take on AOL as the number-one competitor.

Through the 1990s, relations between Microsoft and AOL had moved from wary to hostile to improbably close and back to wary. In 1993, when AOL was a fledgling, cash-strapped start-up, chief executive Steve Case met with Gates in Redmond and received his standard, matter-of-fact analysis of the options before the two companies. "I can buy 20 percent of you or I can buy all of you or I can go into this business myself and bury you," Gates told Case, according to Kara Swisher, my *Wall Street Journal* colleague, in her book *AOL.com*.

In 1995, AOL incited one of Microsoft's many brushes with antitrust authorities when it complained about plans to bundle Microsoft Network, a competitive online service, into Windows 95.

But by 1996, AOL, in a stunning reversal that left Netscape chief executive Jim Barksdale sputtering in anger, adopted Internet Explorer as its Web browser, sealing IE's success in a single stroke.

Through it all, AOL had skillfully managed to avoid becoming Microsoft's primary target. Case understood Microsoft was poorly equipped to fight on anything more than a single front. Some other company had always been at the top of Microsoft's most-wanted list: Borland, Apple, Novell, Netscape, Sun.

In 1995, at PC Forum, an annual gathering of industry bigwigs, AOL honcho Ted Leonsis shared the stage with Russ Siegelman, the head of MSN. Microsoft was preparing to launch Windows 95, bundled with MSN. A member of the audience asked Leonsis about Microsoft's plans.

"Is John Doerr in the audience? John, come on up here," Leonsis called out. Doerr, the most prominent venture capitalist in Silicon Valley, served at the time as a stand-in for Netscape, which was heavily funded by Doerr's firm, Kleiner Perkins Caufield and Byers. When Doerr got on stage, Leonsis grabbed him and made him a human shield against Microsoft, yelling to Siegelman, "Kill him first!"

Silverberg had been a major proponent of killing Netscape first, which put his browser team in conflict with MSN. In 1996, Gates sided with Silverberg and the browser team when he agreed to give AOL placement in Windows in return for AOL's adoption of Internet Explorer. Siegelman, who had hoped to use access to Windows to MSN's advantage, complained the deal was "putting a bullet through MSN's head."

"I think it was just Mr. Siegelman going nonlinear, which he was wanting to do," Silverberg said in his deposition. "It was not a particularly rational debate—it took a while for it to become rational."

MSN flailed through a series of failed strategies and embarrassing mishaps; for a time MSN lost subscribers nearly as fast as AOL gained them. The service was so poor that Gates wrote off tens of millions of dollars for customer accounts that were never billed properly. All told, Microsoft's Internet efforts were losing hundreds of millions of dollars a year. Gates considered the early version of MSN to be one of the few pieces of software he was embarrassed to have released. Even by 1998, he told me later, "MSN was really nowhere."

Still, for years Gates refused to assign his top developers to tackle the problems. Now, with Netscape on the ropes, Silverberg reversed his earlier stance. He wanted to put his browser all-stars on the case and take on AOL directly.

Gates was of two minds. He believed AOL's corporate DNA would ultimately lead more in the direction of media than technology. Even after AOL acquired Netscape in 1998, Gates told Microsoft employees, "AOL doesn't have it in their genes to attack us in the platform space."

At other times, Gates warned that AOL was a potential competitor for all of Microsoft's information management software, since AOL already had a unique capability to run huge amounts of customer data through its massive servers.

He had been gnawing on a similar notion himself. In the technology debates-cum-religious wars, Gates had generally tried to stake out the "decentralized" position. He favored lots of powerful PCs—"clients"—on lots of desktops, where users could install their own software and fiddle with their own setting. Gates regularly derided initiatives from Sun, Oracle, and others as a return to the centralized computing of the mainframe era because they pushed most processing away from desktop PCs and up to the server hardware and software, where they made their money. Microsoft, of course, made its money on clients. There was a fair measure of self-interested dissembling on both sides.

Still, Gates realized that technology fads contain a germ of a good idea. He envisioned the creation of a massive registry of every computer user's digital life, logically centralized but distributed everywhere, accessible on any PC. The data and settings would reside in the "cloud," the network of information infrastructure that users didn't have to worry about, that simply worked. Gates claims to be the earliest internal champion of a project that could only have been named by someone with a particularly tin ear for appearances: "Megaserver."

The ominous name obscured Gates's rather prosaic ambitions. Increasingly, one of the biggest brakes on Microsoft's growth had been the reluctance of customers to upgrade. Any experienced computer user understands the reason: After months of fiddling with settings and controls and drivers and printers and file systems and Internet connections, few want to start all over again with a new operating system that might or might not wipe everything out. Upgrades could consume dozens of hours because of frustrating glitches that would not be tolerated in any other consumer product.

For corporations, the problem is magnified thousands-fold—every computer in every location has to be visited, upgraded, restored to familiar working order, and tested, all without disrupting even a day's worth of productivity of the helpless employee whose entire work environment has just been turned upside down. Many leading corporations, not to mention individual consumers, were only barely containing their rage at the cost and complexity of personal computers.

Megaserver would take care of all of that—managing computers and installing Microsoft's software upgrades, without ever bothering the user. That would make it possible to offer what Gates called Windows Tone, or "Wintone," a kind of PC dial tone. Customers wouldn't manage their computers at all. Microsoft would back up software and data and remotely upgrade its customers' machines. Customers would be able to count on a machine that was available and ready to use, with the latest patches and software. For a fee. That's what made the idea particularly appealing to Microsoft—predictable revenues from regular fees.

A recurring revenue stream. That was the new model. Many big corporate customers were already paying Microsoft an annual licensing fee for a software package, valuing the predictability of their software bill over any concerns that Gates might nickel or dime them around the edges. Add a trouble-free service guarantee and maybe this was the way to finally crack the stubborn consumer market as well.

"That idea of thinking of it more like a magazine where somebody signs up for 12 months to get all the bits we can send, all the support we can send . . . we see that as the future of the business," Gates told analysts in July 1997.

The devil was in the details. For users to be able to replicate their computer "state" on various devices on various networks, there needed to be repositories distributed around the network, all synchronized with each other and with all devices. And if users were really going to trust the service, it would have to grapple with all the problems of reliability and security of the most hardened computer installations.

What do you think about Megaserver? Gates asked Silverberg. The e-mail exchange between the two men turned into a torrent. Maritz was brought into the discussion.

Silverberg began to feel the first stirrings of excitement. There was a way to make it work if people just engaged it, he knew. If the company put its mind to it, it could still change the world. Everybody could get off to a fresh start.

Not so fast. Allchin raised an objection. He saw Megaserver, once again, as a competing platform that could overshadow Windows. If Silverberg were in charge of Megaserver, the ties to Windows would likely be loose. Silverberg would simply choose whatever technology worked best. Megaserver would not be compatible with the NT architecture. Separate code would confuse PC makers about what to put on their machines. Megaserver would need all sorts of base-level functions, such as caching, so information could be called up quickly, and synchronization, to keep all the information updated. That sounded like work for Windows to him. Most alarming, Allchin worried that Silverberg's code would be where the innovation would take place.

"To drive technical and strategic synergy, he thought Megaserver should simply be part of Windows," said Dunie, vice president of the Windows division under Allchin. "Jim was very concerned that if such a team existed somewhere else, they would create a new platform. That's why Jim was very keen on getting ownership of this team."

Maritz made his call. We're going to do Megaserver, he said, but Allchin will be in charge.

Silverberg complained to Gates, who overruled Maritz. Silverberg was assigned to develop Megaserver. By December 1997, three months after he had turned down Gates's previous job offer, he was back at Microsoft part time, laying plans and reassembling his team.

But there was another catch. To create the next great Internet user experience, Silverberg needed control of the browser, which was the point of engagement with computer end-users. The only way to build a compelling experience was to control the complete user environment. He would need e-mail and instant messaging and search and multimedia, but the effort would start with the browser.

The browser was destined to become the company's main user interface and shell. Silverberg's intention was for the new MSN browser to assume many of the responsibilities of the shell. The Windows shell would be left with the traditional Windows-only tasks, but all of the new cool stuff would be in the new browser. The browser, on a faster release schedule and without the burden of the rest of Windows' responsibilities, would quickly overtake the operating system as the target for software developers.

He had no problem in sharing the underlying Internet technology with the Windows team, but he couldn't depend on anyone else for such a critical piece of software. Megaserver was a set of back-end services; the browser was the client software to gain access to those services. He needed end-to-end control.

Most important, he needed his team. MSN was held in such low repute inside Microsoft he knew he would never be able to recruit the talent he needed. With Ludwig and Cole and Chase on his team again, he'd have critical mass. If Silverberg was going to take on the responsibility, he needed to have the authority and resources to be successful. He was not going to take a job that was doomed to failure from the start. The fate of the browser team was the central issue, the deal-maker or -breaker.

Allchin was grumbling. He had been through it all before and could see clearly how things would play out. He was just as unwilling as Silverberg to be dependent on others for a key component of his product. In software, the small everyday decisions are often more crucial than the big strategic ones. The day would come when Silverberg's browser team needed to make a change to counter a move by AOL, just when Allchin needed something else for his Windows user interface. Who would win?

Maritz tried to broker a deal. Ludwig and Chase, firm Silverberg supporters, and Allchin himself engaged in a round-robin discussion. A swing vote was Bob Muglia, a rising star and protégé of Maritz's who had worked under both Silverberg and Allchin. "I was somewhere in the middle," Muglia told me. "I saw the benefit in both positions. I was easily swayed."

A proposal was taking shape. Silverberg would honcho Megaserver and take over parts of MSN. The current head of MSN, Pete Higgins, would keep control of the "content" of the online service, but Silverberg would be responsible for the end-user Internet experience that went head-to-head with AOL's software. Maritz brokered another split-the-difference compromise to allow Silverberg to retain control of the Internet Explorer code and the browser team. The underlying Internet technology would go in Windows, which would continue to include a browser and could even keep the Internet Explorer brand name. After about a year, the browser would finally be transferred to Allchin's Windows group, which was so busy trying to get Windows 2000 done that he wouldn't be able to devote much attention to the browser effort anyway. Silverberg would have time to assemble the tools and the team he needed, and to make the argument that AOL was indeed the next big competitor.

"He and I worked out a scenario under which he would come back," Maritz told me.

It was a deal, but it was fragile. Maritz fretted that there was no consensus. It was a defer-the-decision kind of deal. Anything less and Silverberg would walk away; anything more and Allchin just might do the same. This at least kept everybody on board for the moment. And Gates would get his Megaserver.

Maritz wanted Gates to explicitly bless the arrangement so there would be no confusion.

On December 22, 1997, Allchin, Silverberg, and Maritz filed into the small conference room known simply as "2059" in Gates's executive suite in Building 8. Maritz laid out the pros and cons. Gates went around the room until everyone had had their say. Silverberg was sullen and barely participated in the meeting. Allchin was surly. He disagreed with the compromise plan for both technical and business reasons.

Which pieces went with the browser and which went with Windows? he wanted to know. Outlook Express for e-mail might not be a core part of the operating system. But what about Trident, the dynamic HTML engine in Internet Explorer? The Trident team was out to replace key parts of Windows—surely they belonged in the operating system group.

Maritz explained that it would be difficult to split Trident from the rest of the browser team. Thus, Trident would also stay with Silverberg.

"I've heard all the arguments," Gates said. "Unless the Windows team can prove that moving the browser will materially advance the delivery of NT 5, the browser stays with Brad."

Silverberg's Internet team was back in business with a new mandate from Bill Gates: Take on America Online and establish a new platform for Internet services. He had won the battle to keep his handpicked team together.

Rather than elation, however, he felt dread. Silverberg had enjoyed his leave. The process of negotiating the compromise reminded him of all the reasons he had been happy to be away from Microsoft. For the holidays, he went to Whistler, in British Columbia, the major ski resort nearest to Seattle. A longtime skier, he had tackled snowboarding in typically extreme style, ferrying to the peaks by helicopter to carve the virgin slopes of glaciers. In the mountains, he wrestled with mixed feelings about returning to the corporate fray.

Gates says the decision to go with Silverberg was simply the kind of routine strategy call he makes all the time. "It's not like you have an election, OK? Where people line up and people say, 'I have this point of view, you have that point of view,' and people debate it for six months. It's not like you can have a faction that says, 'OK, we're ascendant,' or 'No, we're ascendant.'

"There was never any set-piece, where people came onto the field and had two different points of view—that never happened," he explained to me when I asked him about his decision. "Or you could say, it happened every minute. Every week, you're making trade-offs: This goes with this group. Make this decision this way. Then new things happen in the market and you make decisions that way."

The obvious role for the browser, he said, was "both." The browser was both the "shell" for Windows and the "carrier" for Microsoft Network. How that would be worked out in practice was just part of running the business. Gates repeatedly reminded everybody they all had options in the same company.

"There's never been any question in this company who's in charge of the technical strategy. The technical strategy of the company has always been set by me. Still is set by me. Every trade-off that I made right in terms of how the two groups work together—to some degree that came together because there's one brain that it's supposed to be able to fit all into.

"Every mistake you can lay at my feet."

4

Citizen Gates

Kane: If I hadn't been very rich, I might have been a really
   great man.
Thatcher: Don't you think you are, Mr. Kane?
Kane: I think I did pretty well under the circumstances.
Thatcher: What would you like to have been?
Kane: Everything you hate.

—*Citizen Kane*

HARDBALL

Two weeks before the tense meeting with Allchin and Silverberg in December 1997, Gates made a two-day trip to China. It was a brief respite from the problems, internal and external, Microsoft faced back home. In Beijing, Gates was mobbed by children on his way to deliver a speech at a conference of Chinese Windows developers. He was also a hit with students the next day at Qinghua University. A government official declared Gates "almost a god to a generation of Chinese youths." The world's leading capitalist was a superstar in communist China.

It was his fifth visit to China in three years. He was treated as a virtual head of state, twice meeting with Communist Party chief Jiang Zemin. Gates and his wife, Melinda, along with fellow billionaires Warren and Susan Buffett and another couple, had toured the country by train in 1995. His book *The Road Ahead* was a runaway bestseller. Chinese leaders declared Windows 95 to be the country's "official operating system."

In the long term, investment in China was a no-brainer, track-the-inevitable bet for Microsoft. Although India had a head start in training software engineers, Gates assured local reporters that the "worldwide shortage of computer skills will make people come to China to look for people."

The long-term opportunity made Gates content to talk loudly and carry a small stick about the rampant software piracy in China. More than 90 percent of Windows and Office users in China used illegally copied counterfeit software. Microsoft estimated the value of stolen sales at billions of dollars in lost revenues each year. For all the tough rhetoric, though, Microsoft's global campaign against stolen software was carefully calibrated to the realities of a given market. China's was not quite "ripe" for aggressive enforcement.

According to Microsoft's "yellow book" of global sales, China's annual PC sales made it the second-largest market in Asia, behind only Japan. But dollars-per-desktop in China were tiny, even compared to developing countries such as India and Brazil. Economic development and the emergence of "knowledge workers" were far more important factors than piracy. Current sales, even if all current Windows users actually paid in full, were only a tiny fraction of future revenues. Market share, even of stolen software, was a higher priority than immediate collection. In piracy as in Internet software, Microsoft valued volume and market share over profits. Like free Internet software, pirated Windows was a loss leader.

"China's growth should be significant for us and well worth what we are doing," Gates said.

Gates's triumphant visit to China was interrupted by a call from Microsoft's in-house antitrust lawyer, David Heiner. The news: U.S. District Court Judge Thomas Penfield Jackson had sided with the government and ordered Microsoft to stop tying its Internet Explorer browser to Windows. At a news conference in China, Gates declined to comment on the case. He hurried home.

To Microsoft executives, the implications of the order were as foggy as the Seattle weather that Thursday afternoon in December 1997. The good news was that Jackson denied the government's request for a contempt citation. The consent decree and Microsoft's behavior, he said, were both too ambiguous to support such a ruling.

However, on his own, *sua sponte*, Jackson moved to enforce the 1995 consent decree Microsoft had negotiated with the Justice Department and European antitrust authorities. At issue was the section of the decree barring Microsoft from forcing PC makers to take an "other product"—in this case, the browser—as a condition of licensing Windows. For monopolies, this kind of "tying" is a no-no. It is considered inherently anticompetitive. If customers genuinely wanted the other product, there would be no need to force them; if they didn't want it, they shouldn't be forced to take it in order to get the product they need.

Any ambiguity came from a proviso that had been negotiated into the 1995 consent decree almost as an afterthought. Now the proviso became the heart of the matter. The consent decree's anti-tying clause, the proviso clarified, "shall not be construed to prohibit Microsoft from developing integrated products." The loophole appeared to give Microsoft an out.

It was Gates himself who had insisted on the loophole in late-night negotiations in 1994 with Joel Klein's predecessor as Clinton's antitrust chief, Anne Bingaman. In the talks, Microsoft's attorneys at first suggested a more limited proviso to the anti-tying clause: Microsoft would not be prohibited from developing integrated products "which offer technological advantages." But that restriction was unacceptable to Gates, who refused to give bureaucrats the authority to decide whether changes to Windows delivered such advantages; he directed his lawyers to remove the last four words. Gates was emphatic that Microsoft would not accept *any* limitations on its rights to design its products as it saw fit. Microsoft signed the consent decree, its lawyers said, only after ensuring its "unfettered right to incorporate new features into its operating systems," according to a declaration by Microsoft's outside counsel, Richard Urowsky of Sullivan & Cromwell.

At the last minute, negotiators agreed to drop another phrase from the proviso. The original wording of the phrase was ". . . shall not be construed to prohibit Microsoft from developing integrated products *nor necessarily permit it to do so.*" The negotiators later explained their thinking: They were simply deferring any definition of "integrated" to a later day, not rewriting antitrust law. Yet, as it stood, Gates apparently believed he had outfoxed the government.

Throughout the summer and fall of 1997, Microsoft's attorneys insisted in a series of meetings with Justice Department attorneys that the "integrated products" proviso gave Microsoft a free pass to add Internet Explorer to Windows. The government was welcome to try its luck with a full-blown Sherman Act antitrust case, they said. But with the language of the proviso, Klein might as well give up any thought of a quick victory with a narrow case under the consent decree, Microsoft's lawyers said. "Don't waste your time on the consent decree. Look at the language," Bill Neukom, Microsoft's dapper general counsel, told Klein's lawyers.

To Microsoft, the proviso blessed the company's right to add any features it chose to its operating system, just as the company had been doing for sixteen years. Microsoft defined "integrated" the way *Webster's Third New International Dictionary* defined it—"combined," "united," or "incorporated into." Under the company's definition, a product is integrated simply because Microsoft says it is. In discussions with the government, Microsoft's attorneys famously argued, were it not for a lack of marketplace demand, the company was free to bundle a ham sandwich into Windows.

Now Microsoft's confidence was shaken by a federal court judge. "Microsoft's 'unfettered liberty' to impose its idea of what has been 'integrated' into its operating systems stops at least at the point at which it would violate established antitrust law," Jackson wrote. To enforce the point, he issued a preliminary injunction ordering Microsoft to drop its requirement that PC makers preinstall Microsoft's Internet browser as a condition of licensing Windows. Even more alarming, the judge's order covered successors to Windows 95. It was the first time Windows 98 had been formally dragged into the company's antitrust troubles. Microsoft had even grander plans for using the market power of Windows 98 to boost Internet Explorer.

Nobody had thought it would go that far. "His last paragraph there was very broad and sweeping, which stunned us," Allchin recalled.

Maritz said, "There were a lot of things in there that I personally found confusing."

The company's high command faced a long weekend of work. Neukom was nominally in charge of the company's legal strategy. But it was David Heiner who was the workhorse, serving as project manager for dealing with the Justice Department and as referee for Microsoft's loud and fast-talking executives. Heiner took over the boardroom across the hall from Gates's office in Building 8 and turned it into the war room for gathering input and plotting strategy.

For those who gathered in the boardroom, the legal discussion was a test of their ability to compartmentalize, a highly prized and necessary skill at Microsoft. The technology tug-of-war between Allchin and Silverberg and the legal imbroglio with the government were running in parallel. The two fronts involved the same set of issues: the relationship of the new phase of technology evolution, centered on the Internet, with the old phase, centered around Windows.

Throughout the fall, many of the same people—Maritz, Allchin, Chase, Cole, and of course Gates—were deeply involved in both sets of discussions. Silverberg, who remained officially on leave, was absent from the legal discussions.

The group pored over the ruling. In Gates's absence, Steve Ballmer peppered Heiner with dozens of questions. There were procedural problems with Jackson's orders, the lawyers explained. When Jackson threw out the contempt claim, that should have been the end of it. But Jackson had moved on his own to issue a preliminary injunction. And he had appointed a "special master," a law professor from Harvard named Lawrence Lessig, to help sort out the issues in what might well turn into a mini-trial of its own, possibly leading to permanent remedies. Lessig was beginning to make a name for himself applying constitutional principles to cyberspace policy disputes. He looked like bad news to Microsoft.

But all that could be taken up later. The preliminary injunction demanded an immediate response. The group quickly dispatched with the implications for Windows 98 by deciding to ignore them. There was plenty of time to challenge them in the six months or so before the expected release of the new operating system. "We had a discussion that said we specifically weren't going to think about this," Allchin later told government lawyers. "We're not thinking about it. March on. In our business we could disrupt a lot of people for nothing in a situation where time is slipping away on us."

It was not as easy to dismiss the implications for Windows 95. The group considered a number of ways to easily deactivate Internet Explorer. Microsoft's own Web sites boasted that "IE uninstalls easily." Perhaps Microsoft could offer PC makers a version of Windows 95 with the Internet Explorer icon removed from the desktop and other program menus. Or it could let PC makers use Windows' own "uninstall" program to remove the browser in the same way a customer might. That, after all, was what the PC makers were seeking from the beginning.

Ballmer's first instinct was to strike a pose of humility and try to avoid direct confrontation with the government. Chase, too, favored taking the high road in the hopes of gradually winning over the company's adversaries with charm and what he was sure were the merits of Microsoft's arguments. Justice Department officials were saying they expected to meet with Microsoft's lawyers within a few days to agree on an approach to satisfy the order. Something could be worked out.

It was spin-control time. The company's first response was striking in its moderation. A Microsoft flak, Adam Sohn, a damage-control veteran from the 1992 Clinton presidential campaign, spread good news to reporters. "We think it's a pretty balanced decision and we're grateful," he said.

Microsoft's press release also accentuated the positive. The company was "gratified" Jackson did not find the company in contempt. It was "looking forward" to presenting more evidence. It was "confident" it would prevail. The press release dismissed as a minor issue the order that Microsoft offer a browser-free Windows. Microsoft could continue to license Windows 95, the release stressed, as long as each PC maker "has the option of installing the portion of Windows 95 that does not include Internet Explorer 3.0 or 4.0 files." Over the weekend, one Microsoft spokesman told the *Wall Street Journal* the company expected to find ways to let PC makers delete Internet Explorer 3.0 and 4.0 files and still allow Windows to function.

When Gates returned from China, he turned the group around and changed the conciliatory tone. To him, a milquetoast response put Microsoft on the slippery slope to bankruptcy. The government's suit was an attack on the company's ability to add features in Windows. Integration was not only a fundamental principle, it was the basic business strategy Microsoft had pursued since it licensed its first operating system sixteen years earlier. If PC makers could pick and choose which parts of Windows to offer and what features to promote on the desktop screen, they could cut deals with Microsoft's competitors to gradually displace Windows.

That was why he had pushed so hard in the negotiations over the 1995 consent decree to secure the exception for integrated products in the first place. Now it was time to take advantage of his foresight.

At stake were all the company's plans for Windows Everywhere. It wasn't only about the browser war, where the momentum had shifted in Microsoft's favor such that the company could probably afford to let PC makers delete the Internet Explorer icon, or even the browser itself, without significant harm. But what about the Windows media player, which competed with the streaming video player from Real Networks? Or voice recognition, where IBM was strong? Or some other technology in the future? "Their position is that every major thing we've done, every major thing we're planning to do, should be blocked," Gates said later.

Gates considered the alternatives. At the end of his sixteen-page memorandum, Jackson's one-paragraph order was vague on exactly what Microsoft was required to do. All it said was that Microsoft must stop its practice of licensing Windows on the condition PC makers also license and install "any Microsoft Internet browser software."

Jackson, in his longer memorandum, though not in the order itself, referred to the "software code that Microsoft itself now separately distributes at retail as Internet Explorer 3.0." Government prosecutors also referred to the retail product in their request for action. The government's imprecision in defining exactly what it meant by "browser" was to be a recurring issue in the case. David Cole had submitted an affidavit attesting to the fact that IE 3 and Windows 95 shared a number of files needed by the operating system even to boot up, or start, properly. Removing all of the IE 3 files would "break" Windows, he had said.

Gates wanted to know what would happen if Microsoft adopted the most extreme, hyperliteral reading of the order? What if the company were to comply with Jackson's order by offering PC makers a version of Windows stripped of every line of code that also appeared in Internet Explorer? PC makers would have the option of installing a broken version of Windows 95, free of Internet Explorer. Microsoft could comply with the letter of the order and demonstrate the absurdity of the government's position at the same time.

Gates, a lawyer's son, was ferocious in legal debates. Microsoft's attorneys needed all their self-confidence and legal experience in order to keep up with his ability to instantly understand and apply the law. Microsoft's internal discussions are typically fast, loud, and "high-bandwidth"—a phrase borrowed from telecommunications conveying high praise for the volume of information that could be exchanged rapidly.

The pedantic, formal style of Richard Urowsky, Microsoft's outside counsel, couldn't be more different, but Gates had immense respect for his legal abilities. In the boardroom, Urowsky's ponderous voice came over the speakerphone from Washington, D.C.

"Bill." There was a long pause. "Bill." Another pause. "This is Richard." Urowsky's trademark interruption was one of the few ways to slow one of Gates's hundred-mile-per-hour rants. The ploy worked marvelously, shutting Gates up and making him smile at the same time.

Microsoft's lawyers agreed that under the strictest possible interpretation of Jackson's ruling, Microsoft could argue that it was required to offer a version of Windows stripped of *any* of the code also used in the retail version of IE 3.0. Microsoft could argue that the simplest method of "removing" IE was barred under the injunction—simply letting PC makers remove the IE icon, or use the "uninstall" feature, because both of those methods left much of the underlying code in place. If the goal of Microsoft's defense was to protect the principle that Microsoft can integrate new functionality into Windows, why offer alternatives that might not comply with the judge's order but could put fetters on Microsoft's unfettered ability to integrate?

The group also was aware that giving PC makers a choice between the status quo and a commercially worthless product might not have been what Judge Jackson quite had in mind. It was never a good idea to anger a federal judge.

The proposal sat on the boardroom table, like a bomb ready to go off.

"We're going to look terrible. We're going to look terrible. We're going to look terrible," warned some people in the room, Ballmer told me later. "I'm in the group of people who understood, we're not going to look good." Ballmer was still recovering from the fallout that followed his "To heck with Janet Reno!" outburst at a Microsoft sales event a month earlier. Microsoft could take a hard line and make its point, but Ballmer wanted to know, What is the outcome? What is the collateral damage? Ballmer acknowledged, "We agonized over that, looking bad."

Indeed, the Broken Windows approach was far from the most commonsense interpretation of the order. The injunction was simply a cease-and-desist order, a holding action until the court could make a final determination about whether Internet Explorer was a separate product and thus covered by the decree. The most thoughtful analysis of the whole mess came from Lessig, the brainy Harvard law professor. Before Lessig's appointment as Jackson's special master was rescinded by the appeals court on technical grounds, he offered his preliminary opinion in an eleven-page letter to lawyers on both sides.

Lessig found that the terms of the original decree were the real guide to what was and was not allowed; Jackson's injunction was simply meant to enforce the decree. And the plain meaning of the consent decree was to give PC makers a "zone of sovereignty" from Microsoft, protection for their freedom to choose competing products. Thus, Microsoft could have met the zone of sovereignty test,

Lessig wrote, by lifting the provisions that restricted the freedom of PC makers to remove or disable the code that enabled the browser's functions. "If Microsoft simply said, with respect to IE, 'You are free,' Microsoft would be in compliance."

In contrast, Microsoft's all-or-nothing stance did nothing to set PC makers free. Microsoft interpreted the injunction that PC makers couldn't be forced to take all of Internet Explorer as meaning they couldn't take any of it, even the parts required to make Windows work. The requirement that PC makers either take the full Internet Explorer/Windows 95 bundle or remove every last bit of code didn't leave PC makers "free to choose about the package of products they will offer to customers," the plain meaning of the consent decree, Lessig wrote.

Setting PC makers free was the last thing Microsoft wanted to do. The "IBM-compatible" PC industry grew up around Microsoft's central role in defining the operating system platform; Microsoft treated PC makers less as partners and more as mere distributors for Windows. Now the PC makers wanted to rebalance the relationships with Microsoft, promote their brands as unique, and take advantage of their relationships with customers to expand their razor-thin profit margins. Microsoft would become just one of several parts suppliers for their PCs.

From Microsoft's perspective, any new relationship that let PC makers go their own way would weaken Microsoft's hold on software developers, who wrote programs for Windows because it was installed so widely. "The minute we give up the contractual hooks, we fragment the platform and we lose the value of the unified platform," Raikes, then the number-two sales executive, told me later.

Maybe there was room for compromise. As the weekend wore on, Maritz and others jumped in, favoring moderation. Maybe hard core wasn't the right approach in this situation, they said. This is a federal judge, not a software competitor. Things could get worse, a lot worse. At a minimum, the company was looking at three months of disastrous PR. Can't we just get this over with? some executives pleaded.

"It was an incredibly awkward, no-win situation," remembers Chase.

Gates continued to argue for the high-risk, high-reward response. If Windows and IE were "integrated," they were home free. To him, there was no better way to prove Windows is an integrated product than to show that it broke when Internet Explorer was removed. "We have to maintain the absolute right to design software as we see fit," he argued. This was a great way to slam home that point.

Gates's proposal drew supporters, including Allchin. Ballmer insisted later that Gates's viewpoint was not "substantively different" than that of the rest of the group. Nobody argued that the Broken Windows approach wasn't risky. Everybody knew the company would certainly take a public relations hit.

Still, Gates said, "I want to go for this." The clincher in his argument: If Microsoft followed the letter of the ruling, it would help its case on appeal.

"We all agreed with Bill and braced ourselves for the fallout," said one participant.

On Monday morning, Microsoft offered the stripped-down version of Windows. To soften its stance, the company also agreed to make available a two-year-old version of Windows 95 that was released at retail before Internet Explorer was added to the product. PC makers would not be given any new flexibility to use the more commonplace methods to remove the browser functions or the icon.

The fallout was immediate. Dan Gillmor, in his column in the *San Jose Mercury News*, called it "compliance with a raised middle finger." The Justice Department claimed the response made an "absolute mockery" of the preliminary injunction and went back to court to again seek a contempt citation. Microsoft employees visiting home for the holidays were suddenly forced to defend the integrity of what had long been one of the country's most respected companies. "It's very painful when you go home and your son asks, 'Daddy, why is the government suing Microsoft?' " said Anthony Bay, one of the middle managers who had attended the Power Lab workshop.

Ballmer acknowledged the damage. "It left us in a position where a lot of people are questioning our company, whether it's a moral company, a proper company, respectful company," he told me. The negative feeling from customers and others in the industry was clear "and has certainly not been lost on any of us," he said. The company convened focus groups and found a noticeable negative turn. "The number of people enthusiastic about the company, the products, who would recommend, or would buy them, has clearly taken a dip. It's not cataclysmic. But it's clear."

The response also damaged Microsoft's credibility with Judge Jackson. He had ordered Microsoft only to "cease and desist" from the company's own practice. He hadn't prescribed the particulars of the new licensing terms the company should adopt. He later said he considered Microsoft's response so "untrustworthy" it colored his view of the company for the next two years.

"I found their compliance to be less than genuine," he said.

Cole was deployed to receive Jackson's wrath. In court a few weeks later, Jackson asked incredulously, "It seemed absolutely clear to you that I entered an order that required you distribute a product that would not work? Is that what you're telling me?"

Cole was a good soldier. "In plain English, yes," Cole told Jackson. "We followed that order. It wasn't my place to consider the consequences of that."

Gates insisted that he had had no choice but to remove every line of code that also appeared in the retail version of the browser. And the court of appeals later found that Microsoft's interpretation was indeed plausible.

"We did exactly what the order said to do. There was no freedom or flexibility," Gates said at a public event a month after the episode. "What did people say about that? How were we treated on that? Brutally, just brutally."

"I was not sitting there going, 'Ha, ha, I'll do what I want.' I was sitting there going, 'This is the worst thing that's ever happened to me. When can I get back to just focusing on developing software?' And then to have the press come out and say, you know, what it said, that felt bad."

SECOND THOUGHTS

The 1997 holiday season was less than joyous at Microsoft. Even on Internet time, the pace of life slows and the mood grows reflective with the short days and the many Christmas parties. Most of the company's senior management had devoted their twenties and much of their thirties to the company. Now, as they started to turn forty, their children, their marriages, and their health were starting to seem more important. But just as the time had come to turn inward, all hell was breaking loose.

Allchin's private view was that the legal mess reflected Microsoft's larger confusion over technology strategy. In public, the company staunchly defended the notion that there was no meaningful distinction between Windows and the browser. But the strategy debates and factional rivalries inside Microsoft belied that claim.

Prosecutors considered whether to make a big deal out of the issues raised by Microsoft's internal organization. The wording of the key phrase in the consent decree, after all, preserved only Microsoft's right to "develop" integrated products. But since the summer of 1995, development of the browser, under Silverberg, and development of Windows, under Allchin, occurred in separate organizations. For two and a half years, Silverberg and Allchin wrestled for control over the evolution of Microsoft's primary computing platform. As Allchin loudly pointed out in his e-mails, the two efforts were at minimum uncoordinated and more often contradictory and competitive as well. The organizational split, he complained, meant little work was being done to integrate IE 4.0 and Windows 98.

Gates had blessed the deal to leave the browser and Windows in two separate teams with separate strategic mandates. Thus, at the very time Microsoft was arguing in Washington, D.C., that IE 4.0 and Windows were a single product, back in Redmond Gates was confirming that separate code and separate development was the optimal strategy for the company. Soon after his controversial decision to tough out the preliminary injunction, Gates had handed down his Solomonic judgment regarding the future of the browser team in the meeting with Maritz, Silverberg, and Allchin. Windows and Internet Explorer would remain split.

The contradictions were becoming harder to explain. The day after the meeting, Microsoft was due back in court, and was going to argue once again that Windows and Internet Explorer were inseparable. Technical integration was clearly the company's main legal claim, but now that was increasingly contradicted by the company's management structure. Gates's decision to keep the browser code and development team organizationally separate from the Windows organization seemed to be shooting the company's legal strategy in the foot.

In Allchin's view, Microsoft's half-in, half-out strategy could help prosecutors convince a federal judge, at least provisionally, that the two technologies were separate. The lawsuit had hardened his thinking about the importance of making the organizational change.

Indeed, government prosecutors later said if Microsoft had followed Allchin's integration strategy from the beginning, and had never marketed the browser separately, they would have been unable to file suit under the consent decree. Even under broader antitrust laws, proving violations would have been much more difficult. But if the browser was indeed shown to be separate from Windows, then Microsoft's marketing tactics were on shaky legal ground.

The company had gone beyond merely tying a separate application, the browser, to the operating system. Rather, it tied its new platform, Internet Explorer, to its old platform, Windows. The new competitors to Windows were not other operating systems but any shell—such as a browser—that could run the new software applications being written—that is to say, Web sites. The browser was obviously the next-generation operating system shell. To the extent Microsoft's shell matched or beat the competition, no competitor could "pull a Windows" on Windows. The way to leverage the old operating system monopoly into the new operating system monopoly—legally—was for the new features to be part of Windows, not a separate product.

Allchin didn't—couldn't—raise such antitrust considerations with Gates. At Microsoft, by design, technology strategy and courtroom strategy were to be "orthogonal," a geometric term to describe two lines that don't intersect at all. For any Microsoft executive, playing the antitrust card was the quickest way to lose a technology argument with Gates. Gates made it abundantly clear that letting legal considerations drive business decisions was the surest way to fall prey to "IBM disease," the paralysis and indecision that gripped the computer giant in the 1970s and 1980s as it faced its own antitrust nightmare. Gates, the legal logistician, would likely have rejected any advice that dictated his technology strategy. It was an article of faith at Microsoft that Bill Gates was hard-core technically; he would never fail to do the right thing for the sake of legal appearances.

Under Microsoft's definition of "integrated," it didn't matter what particular group developed the software. It was all Microsoft. Gates could list dozens of improvements to Windows that came from the Office group and elsewhere and were later adopted and integrated into the platform. Windows was what Microsoft said it was. With that understanding, Gates was free to shuffle teams as conditions demanded.

If Gates himself could ignore legal considerations, Microsoft's lawyers couldn't. The day after the meeting, Microsoft's lawyers were back at the federal courthouse in Washington, D.C., for another bad day in front of Judge Jackson. In his chambers, the judge's assistant demonstrated an easy way to uninstall Internet Explorer in less than ninety seconds. The method left some of the underlying code intact, but Jackson wasn't interested in the nuances. To him, his preliminary injunction had met the test of common sense.

That night, Allchin sent an e-mail to a half-dozen Microsoft vice presidents, expressing his disappointment about the previous day's meeting with Gates. The e-mail reflected the arguments that Allchin had been making all year. This time, however, Allchin discreetly linked Microsoft's internal politics with the escalating external attack. Allchin was worried his proposal might be interpreted as intended to make Microsoft's strategy look better in court. In his e-mail, he mentioned the "perception issue of the DOJ" but just as quickly urged that it be ignored. Allchin wanted it known his rationale was business, not legal.

"The plan that was discussed was that IE stays with Bradsi" for about a year, Allchin wrote, using Silverberg's internal e-mail name. "I personally disagree with this strategy." Microsoft needed more "technical synergy," he argued. "How do we really get a unified user interface if things are split?"

In its zeal to compete head-to-head with Netscape, Microsoft had mistakenly positioned the browser in the market as separate from Windows, Allchin argued. Even the branding was separate—Internet Explorer's spinning "e" rather than the Windows flag appeared in the browser's upper right corner. The press releases trumpeted separate measures of success—for the browser the goal was market share rather than sales of Windows. Microsoft insisted on separate license agreements for Internet Explorer and for Windows. The browser effort was on a separate strategy: Internet Explorer was available not only for Macintosh and Unix computers but for older versions of Windows, such as the millions still using Windows 3.1. In Allchin's view, giving away the browser as an enhancement to versions of Windows that customers had already bought undermined the incentives for customers—paying customers—to upgrade to the next Windows release.

As Allchin saw it, simple things like the brief description of Internet Explorer in Windows 98 itself made the browser appear as a separate product. Or the fact that IE, like other Microsoft products, had its own site on Microsoft.com, the company's heavily trafficked corporate Web site. Why wasn't it a branch under the Windows page, like other Windows features? He told colleagues Silverberg's strategy was giving ammunition to Microsoft's critics.

He concluded Microsoft needed more, not less, integration with

Windows, in both technical and marketing terms. "I see this as critical. This is a hard balance, but I feel that we need to slant things much
more toward Windows while we still accomplish the other goal
against Netscape." He said the split organization that Gates had approved would be tough to explain to his troops. "I believe they will
laugh at management again for not making the hard call."

In his e-mail Allchin urged anyone who agreed with him about the
fate of the browser to weigh in by sending e-mail to Gates and
Maritz. The senior technical team was being forced to choose sides in
what seemed like a final showdown. Silverberg was threatening to
quit if he didn't get his way. Friends had told Allchin to raise the
stakes as well.

Over the Christmas break, Muglia, who claimed to be a fence-
sitter, came down on Allchin's side. He had a finely tuned sense of the
direction of Microsoft's political winds. He lobbied Maritz that the
browser belonged with Windows. The decision was a test of Maritz
as a manager, Muglia said. Was he going to build an organization
around personalities or logic? Personalities aside, the issue was simple: The browser team was doing the new user interface for Windows; thus, it should be part of the Windows organization. Was he
going to cave in to Silverberg or do the "right thing"?

Maritz understood such arguments and began to come around. In
1990, he had tried to rationalize Microsoft's tortured relationship
with IBM. The two companies were jointly developing OS/2, a successor operating system to DOS. The organization of the project was
a mess—two teams with two management structures that came together only at the top of the two companies. It was an inefficient,
error-prone way of creating software that in Maritz's view wasn't
going anywhere good for either company. He pushed for Microsoft
to go its own way.

The lesson from the IBM experience became what could be called
the Maritz Doctrine: Without workable management structures and
clear business goals, you're not going to succeed. Software development is complicated enough as it is. Maritz, a conflict avoider,
dreaded the prospect of mediating another round of internecine war-
fare. "There comes a time when you really have to recognize you've
allowed things to become too complicated or unworkable," he told
me. "Then you've got to make some hard decisions."

The internal organizational issues, however, had been on the table
for months. What was new was the argument about the appearance

Microsoft's organizational chart might make in Judge Jackson's court. Gates may have been able to make technology decisions free of legal considerations, but Maritz had no such luxury. It was clear that appearances were going to matter hugely. Any lawyer would provide a client in such a situation with prudent advice: Clean up your company's organizational structure before going in front of the judge. Microsoft would be better off if the "facts on the ground" supported their story in court.

Between Christmas and New Year's, Maritz had second thoughts about the critical question of who should control the browser team, which had seemed to be resolved in favor of Silverberg in the December 22 meeting. He told Gates he had changed his mind; he now believed the team and the software code should go to Allchin, not Silverberg. He later told me the preliminary injunction was not a "major" reason for his reversal. Instead, Maritz said he felt it was more important to weld the groups together at a low level in the organization rather than have them welded together at a high level. Whatever his reasons, they were good enough to outweigh the unavoidable consequences: Silverberg would quit. Maritz wondered whether he had done the right thing.

The plan to keep Silverberg had been motivated by more than mere loyalty. The Megaserver project was important to Gates. Silverberg, with his aggressiveness and focus on the competition, was the right guy to spearhead the initiative. And if Microsoft lost him, Silverberg would be immensely valuable to any competitor seeking to challenge Microsoft.

But nobody was indispensable. Gates had already overruled Maritz once. He couldn't make it a pattern.

On the first day back in the office after New Year's, Maritz called in Silverberg's lieutenants, Ludwig and Cole, before telling Silverberg himself. Near five o'clock, past sundown in the dark Northwest winter, Cole went to see Silverberg. "Have you talked to Maritz today?" he asked.

No, Silverberg said. He had an appointment in the morning.

"Uh, you should go see him," Cole said.

Silverberg didn't need to ask Maritz what was going on. He knew instantly what had happened.

Gates received Silverberg's e-mail that night. As Silverberg saw it, Gates had reneged on his promise, Silverberg said. It was a question of trust. He gave Gates a day to change his mind, or he was gone.

The next day, Silverberg went to Maritz's office; Maritz confirmed he had changed his mind on the browser deal. Silverberg might think the browser team was critical to his new role, but Maritz didn't think so.

"This is one of the most dishonorable things I've ever seen," Silverberg said. "We agreed. You knew this was our agreement. You had plenty of time to work things out. Once you make an agreement, you have to stand by it."

"This is where I think it belongs," Maritz told him. "And I hope you'll stay."

Silverberg cursed at him and walked out. The two wouldn't talk again for eighteen months.

When Silverberg saw Gates, Gates stood behind Maritz. We think this is the right thing to do, he told Silverberg. I get to make the hard calls, and this is my call.

With the browser now under his control, Allchin wasted little time in enforcing the new regime. He ordered a sweep of the Internet Explorer Web site, "where we ensure it is clear that IE is just a capability of Windows."

"I am very concerned about how Internet Explorer is presented in Windows 98," he wrote to Yusuf Mehdi, who with Silverberg's exit transferred into Allchin's group. "Even simple things . . . make it appear separate. I think it is critical that someone does a thorough walk-through looking for places in the user interface that can be corrected (hopefully just text) easily *before* Windows 98 ships."

Mehdi, an easygoing optimist, had been one of the strongest advocates for Silverberg's return. But now that he was out, Mehdi was eager to get on with the new program. Silverberg and Ludwig encouraged him to take the new job. "He's a smart guy, you'll learn a lot," they told him.

Mehdi quickly replied to Allchin's e-mail. A review was already set for the Windows 98 team, he wrote. "Someone from legal staff and we will ensure Internet Explorer is properly presented."

Mehdi's boss, Brad Chase, Silverberg's longtime ally, also agreed to work under Allchin, surprising many people inside Microsoft. Chase, a company loyalist, resigned himself to the fact that the Internet platform strategy would have to wait.

"We just didn't convince enough people," he said.

• • •

Out of Control

Bill Gates doesn't like to make complex decisions. He sees all shades of gray; nothing is ever black or white. He integrates, endlessly computing and recomputing against any new information to come up with a dynamic synthesis. All the arguments, all the implications of future events discounted back to the present. He hates trade-offs. Rather than make them, he prefers to leave decisions open, gather more data, make sure he's not wrong. He ducks as long as he can.

Now he had been forced to choose. Legal necessity had pushed Gates to assert the unity of Windows and the browser; now he was unable to set the browser and the browser team free to form the foundation of the new Internet platform that was clearly the future of computing.

No Microsoft executive confirms that legal appearances were the reason for the pullback from the 1997 plan to build a new Internet platform, though many people familiar with the internal discussions have that suspicion.

Microsoft's stubborn stance seemed to be: We have the absolute legal right to pursue the wrong strategy.

Gates had held the Internet's future in his hands and considered the choice between opportunity and fear. To embrace opportunity, he had to trust. Trust that he could retain the loyalty of developers who were free to switch to rival offerings once Microsoft let go of the hooks that kept software developers and users tied to Windows. Trust that Microsoft's development team was indeed the best in the world and could build better software and compete on the merits of quality and price. Trust that increased volume, once again, would make up for the drop in market share and profit margins in a world of heterogeneous and open software.

Gates prided himself on not spending "one second" being concerned about shareholder value. It is more important, he insisted, to make long-term investments that might not pay off for five or ten years or ever. "You have to be ready to take the criticism, or lower valuation, for that length of time," he says.

But when forced to choose, he opted for fear. For all his bravado, he wasn't willing to bet the company.

At the moment of his greatest opportunity, Gates chose to retrench. Rather than rising to the challenges of the new Internet model, he chose to resist them. Rather than embracing the new wave of innovation, he sought to slow it down in order to preserve Microsoft's old dominance.

A line had been crossed. The precise reasons for the reversal are less important than what the splintering of the browser team came to represent within the company. The dissonance between Microsoft's self-conception and its new reality demoralized even those who still loved the company. Microsoft was tied in knots. It wasn't the legal attacks themselves, but rather the company's response, that slowly sapped Microsoft's energy.

"We stalled and became a muddled mess," said Tod Nielsen. "It wasn't a clear Microsoft message. We never made the bet on the new paradigm. Confusion reigned."

The internal divisions and external attacks were taking a toll on Gates himself. The company's eight-member executive committee, always unwieldy, had broken down, leaving pretty much everything on Gates's shoulders. He was keeping up his grueling travel schedule, delivering keynote addresses, meeting fellow chief executives of major customers, hosting visiting politicians, reviewing the product groups, and seeking to soften his harsh public image. In late January, he hastily agreed to a longstanding request for an interview with ABC's Barbara Walters. During Walters's visit to Hood Canal, she asked Gates what he sang to his daughter, Jennifer Katherine, then nearly two. He broke into "Twinkle Twinkle Little Star."

Gates was never as good as Ballmer at managing his time. Now, the legal issues were taking a huge chunk of an already booked calendar.

"Bill got so tied up with other things, he was not managing the company," said David Marquardt, a venture capitalist who has been on Microsoft's board since he made the original investment in Microsoft in 1981.

The independence of Microsoft's board of directors had never been seriously tested. Microsoft had always been Gates's company. The primary responsibility of any board is to decide when it's time for the chief executive to go; for Microsoft that was out of the question. From the beginning, Gates *was* Microsoft. Everybody else used the pronoun "we" when they discussed Microsoft. Gates used the first person: I did that, my strategy is this.

Board members were reluctant to stand up to Gates. Direct challenges rarely succeeded and were always painful. Dealing with him presented a difficult contradiction—he didn't invite challenges, but you couldn't earn his respect without challenging him. Not many of the board members had the stamina to endure the brutal treatment Gates could mete out.

Jon Shirley, Microsoft's former president, helped rationalize the company's operations in its early days and built the company from $50 million in revenues to its first billion-dollar year. But Shirley was a numbers guy, not a products or strategy guy. And Microsoft had long since moved into a realm in which Shirley realized he had little experience. Paul Allen, Microsoft's cofounder who had been on and off the board since he relinquished his operational role at the company, occasionally challenged Gates's thinking on high-level strategy, but Gates knew Allen's moves intimately. He countered by delving deeper into specifics until even Allen could no longer follow him. Richard Hackborn, a longtime Hewlett-Packard executive, was averse to conflict and never established an easy rapport with Gates. The other members of the board were Jill Barad, the embattled then-chief executive of Mattel, and William G. Reed, a retired Seattle lumber industry executive. Gates didn't nurture close board relationships.

Marquardt tried to raise the difficult issues delicately. "You have to penetrate the hide, then back off and let it fester," he said.

He and other board members spent days in Redmond in late 1997 and early 1998 talking with key people at the company, trying to understand what was wrong and how they could help.

Since the founding of Microsoft, Gates had been its single point of integration. Now the board found that he had become the single point of failure. Gates was losing control of Microsoft. The Windows 2000 effort was in danger of collapsing under the weight of its own staggering complexity. Other products were late as well, and were not being defined crisply. Real Networks had jumped to a commanding lead in streaming technology. Palm had a stronghold on personal digital assistants. The company let drift its contentious relationship with Sun over Java. Microsoft might well have sued Sun for breach of contract; instead, Sun struck first and filed suit against Microsoft. Customers were flocking to the Internet while Microsoft preached Windows, Windows, Windows.

"There were no signs of wins anywhere," Marquardt said.

Control, for Gates, is not a matter of status or ego. It is more like breathing—essential to his very functioning. From his first forays into business as a teenager, he had told his partners, I'm much easier to deal with if I'm in charge. Now, the centralized structure was no

longer working. He had allowed the company to drift in a kind of
haze, deferring the tough strategic questions. Other companies were
spinning off units, "delayering" to make themselves more nimble.
Loosely coupled "holding companies" were gaining favor on Wall
Street. Microsoft remained tightly integrated, with all decisions
flowing through Gates.

At several successive board meetings, Gates seemed emotionally
drained and exhausted. His mood darkened in the weeks after the
showdown with the government, which ended with a settlement
under which Microsoft allowed PC makers to hide the browser icon
on the Windows desktop, the concession he had so adamantly sought
to avoid.

At the quarterly board meeting in January 1998, after dispatching
the routine agenda items, Gates launched into a remarkable rambling
discourse, alternately lashing out at his detractors and descend-
ing into self-pity. He was drowning, he said. He was having trouble
sleeping, and his stomach was bothering him. Melinda was worried
about his health. The weight of expectations, the problems piled
on him from inside and outside the company, was overwhelming
him. He lost his composure, and it took him several minutes to recover.

"It was a plea for help," Marquardt said. He and the other board
members were stunned. They had never seen Bill Gates like this before. Gates almost never asked for help, regarding it as a sign of weak-
ness. He had always seemed totally in control.

MANY Microsoft managers groaned when they heard the official
reason why Gates was handing off business responsibilities to
Ballmer: He wanted to spend more time with Microsoft's product
groups. To them, that was precisely the wrong direction. His new
role would give him even more time to scream at and disrupt their
teams.

Newcomers hired into senior positions were initiated into the
basic precepts of "Bill management" almost as soon as they learned
to navigate the dozens of buildings on Microsoft's campus. One key
piece of advice was: Keep Bill as far away from your project as possible.

The conventional wisdom was that the more deeply Gates was involved, the more likely a project was to fail. To rational-minded engineers, evidence was everything. They noted the inverse correlation

between software projects in which Gates took a strong personal interest and success. At the top of the list was Allchin's Cairo project, the ambitious next-generation operating system that was hugely hyped and then quietly dumped. Also on the list of failures was much of Myhrvold's early work on interactive television, the early MSN efforts, the Windows at Work attempt to modify the operating system for copiers and fax machines, and of course Bob, the "social interface" to help beginning computer users, whose time, Gates still insists, will come. In contrast, Gates's involvement was relatively small in Windows 95, Office, and even Windows NT.

Gates had lost the technical respect of many of Microsoft's key managers. Even supporters acknowledge that his direct "value add" in the Internet era was not nearly as high as in the PC era. In the very meritocracy he had created, Gates was slowly being marginalized. For five years or so, he had been largely irrelevant to much of what Microsoft was doing. Gates was simply too far removed from the trenches.

He was still accustomed to quickly absorbing everything in his regular product reviews, asking his usual rat-a-tat-tat series of incisive questions, issuing his peremptory orders, and moving on to the next appointment on his too-busy calendar. But his method wasn't working as well as it had.

"For many years, he could grok it end-to-end and give people instant feedback," Maritz told me. The new set of problems needed more careful thought. Even for someone as smart as Gates, Maritz said, "There's enough existing thinking, you need to digest it all before you can engage."

Those most adept at handling Gates were able to ignore his suggestions without incurring his wrath. "All the senior managers know how to manage Bill," said a former vice president who was considered a master of the art, which included keeping his name out of print. The key is to resist his suggestions gently or to frame them in the context of the kinds of trade-offs Gates hates to make. Suggested lines of defense include: Customers don't want it. It will make the system slow. It can't be done in the time left before we ship. We don't have the people to assign to that problem. If Gates's idea is good, agree to put it in the next version, or add a placeholder as a nod in Gates's direction.

Microsoft's three-year planning process provided another convenient way to subtly shine on Gates's pet priorities. The concrete goals in the plan's first year invariably took eighteen months to complete.

Before the time ever came to implement Year Three objectives, it was time to make another plan.

With Gates under increasing pressure, the problems were getting worse, not better. Managers felt their authority undermined by Gates's abusive behavior. "He will debate you and destroy you in front of all the people who work for you," the former vice president said. "After the tenth time that happens, when you've got more money than you could ever spend, you say, 'I think I'll just pass on the next one.' "

Gates invariably pressed the same point: Be more "strategic." He demanded hooks to lock in customers. The goal was to drive interdependencies between various Microsoft products and thus make it more painful for customers to switch to a competitor for any individual feature.

Gates was nervous about the ephemeral quality of popularity. His managers felt he didn't think Microsoft could win just by producing good software. He didn't want to grind out business without a lock-in strategy. If the competitive situation hinged on a product being "better," Gates feared there was nothing to stop customers from adopting the next-better thing that comes along. The imposition of what is referred to at Microsoft as the "strategy tax," or sometimes the "Windows tax," was inherently demoralizing; the teams preferred to see themselves as winners on the merits.

Microsoft insiders acknowledged there was a grain of truth to the criticism from competitors that Microsoft routinely breached the "Chinese wall" executives had claimed separated developers of application software, such as Office, from the Windows operating system, or platform side of the business. But the critics had it backwards. The edge came not from inside information about secret features. It came from better intelligence about what part of the "vaporware" from other parts of the company to ignore, whose ideas were dumb, and when things would realistically ship. Competitors, even after being burned repeatedly, invariably put too much stock in Microsoft's public announcements.

Many managers actively postponed Gates's reviews of the products. Others learned not to let their supervisors attend "BillG reviews" to prevent them from insisting on changes to satisfy his concerns in order to further their own ambitions.

Gates had an inkling that he was sometimes ignored. "It would be usual within Microsoft that if you asked a question, you would receive an answer; is that fair, sir?" government lawyers asked him in his deposition.

"No. There's no—there's lots of questions I ask I don't get answers to," Gates said. "But well over 50 percent, I do."

"When you say that there are lots of questions that you ask people of Microsoft that you don't get answers to, do you mean you don't get any answer at all, they just ignore it?"

"That happens," Gates said.

GATES was losing control of the legal situation as well. When financier J. P. Morgan was facing his own antitrust suit early in the twentieth century, he felt confident enough to offhandedly instruct President Teddy Roosevelt, "Send your man to my man and they can fix it up." Gates possessed no such ability to finesse his legal problems. Through 1997 and 1998, Microsoft was badly outmaneuvered by a high-powered legal and lobbying campaign funded by competitors Netscape, Sun, Oracle, and others.

The competitors danced delicately around an obvious contradiction. In the marketplace, they loudly proclaimed that Microsoft was doomed, the victim of a sea change in computing that was making the PC obsolete. Larry Ellison, the mercurial chief of Oracle, called the PC a "ridiculous device." Sun's Scott McNealy derided Office as a "hairball."

In court, however, without a trace of irony, they painted Microsoft as invincible, a permanent obstacle to fair competition.

In truth, the legal attack on Microsoft was simply another front of the industry's geopolitical battle for dominance. An internal IBM strategy memo circulated in July 1998 exhorted, "The entire industry must behave like a single, focused competitor to Microsoft."

Microsoft's competitors were similarly united in their lobbying efforts. In 1997, Microsoft was effectively shut out of the founding of Technology Network, or TechNet, a bipartisan industry lobby. TechNet served as a fund-raising machine, to tap the fountain of technology money and boost the industry's clout in Washington. It was set up by John Doerr, the most prominent partner in the most prominent venture capital firm in Silicon Valley. The new organization formalized the efforts of a group of CEOs who had met with Vice President Al Gore eight times since January and in June 1997 had a seventy-five-minute meeting with President Clinton at the San Francisco home of investment banker Sandy Robertson. The Clinton Administration was eager to rebuild relations with Silicon Valley, which had become cozy during the 1992 campaign. By 1995, the courtship had chilled completely with Clinton's veto, later overridden, of a securities-litigation overhaul sought by the industry to limit shareholder lawsuits.

Doerr was a registered Republican, but he became so close to Gore and was such a "new economy" superstar that for a time it was popular in the Valley to talk about "Gore and Doerr in '04." Netscape's CEO, Jim Barksdale, a more traditional Republican, served as cochairman of TechNet.

Doerr insisted he bore no animus toward Microsoft, offering as proof his own large stockholdings in the company. Still, he was the leading figure in bringing together a *keiretsu* of companies, led by Netscape, that formed the only effective counterweight to Microsoft's increasing domination of technology standards. Doerr's public posture was that TechNet would stay away from antitrust and pursue such consensus issues as litigation reform.

So where was Bill Gates? He's definitely going to be part of Tech-Net, Doerr told me. There's nobody more influential in the new economy than Bill Gates, he said. Doerr indicated he'd be calling Gates right away. A couple of weeks later, I asked Doerr again. He still hadn't called, but he would do so soon. Six weeks later, Gates told me he still hadn't heard from Doerr. (Several months later, Microsoft did join TechNet.)

TechNet's fund-raising clout provided influence to members who used the group's fund-raising events to make clear their interest in action against Microsoft, even though the issue was not on the group's official agenda. In private conversations, the executives tried to recast the antitrust debate, not as an attack on Microsoft's success, but as a new economy issue of preserving open competition. Floyd Kvamme, another partner at Doerr's firm, Kleiner Perkins Caufield & Byers, helped enlist conservatives in the get-Microsoft effort. In December 1997, he wrote to Jack Kemp, a member of Oracle's board of directors, asking him to "consider joining conservatives who will look at this as a real issue for the health of a market-based economy."

Microsoft's competitors did line up a Murderer's Row of conservatives: former Senate leader and presidential candidate Bob Dole; Senator Orrin Hatch, the Republican from Utah and chairman of the

Senate Judiciary Committee; and Robert Bork, Reagan's failed nom-inee to the Supreme Court, intellectual leader of the free-market "Chicago School" of antitrust policy, and author of the conservative legal classic *The Antitrust Paradox*. Bork, now a lobbyist and consult-ant, was hired by Netscape. Allowing Microsoft to be badly out-flanked on the right side of the political spectrum was arguably Gates's biggest tactical mistake. Competitors had neatly denied Mi-crosoft its easiest argument: antitrust scrutiny as the unwarranted in-trusion of big-government regulators.

Dole, of counsel to the Washington law firm of Verner, Liipfert, Bernhard, McPherson and Hand, came aboard after Netscape re-tained another Washington operative, Mike Pettit, a former Dole staffer. Dole wrote letters soliciting corporations for $250,000 mem-berships in the anti-Microsoft coalition. For his temerity, Microsoft produced a humorous video for Gates's Comdex speech that lam-pooned Dole's appearance in a TV commercial endorsing Viagra; in the spoof, actor Leslie Nielsen, playing Dole, solemnly described the embarrassment of "hard drive dysfunction."

"Nothing is more embarrassing about booting up your computer and having your hard drive freeze up on you, if you know what I mean," says Nielsen. "I have learned that a properly functioning hard drive is important to all of us."

Hatch's first big opportunity to help pry open the floodgates of tech-money campaign contributions came in June 1997, as he han-dled confirmation hearings for Klein's nomination as antitrust chief. Hatch was active in trying to persuade his Republican colleagues not to block Klein. As Bingaman's deputy, Klein was thought to be a weak antitrust enforcer, based on his role in letting big telecommu-nications mergers go through easily. Microsoft, ironically, lobbied on behalf of Klein's nomination; Netscape worked against him. He was considered likely to go easy on the software giant. The anti-Microsoft coalition generated hundreds of letters of complaint about Microsoft's tactics to Montana Senator Conrad Burns, a Republican member of the Judiciary Committee. Only after Klein committed to an aggressive investigation of Microsoft did Burns lift his hold on the nomination.

A few months later, Mike Hirshland, a Hatch aide, waded through the anti-Microsoft evidence provided by its competitors. Netscape chairman Jim Clark had come into his office, browser software in hand. As Hirshland, a former clerk to Justice Anthony Kennedy at the U.S. Supreme Court, examined the evidence of Microsoft's heavy-handed dealings with PC makers, he recalled a passage in Bork's book, the Republican antitrust Bible, describing the rare circumstances in which "exclusive dealing" called for antitrust action. To Hirshland, the terms of Microsoft's deals with PC makers "fit the Bork hypothetical to a T."

Klein, who had earlier served President Bill Clinton as deputy White House counsel, was weighing the odds of winning a full Sherman antitrust case against Microsoft. The debate inside the Justice Department seesawed between conservatives and risk-takers. Staff lawyers were confident they had a winnable case, but the conflict needed the right framing. If Microsoft was seen by the public as winning market share with better technology and lower prices, the government was a loser. More subtly, the government would also lose if it was seen by the public to be punishing Microsoft because it threatened the revenue streams of major oligopolists and campaign contributors such as cable operators, broadcasters, airlines, and banks.

But if Microsoft could be charged with monopolizing the Internet—that could be a winner.

Hatch scheduled a hearing for March 1998 on competitiveness in the software industry. The goal was to test the political winds and send a signal that mainstream Republicans wouldn't beat up the Clinton administration for taking on high-tech's biggest icon.

A month before the hearing, Gates ran into Hatch in Davos, the city in the Swiss Alps that plays host to the political and business elite who gather every year at the invitation of the World Economic Forum to discuss big-think issues of globalization and technological change.

"Hi, Bill. How are you?" Hatch asked cheerfully.

"Not very well, thanks to you," Gates scowled.

When Gates played bridge, or even Monopoly, he knew every nuance of the rules, the better to push them right to their limits. In the software industry, Gates knew how to play the game better than anybody. Now he was in a game where the rules were obscure and, more alarmingly, always changing.

Before agreeing to appear at the Senate hearing, Gates demanded that Hatch put on the witness panel some of his computer industry allies to balance Netscape's Barksdale and Sun's McNealy. An executive from Compaq was the most obvious choice. Despite the spat over the browser icon in 1996, Compaq was Microsoft's closest PC partner. The companies had kissed and made up with an agreement guaranteeing Compaq the industry's lowest prices for Windows. Even a cost savings of a few dollars—at Microsoft's discretion—gave Compaq a concrete advantage over other PC makers. But Compaq's upper management was in its own turmoil. Among other major PC makers, Microsoft had chilly relations with IBM and Gateway; those companies paid higher prices for Windows.

Gates turned to Michael Dell, the boyish billionaire founder of Dell Computer. Dell's assigned role at the hearing was to testify to the benefits to PC makers of an industry-standard operating system like Windows. Like all PC makers, Dell's fundamental interests were split. Later, Dell would take advantage of the increased freedom from Microsoft gained by PC makers as a result of the company's legal mess. So perhaps it shouldn't have been a surprise that Dell's performance at the hearing recalled the Marlene Dietrich character in the 1957 movie *Witness for the Prosecution*, who dramatically testifies against her husband.

In his testimony, Dell claimed his company freely distributed Netscape's browser as well as Microsoft's. Hirshland had evidence to the contrary. He had used Dell's 800 number to try to order a PC with Netscape's browser. In his questioning, Hatch recounted the conversations with Dell's customer service representatives— "George, Brad, Jason, Bobby, and Jeff." None of them would agree to configure a PC with Netscape's software.

The Hatch hearings were a tryout for Gates on the witness stand. The proceedings were not a trial, but Gates was clearly "in the bull's-eye," as Senator Edward M. Kennedy, the ranking Democratic senator on the committee, put it. Hatch thought he had the goods on Microsoft's contracts with Internet publishers who wanted a place on the Windows desktop. From reporters, challenges to Gates rarely went beyond an opening salvo and perhaps a follow-up question. Hatch went five rounds with the reigning champion. Hatch was a Senate committee chairman; in Washington, D.C., that position carried more power than the title of world's richest man.

In Hatch's view, Microsoft's strong-arming of PC makers was more legally significant than the restrictive marketing contracts. Microsoft's influence over what software ostensibly independent PC companies did or didn't sell went straight to the heart of antitrust doctrine on exclusive dealing. But the people with firsthand knowledge of such dealings were staunchly resistant to going public, much less testifying. The marketing contracts were in writing, unlike the tactics used against PC makers.

"Mr. Gates, you have been somewhat hard to nail down on a very specific question, and I would appreciate just a yes or no, if you can," Hatch pressed. "Does Microsoft limit the ability of its content providers to advertise or promote Netscape?"

Gates answered narrowly. "Every Internet content provider that has a business relationship with Microsoft is free to develop content that uses competitors' platforms and standards."

Hatch pressed on. "But my question is do you put any limitations on content providers?"

Gates again answered obliquely. He said that Netscape signed up Web publishers as well.

"How about Microsoft: Do they put limitations or restrictions on people from advertising and promoting Netscape?"

"I am not aware of any limitation that prevents them from doing content that promotes Netscape."

"Do you use your exclusive arrangement with the companies—do you use that as leverage to stop them from advertising or promoting Netscape?"

Gates stumbled. "I don't—we don't—"

Finally, after another try from Hatch, Gates confirmed a minor restriction on the publishers but neglected to mention, to Hatch's later ire, that Microsoft's contracts did indeed restrict content publishers from paying Netscape for placement on its market-leading browser—a preemptive strike that shut down a potential source of revenue for a competitor who was not subsidized by Windows licensing fees.

Brad Chase had similarly insisted publicly that Microsoft's contracts with Web publishers for a place on Windows' Active Desktop were not "exclusive." But he had refused to disclose the terms. When the contracts later became public in the legal proceedings, it appeared the provisions skirted the line. PointCast, for example, agreed it "will not, directly or indirectly, market, promote, distribute or license for distribution" its network of content to any company producing "Other Browsers." Microsoft charged PointCast $10 million a year for placement on the Active Desktop—and credited PointCast $10 million, $4 million for adapting its content to use features of Internet Explorer and $6 million to promote Microsoft's browser.

Microsoft's contract with Disney similarly barred them from paying Netscape. The contract also limited promotion of Netscape to no more than one-quarter of all Disney Web sites. The contract further required that Disney's listing on Netscape's channel bar be nothing more than a text-only listing, stripped of Disney's distinctive logos or characters.

Microsoft was serious. In October 1997, a Microsoft representative threatened to yank Disney from the channel bar because its Netscape listing was rendered in Disney's trademark script rather than in generic text, according to a Disney executive. The executive protested to his colleagues that he "didn't like being strong-armed," but feared Disney would lose substantial value without the spot in Windows. "We are being roughed up by the 1,000-lb. gorilla of the industry," he wrote.

Gates was deeply immersed in the details of Microsoft's marketing strategies. On a Saturday evening two weeks before going to Washington to testify before Hatch's committee, Gates took time from his weekend to send e-mail to nine of Microsoft's most senior executives, including Ballmer, Maritz, Allchin, and Chase. Gates underlined the importance of driving PC customers straight from the forthcoming Windows 98 to Microsoft's browser, e-mail, and online services.

"I hope everyone is agreed on the registration/signup/hotmail/ MSN issues," Gates wrote. "These are the areas I know where we would hold up the product unless we have a clear plan that supports our objectives."

Laura Jennings, who was then running MSN, reported back to Gates that the teams were indeed pursuing the objectives. Microsoft, operating in the hazy zone between exclusive dealing and free choice, required Internet services that wanted to be included in the sign-up feature in Windows to demonstrate that 75 percent of their subscribers used Internet Explorer. Plans were also underway to tie "Start," Microsoft's latest answer to Yahoo!, to the sign-up service.

But Jennings told Gates she was concerned by the potential legal and PR fallout from the portal tie-in, "or at least there may be timing issues related to your appearance at Senator Hatch's hearings?" The plan was dropped.

"The PR groups thought it would be controversial, and we didn't see the benefit as being worth having that controversy," Gates said later.

The particulars of the dealings quickly became irrelevant—the Windows "channel bar" never generated any interest and was quickly dropped; plans for Start soon morphed into the next twist in MSN's strategy. The issue was control itself. That the stakes for Microsoft were so low was precisely what made Gates's exchange with Hatch remarkable. Gates was unwilling to budge on Microsoft's right to drive nakedly self-serving deals—even ones that he later mocked as worthless. In full public view, Gates was revealing himself as obnoxiously literal if not actually dissembling, even on points that he could easily have conceded.

Gates fared little better when he again flew to Washington a month later to personally try to back off Klein and the Justice Department. At the meeting, at the offices of Microsoft's law firm, Sullivan & Cromwell, Gates tried charm, anger, humor, and vehemence but offered little that was new. "I've never worked for anybody as rich as Gates," said David Boies, the star litigator signed by the government to argue the case in court. "But I've worked with a few billionaires. And the thing they all have in common is that they think if they can get in there personally, they can convince anybody of anything."

Boies considered it likely that one of the reasons Klein hired him was so that Microsoft couldn't. Boies, after all, had cut his teeth defending IBM from government antitrust charges. He garnered more glory beating back a libel suit against CBS brought by retired General William Westmoreland and pressuring junk-bond financier Michael Milken into a $1 billion settlement to help sort out the savings-and-loan debacle. Much later, he would lead Vice President Al Gore's efforts to force a hand recount of the vote in Florida in the 2000 presidential election.

In the meeting, Gates continued to insist that Microsoft was not a monopoly. "He was in battle mode," Boies said. "It's a dangerous mentality to get into."

The absence of a creative legal strategy on Microsoft's part was surprising, given the company's creativity in business strategies. Gates's lawyers seemed resigned to a long battle of attrition. With his silver hair and bow ties, Neukom set the courtly tone. Microsoft's general counsel had come from Gates's father's law firm and had enjoyed tremendous wealth as a result of the move.

Boies anticipated something bold. Had Boies worked for Gates, *U.S. v. Microsoft* might well have taken a very different course. For starters, Boies would have abandoned the effort to contest the monopoly designation. Refuting the obvious evidence of market power was an unproductive and distracting burden. "If I had been doing the Microsoft case, I like to think I would have the client confidence to take that approach," Boies said.

There were many ways in which Microsoft might have seized the initiative. In litigation, you have to be willing to offer to do a few things you don't think will happen, just to scramble the deck and throw your opponent off balance. Microsoft, for example, could have established a separate price for its browser, say forty-nine dollars, the same price Netscape charged for its browser before it was forced to match Microsoft's giveaway. Such a move would have had the public howling at the government for forcing them to now pay for something they had earlier gotten for free. The public would have run the Justice Department off with its tail between its legs.

But Microsoft offered nothing of the sort. In May 1998, when the government's deadline for filing the case was delayed a few days for a last-ditch attempt to find a settlement, Gates continued to stubbornly insist on leading his company into its worst crisis. In a late-night call to Klein, Gates seemed to offer flexibility about relaxing the "first screen" restrictions Microsoft placed on PC makers. Klein held up the filing to pursue negotiations with Neukom in Washington, D.C. Two days later, the flexibility evaporated. Klein moved forward to file the suit, without even a final phone call with Gates. Gates's curious reversal in the last-minute discussions gave government lawyers a new understanding of the experience of Microsoft's partners in negotiations with the company.

Whether or not Gates intended to cross the line into business practices that would bring down the wrath of antitrust prosecutors, there is no question that he pushed Microsoft right up to that line. Now that it was clear he had miscalculated, he was unwilling to take any significant steps back from that line. Microsoft insiders glumly added the legal situation to the list of projects that, under Gates's close supervision, went dramatically awry.

Microsoft's executives gamely tried to spin Gates's state of mind. "Bill is focused in on what we are doing in our technologies," Raikes told me at the time. Gates was such a quick study that the lawsuit didn't require much of his time, Neukom added. "Bill is the leader of this company. He is not going to let himself or anybody else get distracted by this litigation," Neukom said. "The notion that this company would get distracted from its mission, that's just unrealistic in our culture."

In reality, however, Gates was obsessed with the case, telling associates that his mind wandered to it six or seven times a day.

Either way, when Microsoft most needed its leader to defend it, Bill Gates was a no-show.

WIN, PLACE, OR SHOW

As the Justice Department's case against Microsoft got under way, a government lawyer gave me a simple guideline for judging whether the action had been effective. "If their profit margins go down, you'll know we've done our job," he told me. That statement contained so much common sense, but so little legal basis, that the official insisted I not use his name.

Microsoft had the misfortune of seeing its profit margins sky-rocket just as its business practices came under intense legal scrutiny. In April 1998, the company's third-quarter earnings had shown that operating profits, already among the highest of any major U.S. company, had climbed past the mark where more than half of every dollar of sales came down as before-tax profits. "I would defy you to come up with any major company in any major industry that makes that kind of money," Senator Herb Kohl of Wisconsin, a member of the Judiciary Committee, had said at Hatch's hearings.

There has long been an odd disconnect between Wall Street's financial analysis of corporate performance and antitrust analysis of market power by economists and lawyers. PC hardware prices were in free fall, but the prices Microsoft received for Windows and Office were stable, if not increasing. To Wall Street, that was a good thing. Microsoft's market power was richly rewarded with a sustained boost to its share price—a monopoly premium.

Antitrust economists also use profit margins as a crude, but useful, measure of monopoly power. Sustained fat profit margins are prima facie evidence of monopoly power, because without it hungry new entrants would undoubtedly nibble away at them. Microsoft's margins were not consistent with competition, Garth Saloner, an economics professor at Stanford's business school, told me. To antitrust regulators, that's a bad thing.

In my articles in the *Wall Street Journal* on Microsoft's quarterly earnings reports, I generally applied Wall Street's analysis to the company's results. In his column in the *San Jose Mercury News*, my friend Dan Gillmor chided me for the repetitive drumbeat of such stories, in which I characterized profits as "beating analysts' expectations" (October 1997), "surprisingly robust" (January 1998), "higher than analysts' consensus" (April 1998), "topped Wall Street estimates" (July 1998), "handily beat the expectations of Wall Street analysts" (October 1998), and "blew past the consensus Wall Street estimates" (January 1999).

But in April 1998, I suggested Microsoft's profit margins "may prove an embarrassment of riches" in the context of the looming antitrust action. In response I quoted Maffei, the chief financial officer, who dismissed any relationship between the financial results and the antitrust actions. "Intellectual property businesses generate high profit margins when they're successful," Maffei said. "The way to measure them is not against Senator Kohl's grocery-store chain." When Maffei's deputy, Jerry Masters, read the article the next morning, he sputtered to Microsoft's public relations handlers, "The story makes me sick."

The issue of its outsized profit margins would bite Microsoft again during the trial. Boies wanted to use Microsoft's profit margins as evidence of its monopoly power. But he was on uncertain legal ground. The government's own expert economist, Franklin Fisher, had published articles pointing out the difficulties of using that analysis. But Fisher was already off the witness stand and unlikely to be recalled.

Microsoft's economist, MIT professor Richard Schmalensee, testified that profits were not a reliable indicator of monopoly power. During his cross-examination, Boies introduced an article he had written sixteen years earlier in the *Harvard Law Review* in which he said, "persistent excess profits provide a good indication of long-run power." When confronted with the contradiction, Schmalensee uttered one of the trial's most memorable lines: "What could I have been thinking?" He added that the article no longer reflected his current views.

Nonetheless, "he became the 'What could I have been thinking of' witness," Boies said later. "Microsoft's case became the 'What could I have been thinking' case."

Microsoft was unable to effectively make the argument that it more often played the role, not of price-gouger, but of price-buster. If the "evil" Microsoft operates like a predatory monopolist when it commands more than 90 percent of the market, its "good twin" behaves like a tireless challenger when it has less than 30 percent. Microsoft's good twin runs circles around entrenched incumbents and breaks open their strongholds. In the database software market, for example, the company attacked Oracle with a classic price-busting strategy. Microsoft turned once-expensive software into a mass-market commodity. Working through partners, it offered packages at about one-fifth the cost of Oracle's.

As the Internet team had explained in their 1995 strategy memo,

30 percent was the magic number needed to keep any market leader honest. A challenger with 30 percent helps hold down prices, enforce interoperability, and encourage innovation. All the better, if one or more scrappy start-ups hold about 10 percent each with products that can grow into mainstream threats given breakthroughs in technology and business models.

In 1995, Microsoft's initial goal in the browser war had been to get to 30 percent market share within twelve months. When Microsoft reached that mark, developers and publishers would have to adhere to common standards or write off a large share of potential revenues. As a challenger, Microsoft effectively kept browser technology standards open; the advanced features that were unique to each company's versions of the browser by and large failed to catch on.

By 1998, the market had tipped. It was Microsoft's competition that identified 30 percent as its own critical benchmark. In an internal strategy paper, IBM outlined the assistance it was providing to Netscape to maintain at least 30 percent market share.

"If it falls significantly below this level, applications developers will feel less pressure to support Navigator and will optimize to the IE platform by writing to the Microsoft interfaces," the memo warned. "As more and more [independent software developers] drop support, customers will start moving to IE and the battle for the client will be lost."

For the leader, a 60 percent market share makes for a good business. That's enough to drive standards and promote widespread adoption. The economics of fixed development costs and high-volume software sales still work wonders on overall profit margins. A software provider that responds to customers' demand for better integration, greater ease-of-use, and new features can be well rewarded for being faster and better than the competition.

Software won't become free, innovation won't grind to a halt.

But with a strong challenger, any attempt by the market leader to lock in customers or exclude competitors is apt to be punished by customers. The market itself provides a check on coercive behavior. Interoperability becomes self-reinforcing because any market leader who doesn't deliver it will lose customers to the number two or number three player, who surely will deliver what customers want. The market leader won't be able to secure a permanent lock on the market and won't be able to milk monopoly profits.

In *U.S. v. Microsoft*, the public began to grapple with the implications of private actions to close off competition in digital markets. It was a worthy, but flawed, effort. Antitrust law is intended "to preserve, improve, and reinforce the powerful economic mechanisms that compel businesses to respond to consumers," Bork wrote. But antitrust actions are by nature retrospective, reactive exercises against only the worst anticompetitive excesses.

Taking an alternative approach, Gates might have trumped both prosecutors and his critics with a bold proposal for proactive public policy to encourage competition to speed innovation, lower prices, increase interoperability, widen access, and promote greater social inclusion. He might have challenged the entire industry, not just Microsoft, to play by the new rules of openness. He might have championed a vastly expanded common space in software.

The open standards and public protocols at the center of successes such as the Internet and the World Wide Web represent such a digital "commons." The concept of the commons is old, with deep roots in English history and law. Sometimes it is associated with tragedy—when private interests overrun a space that had been preserved for everybody's use. But there are also everyday examples of successful commons all around us. City streets and parks are commons. The presence of a vibrant commons need not detract from private free-market activity; indeed, the greater the commons, the greater the private opportunities.

In the software world, the source of power is control of the key interfaces, both for users and for developers. Each company's first choice is to control a wildly popular interface that many other players depend on. But if they don't have such control, they far prefer to have an open standard than to have a competitor own it all. For each company, the second-best outcome is for key interfaces to be as open as possible, based on open standards or even open-source code, not under the control of any single company.

The best example of such a "second-best" outcome is the Internet itself. The Internet is nothing more than a set of protocols for exchanging data packets. No company owns the protocols, and no permission is needed to use them. As long as data packets adhere to the simple guidelines, computers that adhere to Internet protocols will route them along the network. What people or computers do with the data packets at either end is of no concern to the network. Importantly, the Internet grew up and attained critical mass when the two most likely dominant providers of nationwide digital packet networks, IBM and AT&T, were hamstrung by their own long-running antitrust battles.

Now Gates had a similar opportunity to expand the commons for the next stage of technology development. Open-source code, publicly licensed and available for modification, represented the next evolution toward full interoperability. The success of the open-source Linux operating system provided an object lesson. Since many unrelated programmers are working on the Linux software at the same time, the code has developed along modular, interoperable lines. Developers of new features can easily see how to adapt their software to integrate with existing Linux code.

Most important, as Lessig later explained in a brief for Judge Jackson, no open-source project could come close to violating the anti-tying provisions of antitrust law. "While as a policy matter one might favor such a design architecture, the antitrust laws have not compelled it," he wrote.

All through Microsoft's antitrust troubles, I expected Gates to drop some kind of bombshell to reposition the company far in front of its detractors. Late one night, I wrote Gates a letter, which was, of course, never sent.

"Dear Bill," I wrote. "Do exactly what the government has asked you to do from the very beginning. Separate the core Windows operating system from all the bells and whistles that have been added as part of the Internet Explorer campaign. Then open and release the source code for Windows. Make it completely componentized, readily re-usable and absolutely free. In one swoop, you completely remove the target of the antitrust suit.

"You keep control of the crucial software interfaces that will drive the integration of the Web—now called Internet Explorer. Windows is free. Blame the revenue hit on the government. Charge $19 a year for Internet Explorer service. Volume is awesome.

"If you really play your hand right, Microsoft again defines the platform of the digital age. You simply catch a ride on the next wave up, instead of being overwhelmed by it.

"Just a thought. Warm regards."

FOREVER FREE

Gates wasn't prepared to do anything of that sort. In his twenty-hour, three-day deposition in August 1998, he continued to play the insolent schoolboy. He slouched in his chair and avoided eye contact. Gates was going to make it as uncomfortable as possible for his questioners.

As a legal tactic, Gates's approach backfired. Microsoft's attorneys claim they believed the videotaped deposition would never be played in court. That's plausible, if only because they could hardly have staged the deposition more poorly. In the harshly lit Microsoft conference room, Gates projected a visual image of an evasive smart aleck. It was a win for the government. The video effectively countered Gates's popular persona as Chief Digital Seer.

The raw transcripts reveal a deeper level of psychological truth even than the video. In black-and-white text, Gates is clearly self-censored, his inability to speak a function of his own spectacular success, which had left him unable even to claim as his own the glory that was Microsoft.

About Gates's well-known pledge never to charge for Microsoft's Web browser, Boies asked, "Do you remember using the words, 'Forever free,' those exact two words?"

"I'm sure I used those before I was five years old," Gates said.

Really? Boies asked.

"Forever free," Gates said coolly. "I wanted to be forever free."

Gates tried to stall Boies. While he otherwise had crisp recall of the pros and cons of every strategy debate since Microsoft's inception, he, in his deposition, claimed not to remember whether he did or did not write or receive any of the dozens of e-mails put before him. At one point, Boies showed him an e-mail concerning Microsoft's relationship with IBM. On his way to a different point, he casually asserted that Gates had typed "Importance: High" at the top of the message.

"No, I didn't type that," Gates said.

"Who typed in 'High'?" Boies asked him.

"A computer."

"A computer," Boies repeated. "Why did the computer type in 'High'?"

"It's an attribute of the e-mail."

"And who sets the attribute of the e-mail?"

"Usually the sender sets that attribute."

"Who is the sender here, Mr. Gates?"

"In this case, it appears I'm the sender."

His hard-core competitiveness was neutered. One e-mail from Slivka promised Gates that Microsoft would be "pissing on" an aspect of Sun's Java. Gates claimed not to know what Slivka meant by "pissing on."

"Would it be fair for me to assume that 'pissing on' is not some code word that means saying nice things about you?" Boies asked.

After a few rounds, Gates conceded, "In this case, I think it means what you've suggested it means."

Certainly, Boies was setting him up for a fall. But once Gates opted for the approach of feigned ignorance, Boies gave him plenty of rope to hang himself.

At the end of a long oration by Gates, Boies asked, "May I ask the witness what question is he answering?"

Gates turned to the court recorder. "Can you read back the question?"

"No." Boies stopped her. "Can you tell me, Mr. Gates, what question you're purporting to answer?"

Gates danced. "Your last question."

"Do you know what it is?"

"Could I make it as convoluted as you did? No."

"Can you tell me what question you're answering?"

Gates held firm. "I can't repeat back that convoluted a question."

But it was Gates, not Boies, who decided that rather than try to provide a common sense response to the particulars of the evidence, he would simply stonewall.

Despite Gates's best efforts, a little bit of light escaped. When he quibbled about the difference between "market share" and "usage share," he was telling Boies something about how the software market works, where winning the highest share of usage is a long-term strategic advantage far more valuable than short-term revenues. When he insisted on the distinction between the "Java language" and "Java runtimes," he was telling Boies something about Microsoft's strategy for co-opting the attractive parts of Java language while denying Sun the ability to get its own "lock" on software developers.

Far from being forgetful and detached, Gates was demonstrating that he was fully aware of, and had personally steered, Microsoft's competitive strategies and tactics. But he didn't want to say too much. Of all people, Gates himself knew best that, unplugged, he was liable to be too much of a truth-teller.

After being deposed for two days, Gates flew off to catch up with the cruise liner chartered by Paul Allen with five hundred guests, all in Alaska to cheer Gates up and take his mind off the company's legal problems. His approach didn't change when he returned for the third and final day of his deposition.

In what turned out to be his only chance to influence the trial, Gates had opted for obfuscation rather than clarity. His evasiveness and forgetfulness in the deposition had disqualified him as a witness in the courtroom. The forceful defense he might have later chosen to make would be fatally undermined by his lack of credibility. So Gates effectively gave up his chance to defend Microsoft's strategy as simply the best adapted to the new form of competition in high-technology markets. At the Hatch hearing and again in the deposition, Gates was unable, under questioning, to forthrightly explain Microsoft's business practices.

He would later indirectly, and only partially, admit his mistake. After Jackson's findings and his order to break up the company, Gates acknowledged that he should have chosen to testify in Microsoft's defense. "If we look back, I think it's clear that the whole story of personal computing—how the great things that have been done there and how we created an industry structure that's far more competitive than the computer industry before we came along—that story didn't get out," Gates said on *Good Morning America*. "And I do wonder if I'd taken the time to go back personally and testify, if we might have done a better job in getting that across."

It wasn't lack of time that kept Gates from testifying. How could he explain that he was shackled by Wall Street? That the market, the all-knowing market, agreed and assumed that Microsoft had a monopoly? That Microsoft's astronomical value was predicated precisely on a monopoly premium? And why did Microsoft deserve such a premium? Because Microsoft more than any other company had ferociously defended the "barriers to entry" against any competitor. Gates no longer cared about the money. It had long since become more of a burden than a blessing. It was Wall Street that demanded the monopoly.

How could he tell them that no one could lower the barriers—not Joel Klein, not Brad Silverberg, not even Bill Gates himself—without the whole thing unraveling? That the whole thing was already unraveling? That Microsoft had been trapped on the wrong side, if not of any specific law, then of the long historical trend of technology?

How could he say that he was like a cartoon character who finds himself so high in the air that if he dares to look down he comes crashing to earth?

At the critical moment, he had failed to stand up for his company or for himself. For the founder and chief executive of the company that more than any other defined the rules of the new economy, it was a stunning abdication of leadership.

FOR THE JULY 1998 launch of Windows 98, Microsoft returned to the cavernous warehouse at Fort Mason in San Francisco. This time the hall was outfitted in a salute to the retro world of the automobile. Classic cars were on display, and the backdrop to the stage was a long empty highway, Route 98. As I walked into the hall with a senior Microsoft executive, he looked around to see if anyone was listening and cupped a hand to my ear.

"Do you know the internal marketing pitch for Windows 98?" he asked. I leaned in close.

"Less shitty," he whispered.

Gates's opening speech drew the parallels between the early car industry and the PC industry, both clunky, difficult-to-use contraptions that early on were not even as efficient as the workhorses they later came to replace. The PC industry in 1998 was analogous to the auto industry in 1920, Gates declared.

It was an eerie parallel. Gates well knew that in 1920 the leader of the automobile industry was still Henry Ford, who ruled his company like a personal fiefdom and commanded the dominant share of the automobile market with his single-model, any-color-as-long-as-it's-black approach. Henry Ford's approach was high-volume, low-cost, and he had bootstrapped an industry from infancy to adolescence.

But it was Alfred Sloan, the legendary chief executive of General Motors, who took the auto industry to adulthood. Sloan was the father of the product differentiation, as well as of the modern corporate structure in which managers have considerable independence. Ford forfeited dominance to General Motors because Henry Ford refused to give up the strategy that had made him successful, even after it had outlived its value.

Gates had always vowed to be a Sloan. He was becoming a Ford.

Two weeks later, he handed off many of his duties to Steve Ballmer, who was named president of Microsoft. A year and a half later, in January 2000, Microsoft's board would appoint Ballmer chief executive as well.

Inside Microsoft, associates treated Gates like someone who had just gone through a painful divorce. But it was possible to set him off, even when sticking to safe subjects. Take golf. Gates was deeply ticked that my colleague at the *Wall Street Journal,* John Wilke, had reported on his unsuccessful efforts to gain membership in the famed Augusta National Golf Club, where such CEO pals as Warren Buffett and Jack Welch were members.

"Bill has been through the wringer these last two years," said one executive who worked closely with Gates. "His life work has been picked and picked and picked on."

In his reports to the board, Gates continued to stress that the company had the stronger legal case, and that eventually rationality would prevail. But he was intellectually honest and couldn't ignore the likely results. In December, he finally decided to make an appearance in Washington, D.C., if only by satellite on a large video screen set up in the National Press Club. He reserved particular fury for Boies.

"He really is out to destroy Microsoft," Gates said. "He is really out to make all the good work we've done—and make us—look very bad."

5

Vicious Cycle

BUDDY ACTS

Few chief executives of major American corporations have been eased aside with the sensitivity shown to Bill Gates. But even fewer have been succeeded by best friends as loyal as Steve Ballmer.

As late as 1997, Gates wasn't planning to relinquish the reins anytime soon. He said he expected to head Microsoft for at least another ten years. When he did think about leaving, he considered it unlikely that he would be handing off power to Ballmer. Gates believed Microsoft needed to be run by somebody with deep technical knowledge. Ballmer didn't qualify. In most other companies, Ballmer would count as a techie. In Microsoft's geek culture, he would always be a "business guy."

This was before Gates, for all his genius, badly mishandled the greatest set of crises the company had ever faced.

Microsoft was poorly served by Gates's intransigence in the face of the company's legal challenges. But his inability to avert the courtroom bloodbath was only part of his signal failure. He was equally stubborn in the face of the industry's paradigm shift. When the two realms collided, Microsoft seemed to be pursuing a lose-lose solution, going down in flames in Judge Jackson's courtroom in defense of an outdated technology strategy.

It's not as if it were impossible to run a successful business within the bounds of standing antitrust policy. The two other technology giants that topped Nasdaq's list of market value leaders in the 1990s successfully finessed their own brushes with antitrust authorities. Intel was sued by the Federal Trade Commission over charges it used its monopoly muscle to gain patent licenses from other companies. The suit was settled before it went to trial; without admitting guilt, Intel agreed that it would no longer cut off supplies of chips to companies with whom it had patent or other legal disputes.

Cisco Systems, which dominates the market for network routers nearly as completely as Microsoft does for PC operating systems, also had numerous brushes with the government, but each time the company evaded serious enforcement action. John Chambers, Cisco's chief executive, made it a point to schmooze, rather than antagonize, Joel Klein, the Clinton Justice Department's antitrust chief, and other antitrust enforcers. Cisco trains its employees to avoid incendiary language, such as "kill the competition" and "dominate the market," especially in e-mail. A twelve-minute video presentation about Cisco's internal Web site cites—as an example of what not to do— Allchin's 1996 e-mail urging Microsoft to "leverage Windows" more. And while Microsoft alone controls most of the specifications for the interfaces that allow programs to work with Windows, Cisco with some exceptions adheres to open standards published by industry-wide groups that specify how Internet switches talk to each other.

Of the three companies, only Microsoft blundered into war with government prosecutors.

Two months after the antitrust suit was filed in May 1998, Gates gave up most of his day-to-day responsibilities for running Microsoft. Ballmer was named president; over the next eighteen months he gently, steadily, and forcefully wrested control of the direction of Microsoft from Gates. By November 1999, when Judge Jackson branded Microsoft a "predatory monopolist," Ballmer told me, "I run the company these days."

Jackson's scathing findings of fact from the seventy-eight-day trial left no doubt he held Bill Gates personally responsible for Microsoft's anticompetitive behavior. In his 207-page conclusion, he cited e-mail messages from Gates himself to show that he actively and personally directed the hardball tactics against not only Netscape but putative Microsoft partners such as Intel, IBM, and Apple. Jackson's findings were a direct rebuke to Gates's operating style.

For example, Jackson found that in June 1995, Gates had mounted a personal, three-month campaign to convince Intel's chief executive, Andy Grove, to drop Intel's work on NSP, software developed by Intel to improve the display of Internet multimedia. Microsoft considered NSP a threat to Windows because developers that adopted the technology could more easily adapt their programs for other operating systems. Gates reported that he tried to convince Grove "to basically not ship NSP." More generally, Gates pressed Grove to cut back on the number of people Intel had working on software.

A couple of months later, on August 2, 1995, Gates went to see Grove at Intel's Santa Clara headquarters with an implicit quid pro quo: As long as Intel continued to develop platform-level software that threatened Windows, Intel couldn't count on Microsoft's support for its next generation of microprocessors. Intel's executives knew the company would have trouble selling chips if Microsoft told PC makers it did not support them, the judge wrote. Gates also objected to Intel's work with Sun on Java, which he said undermined cooperation between Intel and Microsoft. The fundamental problem, he told Grove, was that Intel was using microprocessor revenues to fund development of free platform-level software that competed with Microsoft's. That neatly mirrored the core complaint later made against Microsoft—that it used its monopoly Windows profits to fund free software to undermine competitors.

Intel backed down. In October 1995, Gates reported that Intel felt Microsoft had PC makers "on hold with our NSP chill." Still, he wanted Microsoft's executive to remain vigilant. "If Intel is not sticking totally to its part of the deal let me know," he wrote.

The judge found that Gates had also directed the campaign to bring IBM to heel. In July 1995, Gates called an executive of IBM's personal computer division to berate him for IBM's public statements denigrating Windows. A month earlier, IBM had purchased Lotus Development and announced it was bundling Lotus Smart-Suite, rather than Microsoft's Office, on some desktop PCs. As part of the same "IBM First" campaign, Big Blue was also making a last-gasp attempt to market OS/2, its own PC operating system. Still, to remain competitive, it needed a license for Windows 95, which was due to be released in a blockbuster launch in a few weeks.

After Gates's call, Judge Jackson noted ominously, "Microsoft began to retaliate in earnest against the IBM PC company." The retaliation included suspension of negotiations over Windows 95 in order to conduct a lengthy audit of IBM's past royalty obligations.

Microsoft executives told IBM's negotiators they could help clear up the audit by offering a concession acceptable to Gates, such as a moratorium on bundling SmartSuite. In the end, Microsoft didn't grant IBM a license for Windows 95 until fifteen minutes before the product's August 24, 1995, launch event.

Two years later, Jackson found, Gates again served as Microsoft's chief enforcer, this time against Apple. In June 1997, Gates told Microsoft executives in an e-mail that negotiations with Apple "have not been going well at all." Microsoft was seeking to persuade Apple to adopt Microsoft's browser and to drop its threats of a patent lawsuit. Its biggest club was the threat to cancel development of Mac Office, the Apple version of Microsoft's desktop software suite. Cancellation of Mac Office would have meant almost certain death to the Macintosh, which had already lost most of its support from software developers. Gates wrote that he called Gil Amelio, then the chief executive of Apple, to ask "how we should announce the cancellation of Mac Office." When Steve Jobs took over Apple in 1997, Microsoft got its deal.

A week after the judge's ruling in November 1999, Gates walked onto the stage of a Las Vegas ballroom to the refrain from Fatboy Slim's "Praise You." He was there to deliver his annual keynote address at the Comdex computer show. It might have been an awkward moment for him, standing before many of the computer industry players Microsoft stood convicted of coercing. Jackson had painted Microsoft as a powerful industry overlord that rewarded its friends and punished its enemies. He had found, for example, that PC makers such as IBM and Gateway, which resisted Microsoft, paid more for Windows; Microsoft-friendly companies, such as Compaq, Dell, and Hewlett-Packard, paid less. But Gates avoided the substance of the findings altogether and struck a we're-all-in-this-together pose of gentle exasperation. His only acknowledgment of the legal setback was his quip at the start of his talk, "Has anyone heard any good lawyer jokes recently?"

Nonetheless, within two months of the release of Jackson's findings, the other shoe had dropped. In January 2000, Gates turned over to Ballmer the additional title of chief executive.

From the beginning, Microsoft's spinning of the press coverage of Gates's gradual relinquishment of power was masterful. The public relations team prepared Microsoft employees who were scheduled to meet with *New Yorker* reporter Ken Auletta in March 1999 to answer questions such as "How do you think the trial is affecting Bill? Is he demoralized? Frustrated?"

The suggested answer: "Bill's been clear that he's staying focused on his role of running the company and moving the technology forward. That's his passion—why he comes to work every day. None of that has changed."

That Gates hadn't changed was a part of the problem.

Through three years of legal action, Gates never publicly acknowledged a moment of self-doubt about his own actions or the company's practices. On and off the record, he has been consistent that there's nothing, absolutely nothing, he would go back and do differently. Jackson later said Gates's intransigence influenced his order to break up the company.

But as Ballmer took charge, he was less concerned about Microsoft's unraveling in court than he was about the company's unraveling at home.

"Bill has an amazing personal capacity not only to see a lot of things but to keep a lot of things in his head," Ballmer said later. "I'm not bad, but I'm not Bill. And I don't think either Bill or I are up to this company at this point, at this scale. No disrespect . . ."

Among the Friends of Bill eager to offer testimonials to Gates's stewardship of Microsoft is Warren Buffett. Next to Ballmer and Gates, Buffett and Gates formed one of the best billionaire buddy acts in history, a running series of bridge games, train trips, and gags, such as the Microsoft video satire in which the two men go before television's Judge Judy to settle a two-dollar bet.

"We were playing bridge on the Internet. I was cleaning his clock as I always do," Buffett tells the tough-talking judge. "This miserable little cheat unplugged his computer to avoid losing!"

Buffett hadn't fully absorbed the talking points suggested by the PR folks, that Gates would be working as hard as ever at his new job and that his savage treatment at the hands of prosecutors played no role in his decision to step aside.

"Bill is both happiest and most productive, I can tell from talking to him, when he's out at that Think Week. So I think the realization has come to him that that's what he enjoys and is best at. So why not turn Think Week into a full-time job?" Buffett said. "I know the government thing obviously has been no fun. When something isn't much fun, he might look for things that are more fun. It would have happened without the government, but the government thing focused it."

Allowing Gates more time to lead the company's technical strategy was the public reason for relieving him of most of his business responsibilities. That was not quite right. Ballmer needed to give Gates enough time to let go so that others could *change* Microsoft's strategy.

Gates's tightly coupled technology vision had Microsoft tied in knots. His stubborn attachment to Windows Everywhere was causing Microsoft to miss much of the Internet opportunity. Board members wondered whether the company was serving customers or trying to come up with a unified theory to knit together the entire digital universe under Microsoft's banner. Microsoft's marketers were desperate for a message they could sell to developers hungry to exploit the Internet. Tell them to write to Win32! Gates barked until well into 1999.

"Which they did!" he gleefully reported.

As Ballmer dug into his new duties, the evidence he was getting pointed to a disturbing fact: Bill Gates had taken the company down the wrong road.

The management problems that had prompted the board to agree to free Gates from his day-to-day responsibilities in May 1998 were only growing worse. The company was adrift, even as it piled up record earnings and profits. Microsoft, the revolutionary insurgent, had been replaced by Microsoft the defensive incumbent. Innovation had given way to internal politics, teamwork to factional infighting. Gates's technical direction and management style was at the root of the problem.

Ballmer has been Gates's buffer and protector since they first met during their sophomore year at Currier House at Harvard. Legend has it that the responsible Ballmer closed the door and windows after the absentminded Gates left his dorm room wide open to the rain when he went home for Christmas break. After Ballmer's first year at Stanford Business School, Gates asked him to come to Microsoft and help him manage the growing business, which at that time had about thirty employees. Gates and Ballmer like to tell the story of the salary negotiations. Gates, then twenty-four years old, was on vacation in the Caribbean aboard the *Doo Wah Doo Wah*, yelling to Ballmer over a ship-to-shore radio. The deal was fifty thousand dollars in salary and 7 percent of the company. Even with Microsoft's fallen stock price, his stake, now 4.5 percent, was worth nearly $12 billion in January 2000, making Ballmer one of the world's richest men.

The two men forged a bond based as much upon their differences as on their similarities. Gates was an introvert who liked people mainly for the intellectual stimulation they provided. He didn't much like hanging out. Ballmer was an extrovert who enjoyed the pleasures of socializing for its own sake. Now it was becoming clear that to run a company that employed thirty-five thousand people, it helped to like people.

Ballmer had been harder than hard-core in all of Microsoft's most perilous moments. It was Ballmer who steered Microsoft through its first major crisis, the 1990–91 divorce from IBM that led to the success of Windows and the demise of OS/2. The strategy reversal is part of computer industry lore. The divorce put tiny Microsoft, and its untried Windows software, in direct competition with IBM, its former partner and the world's largest computer company.

Ballmer played a small but key role in focusing the company's response to the second major crisis, the Internet. His customers, particularly the U.S. government, were demanding something called TCP/IP. Ballmer didn't know what TCP/IP was exactly, but he was determined to give it to customers and hammered Microsoft's programmers to include what indeed were the basic Internet protocols in the company's software.

Ballmer's day starts at 6:00 A.M., with a run or with hoops on Wednesdays at the Pro Club. The health club, with shuttles from Microsoft's parking lots, effectively functions as the company's fitness facility. The weekly pickup basketball game has been going on for years, a perennial contest between the Generals and the Trotters. Ballmer is usually a Trotter. With his linebacker build, he sets a mean pick.

When he's in town, he takes his oldest son to school in the morning. He cuts off his work day at 5:30 or 6:00 P.M., so he can have dinner with his wife Connie and their three sons. Within a month of each other in 1997, both of Ballmer's parents were diagnosed with lung cancer. His mother died quickly. Ballmer visited his father every night for three years until he, too, succumbed, in 2000.

During the workday his attention never appears to flag. His day is scheduled in half-hour blocks. He moves seamlessly from the first presentation by, say, the designer of the pivot table feature in the Excel spreadsheet program, through the lunch meeting with the Fortune 500 chief executive interested in a partnership, to the day's last review of the divisional vice president's three-year business plan. Some meetings last less than two minutes.

"How does this match the yellow book?" he might thunder.

Ballmer has of course memorized the loose-leaf binder that holds the yellow one-page summaries of the performance and plans for Microsoft's more than two dozen wholly-owned foreign subsidiaries. If the executive doesn't have his answers down, Ballmer doesn't waste time making his subordinate feel better. "Come back when you're ready. You're obviously not ready."

During the eight or nine weeks a year that he's on the road, he is a maniac. On one European trip to review sales operations, he claims that he put in 130 hours of work in 168 hours on the ground.

Ballmer had been passed over for the title of president in 1992 because Microsoft's board of directors felt he wasn't seasoned enough for the job. His titanic energy and aggressive style usually got the job done but sometimes caused collateral damage. "He could be very direct," said Brian Valentine, a Ballmer loyalist who is now senior vice president for Windows. "He would give you his opinion first. It would be hard to have a debate with him, to put it kindly."

Even at his most bombastic, Ballmer's flaw was usually an excess of enthusiasm, not of malice. Even his "to heck with Janet Reno" comment didn't sound so bad in context—a conference for small-business owners at which Ballmer committed Microsoft to deliver for those often overlooked customers, no matter what the government did.

If Microsoft lost a deal, Ballmer might pick up the phone and bellow, "You're either a friend or a foe and you're an enemy now." That was his threat to David Dorman, then Pacific Bell's chief executive and later president of AT&T, when Pacific Bell cut a deal to distribute Netscape's browser rather than Microsoft's. Ballmer backed down after Dorman reminded him that Pacific Bell had thirty-four thousand desktop PCs running Windows and scolded him, "How can you call a corporate customer an enemy?" Ballmer quickly changed his tone and asked how Microsoft could do better the next time.

Ballmer's easy bonhomie and meat-and-potatoes approach to the business seemed to be just what Microsoft needed, the perfect antidote to Gates's enigmatic aloofness.

When he had been passed over in 1992, Ballmer was promised another shot at the job if he took on the challenge of modernizing Microsoft's global sales and marketing operations. By most accounts, sales and marketing were the parts of the company that remained in the best shape through the 1990s. For all the talk that Microsoft's is a culture of engineers, it was Ballmer's global sales force that had the best esprit de corps.

As soon as he was named president, Ballmer dug into the problems with all of his legendary stamina and focus.

The product teams that designed, built, and tested Microsoft's software were in the most disarray. Ballmer blocked out one hundred fifty hours and scheduled one-on-one interviews with a hundred or so programmers and managers working on Windows, Office, and MSN. What do you think is wrong with the company? he wanted to know. How could it be fixed?

He was flattened by what he heard. "Where was I?" he asked colleagues. "How did I let things get so bad?"

The teams were in disarray, demoralized from the infighting and paralysis. The "shippers," specialists in pushing products out the door, resented the "visionaries," who were always dreaming up new features. Similarly, the "entrepreneurs," seeking to capitalize on the immediate needs of the marketplace, disdained the "architects," who focused on grand edifices that tied Microsoft's many initiatives together. "Some people thought it was going well," Ballmer told me later. "Others thought we needed to get back on the right trajectory."

Many of the processes that worked when Microsoft was small didn't "scale" now that it was big. Half of the nearly forty thousand employees had been hired during the previous five years. Internal issues were consuming more and more time—people complained about the need to respond to nearly a hundred e-mail messages a day, to attend endless, repetitive "off-sites," to adjust to yet another reorganization. Don't hire any more people, many employees told Ballmer. Don't make the company any bigger or we're all going to leave.

Both old-timers and newcomers were frustrated by the increasing volume of internal politics. The company seemed slow to respond to the new needs of the market and resistant to change. Decisions were not getting made, and priorities were not getting set. Simple changes, such as moving a small team into a new group, could take as long as nine months. Some employees felt Microsoft was deaf to customers' needs; others thought it was too responsive, promising fully integrated systems requiring synchronized release schedules that tied the product teams in knots.

Ballmer found that few people understood Microsoft's overall strategy. If key employees didn't understand the roadmap, probably no one else did either, he concluded. "People wanted a clearer sense of vision and priorities," he said.

Changes were needed. Many people told Ballmer that the company needed to seize the initiative, any initiative. Everyone noticed that Microsoft had lost its overwhelming dominance. It still dominated the PC, but the PC was becoming a smaller part of the whole. Ballmer knew that Microsoft's long-term health depended on more than selling copies of Windows. It depended on providing the platform that software developers targeted for new and exciting applications. And in that, Windows was slipping markedly. Sure there were still Windows applications, but where was the buzz? The growth? It was on the Web and on a new set of devices like 3Com's PalmPilot or NTT DoCoMo's wireless services, which were all the rage in Japan. In market after market, Microsoft had spotted competitors to huge leads. When Microsoft had seemed poised to dominate, companies were eager to tag along. Now that it seemed clueless, they were more than happy to let it flounder. Microsoft was suffering significant setbacks and making very few gains. The information technology world was losing its fear.

In the first week of December 1998, Ballmer rang the alarm bell. He held a meeting for fifty top executives, so-called "Level 14s," who included general managers and vice presidents. (Ballmer later expanded the number of steps in Microsoft's pay scale to give the company greater flexibility in making promotions; now such meetings of senior staff are known as "Level 68s.")

Ballmer's report, with Gates at his side, was bleak. The company's products were too difficult to use, with features that didn't meet customers' needs. Because the scheduled milestones for Windows were unrealistic and unbelievable, nobody could count on them. The old practice of pitting development teams against each other was a failure, he said, generating needless conflict and squandering resources. Microsoft had to prioritize. Trade-offs had to be made.

Without a drastic reorganization, the rash of employee departures would accelerate, Ballmer said. People won't be building great products, and they won't be having fun. "We will get into what I'd call a vicious downward spiral."

"We're at an important point for the company's long-term health and viability. If we don't do the right thing, we just won't be in a great place three to four years from now."

COUP D'ETAT

In the upper reaches of Microsoft's management, there are "Bill guys" and there are "Steve guys." Like Gates, Bill guys are apt to want to do everything without trade-offs. Like Ballmer, Steve guys think they know how to prioritize ruthlessly and sacrifice the non-essential. Bill guys think winning is mostly about strategy. Steve guys rely more on operational execution. Gates's favorites tend toward technical absolutism. Ballmer loyalists are likely to be more savvy about revenues, marketing, and customer concerns.

Another distinction: Ballmer was an income-statement guy, most concerned about generating new sources of revenue growth; Gates was becoming a balance-sheet guy, increasingly enamored of the scorecard of the company's assets and liabilities that reflected its cash holdings, its investment portfolio and, more generally, its ability to cut deals with the big cable and telecommunications providers.

Greg Maffei, Microsoft's top deal maker and chief financial officer, who had no technology background before joining the company, was a new kind of Bill guy. He helped Microsoft for the first time become a big player in the Wall Street dealmania spurred by the digital convergence of telecommunications, entertainment, and computers. The balance sheet was Microsoft's ace in the hole: no debt, more than $20 billion in cash, and a bulging portfolio of stock market holdings.

But the Steve guys were on the rise. Ballmer considered the dealmania a distraction from the need to build new businesses that sent profits to the bottom line. Unlike Gates, he relished discussions about product pricing and marketing, or the number of sales representatives Microsoft needed in order to capitalize on new opportunities, such as in the telecommunications market or among Web advertisers globally.

Jeff Raikes was a Bill guy when he joined Microsoft from Apple Computer in 1981. Raikes had gone to Stanford to study agricultural economics. He planned to spend ten years at the Department of Agriculture, get frustrated about his ability to change the world through agricultural policy, and return to the family farm near Lincoln, Nebraska. Instead, he got fascinated by software. With corn fetching less per bushel than his family's cost of production, he thinks software is still the better bet.

He headed Microsoft's Word team in the 1980s, during its come-from-behind victory in the word processor market. To prove his competitive passion, he memorized the names and birthdates of all the children of the head of archrival WordPerfect; he can still recite them. His other claim to Microsoft glory: He and his wife, Tricia, a marketing manager who created the corporate logo the company still uses, were the first Microsoft couple to marry.

Raikes's eyeglasses are the same style as Gates's, and his vacation home is only a few doors from Gates's compound on the Hood Canal. But in 1993, Raikes followed Ballmer to the sales side. He became head of worldwide sales when Ballmer was promoted to president. After Ballmer was named chief executive, I asked Raikes whether he was a Bill guy or a Steve guy. He gave me his sly smile. "I'm a chameleon."

Wall Street analysts joked that Raikes's golf handicap was the leading indicator of whether Microsoft had met its quarterly sales goals. Raikes is one of Microsoft's best golfers, scoring in the high seventies or low eighties. When his handicap rose to seven or eight, the analysts figured he was out selling software; the quarter would be good. When he got his handicap down to three or four, they figured he was spending too much time on the golf course and started to worry.

In 1992, Raikes joined a group of local millionaires who helped Nintendo purchase the Seattle Mariners baseball team, defusing the controversy over a Japanese company buying a piece of the national pastime. Raikes's 2 percent stake puts him on the hook for 2 percent of the team's ongoing operating losses, which have topped $150 million. He calls his investment in the Mariners an "unusual form of non-tax-deductible charitable contribution to the community." But there are perks, particularly since the opening of Safeco Field made Mariner home games the place to be seen in Seattle society. The buffet in the owners' box: salmon fillets with fresh dill, wild rice and grilled asparagus, eggplant and peppers with fresh mozzarella. For dessert: key lime cheesecake and caramel apple pie. Sure beats hot dogs and Crackerjack. Raikes points out the owners' box is only the second-best place to watch the game, however. The best? His regular seats behind the Mariners' on-deck circle, fifty-eight feet from home plate. "That's even closer than the pitcher's mound," he says with a wink.

Raikes knows his numbers. When I met with him in June 2000, his handheld PocketPC told him it was his 6,779th day at Microsoft. He ticked off other numbers: 350 million PCs installed around the world. More than 50 percent of Microsoft's revenues from outside the United States. About 4.1 million PC server computers sold each year, nearly two-thirds of them running Windows NT software. Ballmer pioneered the measurement of "dollars per desktop." Raikes has taken it to the next step: dollars per server, with each installation of Windows NT serving as a foundation for selling an SQL Server database and other software. He jokes that he gets management tips from Lou Piniella, the manager of the Mariners, who says the three keys to winning in baseball are pitching, pitching, and pitching. Raikes's top goals, he told me once, were beat Oracle, beat Oracle, beat Oracle.

In 2000, when Raikes took on another assignment from Ballmer, returning to the product side to run the Office group, Microsoft's most reliable moneymaker, he passed the sales baton to another Steve guy.

Orlando Ayala, a hard-charging Colombian, was hired in 1991 to start Microsoft's Latin American division. Ayala pressed the company into taking a more global view. Microsoft had found early success overseas by replicating its North American business practices around the world. For example, the company exported the three-tier distribution system in which Microsoft sells to major software distributors, who in turn service individual customer accounts. When such a distribution system doesn't exist in a particular country, Microsoft helps get it established. But Ayala saw that many of the best sales ideas were coming from the other direction and pressed the company to adopt in the United States practices pioneered by Microsoft's international subsidiaries. In Brazil, for example, Microsoft helped guarantee loans to small businesses for software purchases.

When Thailand, Indonesia, and Mexico suffered financial crises, Ayala insisted that Microsoft increase, not cut, its investments in those countries. His division expanded to cover all developing markets and doubled its revenues every two years. In 1995, Ayala spent five weeks in India to get a firsthand understanding of the market dynamics. That led Microsoft to open sales offices in four additional cities. Its staffing went from thirty people to two hundred.

When Ayala was named to head U.S. sales, on his way to running the entire global sales operation, the handoff was commemorated in one of Raikes's classic sales-meeting videos. "Orro and the Seven Crusades," a take-off on the movie *Zorro*, opens with a sonorous narration: "In a land where great software is threatened by evil men, a fearless defender will make his mark . . ."

Ayala, on his knees, is near tears. "Master, how am I supposed to fight competition with the DOJ breathing down my neck?"

"With this," Raikes says, holding up a black mask.

By the end, Raikes says, "I have taught you well."

"Master," responds Ayala, "I'm ready to kick some ass."

• • •

BALLMER needed Steve guys on the product development side. Over and over again in his interviews, Ballmer heard that the main obstacle to progress anywhere in the company was Windows 2000. The project was billed as the biggest software effort in history and the most important product ever for Microsoft. Windows 2000 was finally to deliver on Gates's major goal of unifying the two strains of Windows, the old one rooted in MS-DOS and Windows 95 and the new one based on NT.

But the project had grown like a B-movie science experiment, threatening to devour all of Microsoft. Critical strategic decisions were on hold in order to get the mammoth project out the door. Windows 2000 consumed an ever-greater portion of Microsoft's human resources, up to two-thirds of all the company's code-creation brainpower.

The low point came in mid-1998, when by earlier predictions the software should have been nearly ready for release. Instead, there was a growing fear it might never be ready. A growing lack of discipline among the coders and repeated requests for new features combined to bloat the project to a staggering 40 million lines of programming, later pared back to 29 million. The number of bugs in the software was exploding, rather than shrinking. In Microsoft's jargon, the product was not converging.

"God, how deep is this crater?" Allchin wondered. He says he considered shaking up the Windows team in the spring of 1998 but backed off.

When Ballmer confronted the situation in December 1998, the shake-up could no longer be put off. The repeated delays in Windows 2000 were causing something close to panic in his old sales and marketing group, who saw competitors such as Sun, Hewlett-Packard, and IBM grabbing the growing server business while Microsoft was sidelined. "Every day you're not shipping is a day people can buy something else," Ballmer told me.

The fastest-growing competitor to Windows 2000 was not an established company at all but Linux, the variant of the Unix operating system that had been improved and debugged by a worldwide army of volunteer hackers, working on the software's open source code under the gentle guidance of a Finnish-born programmer named Linus Torvalds.

What most alarmed Microsoft was not the unorthodox community of developers who fine-tuned the operating system but that
Linux took advantage of the very "PC model" Microsoft had pioneered. Linux, like Windows 2000, ran on inexpensive Intel-based
PCs, rather than the more expensive, proprietary hardware that Sun,
IBM, and H-P sold with their Unix server software. Until Linux,
Unix providers had remained addicted to the profit margins from
their hardware sales. That crippled their ability to create a unified
platform to rival Windows. Led by Sun, they intentionally differenti-
ated their software, splintering Unix into multiple incompatible "fla-
vors" and destroying its early promise of interoperability.

For years, Microsoft feared that a unified Unix market might
achieve the volume economics of the PC industry or, alternatively, a
Unix competitor would ride the volume economics of PC hardware
to eliminate Microsoft's price advantage. Now there was a bona fide,
if unconventional, operating system competitor that did just that. Because Linux, like Microsoft, wasn't pulling along anybody's hardware
business, it escaped the inherent conflict of interest that had hampered Microsoft's traditional competitors.

At the very time Microsoft was preparing to attack Sun and IBM
with a cheaper alternative for network server computers, Linux was
threatening Jim Allchin's Windows 2000 from below.

Publicly, Allchin pooh-poohed Linux as a "handyman special" that
incorporated all of the defects of the thirty-year-old Unix code base.
But he was concerned enough to commission an internal analysis that
suggested Microsoft should take Linux and open-source software
generally very seriously indeed. Two memos were prepared for presentation to Maritz in August 1998 by a young engineer named Vinod
Valloppillil. Open-source software, the first memo said, "poses a direct, short-term revenue and platform threat to Microsoft, particularly in server space."

The report acknowledged that Linux appeared to have what Microsoft was struggling to achieve: rock-solid reliability. By exposing
the source code to view, Linux took advantage of the eagle eyes of
thousands of developers to continually debug the software. "Commercial quality can be achieved/exceeded by open-source software
projects," Valloppillil said.

Most important, the documents made clear that Linux, and open-
source software generally, was as much a cultural as an economic
threat to Microsoft. "The ability of the open-source software process

to collect and harness the collective IQ of thousands of individuals across the Internet is simply amazing," Valloppillil concluded. "Since money is often not the (primary) motivation behind open-source software, understanding the nature of the threat posed requires a deep understanding of the process and motivation of open-source development teams. In other words, to understand how to compete against open-source software, we must target a process rather than a company."

The blunt, analytical report found that the open-source process was in many ways better adapted to the new dynamics of the software market than Microsoft's own centralized structure. Open-source projects easily draw talent from anywhere in the world, he said, scale up as needed, and demobilize just as effortlessly.

The biggest difference between the open-source model and Microsoft's is in the transparency of the underlying programming code, Valloppillil wrote. Outside developers, and many of Microsoft's own programmers, are not able to look at the way Microsoft writes its source code. The company, like most but not all commercial software companies, supplies only the compiled bits in a stream of indecipherable 1s and 0s. The millions Microsoft spends evangelizing its platform is needed in part because developers who rely on Microsoft's interfaces have no choice but to place complete trust in Microsoft. The only information available is a general manual and the technical specification for the interface, not the code itself. That's locked away in a black box.

With open-source code, any developer can enhance interoperability by tweaking the source code on their own and then sharing their improvements with others. Valloppillil summarized the point in perfect Microsoft-speak: "The intrinsic parallelism and free idea exchange in open-source software has benefits that are not replicable with our current licensing model and therefore present a long-term developer mindshare threat."

The contagious enthusiasm of the Linux insurgency contrasted sharply with the ennui that gripped Windows 2000 developers. Ballmer was shocked by the number of people who told him to attend a bug-triage meeting or sit in a build-lab for a day. Microsoft's brute force approach to software creation simply didn't scale with the exponential increase in complexity that came with growth. Ten years earlier, only the largest product teams had more than a hundred engineers. Five years earlier, the big product groups employed seven or eight hundred engineers. Now, Windows 2000 employed more than six thousand engineers. Only one out of every eight people actually wrote code that made it into the finished product. The rest were testers, debuggers, or managers. It was a huge challenge simply to manage assignments, changes, versions, and quality control.

Something had to give. Ballmer briefly toyed with the notion of opening some Windows source code, but the magnitude of the transition made that route impossible. Instead, he brought in somebody who could take the hill the old-fashioned way.

He called in an old chit from Brian Valentine, one of the company's best "shippers" and among the handful of go-to managers who have the luck or misfortune to get assigned Microsoft's most critical and troubled projects.

Valentine joined Microsoft from Intel in 1987, taking a $7,000-a-year pay cut and a loss on his house in Portland. In the early years, his wife, who stayed home with their children while Valentine worked late into the night, told him he was the "dumbest sonofabitch in the world." Valentine went to Ballmer for a pay raise.

"Steve, I just have one point I want to make," he said. "If I'm going to work the hours I'm working, I at least want to be able to give my kids a swing set to play on when Dad's not there."

He got his raise, and Ballmer still teases Valentine about it. "How big a swing set do your kids have now?" he asks.

Valentine, who was friends with the son of a tombstone maker in his hometown of Centralia, Washington, says his own epitaph will read "Reality ended up being larger than his greatest dreams."

Valentine, a burly hockey player, has a reputation for both toughness and humor. Once, hunting in Botswana on vacation, he had bagged two of the big-five game animals, a buffalo and a leopard. Here came the third, a huge fifty-year-old elephant close enough that Valentine could hear his ears flapping. The game scout told him, "If he knows we're here, he's going to charge. So be ready."

"What do you mean by 'Be ready'?" Valentine wanted to know.

A body shot won't stop him, the scout explained. It's got to be a brain shot. Wait until he's ten yards away and puts his head down. Valentine considered the prospect of waiting until the thirteen-thousand-pound bull charging at thirty-five miles an hour was less than thirty feet away. Another scout whispered, "Just don't leave any shells in your gun."

He took his shoes off and stalked the elephant through thick brush until he had a shooting lane. He hit him with two shots, one in the heart and the second in the brain, without ever being charged.

But that didn't stop him from embellishing the anecdote in a speech to a group of software developers. He said the experience would be helpful in dealing with Gates. The next time he was in a meeting and Gates was coming down on him, he would say, "Bill, you've got to work on your intimidation. I've been charged by a bull elephant. It's just not the same anymore."

Valentine showed up at his first meeting with the Windows 2000 team riding a Harley. He was in full leathers, then stripped down to a white Elvis costume to deliver his motivational spiel. It was badly needed. Seeing software project teams careering toward launch date, he later said, is like entering a mobile home filled with neglected children living in squalor. The Windows 2000 team had not gone completely over the edge but could have. "Then you've lost it," he said. "Your talent starts leaving."

Valentine's first question upon taking charge was: How do we know when we're done? "I couldn't get an answer," he says. He deployed a lieutenant to canvass the project and establish detailed benchmarks. Then he set about pruning any remaining projects that were not indispensable. "I just shut down a lot of open issues," he says.

The biggest project he shut down was Gates's own pet: unification of the Windows 95 and NT code bases. Valentine abandoned the plan to market Windows 2000 to consumers as the next operating system for home computers. It simply wasn't going to be possible to make Windows 2000 work reliably with all the older Windows and DOS software and peripheral equipment, such as printers, that home consumers still used. It was hard enough getting Windows 2000 to work with the most popular business applications from the previous version of NT.

Unifying the Windows code bases might be important to Gates's Windows Everywhere strategy, but it had become an obstacle to getting anything else done. Dump it, Ballmer agreed.

Ballmer moved with equal dispatch on other fronts. His extensive interviews had helped him take the measure of his troops' motivation. Ballmer likes sports metaphors; it was time for everyone to step up their game. Are you fired up!? If not, it's time to get out! Not everybody signed up for Ballmer's forced march. Within a few months of Ballmer's takeover, even longtime Microsoft loyalists were finding the door.

Nathan Myhrvold, a quintessential Bill guy, was one who got the message. Gates had already moved his best tech buddy out of product development and given him the title of Chief Technology Officer, with a checkbook to establish Microsoft Research as the successor to the great postwar corporate research labs, such as ATT's Bell Labs and IBM's Watson research center. Myhrvold lured top-flight talent from those places and from elite research universities. But Myhrvold couldn't shake the reputation around the company—unfair, he insisted—that he "missed" the Internet. For a "shipper" that might have been excused, but for a "visionary" it was not.

"If you look at the Internet phenomena, I wouldn't argue the research group helped us there," wrote Jon DeVaan, then head of the Office team in one e-mail. "In general, the Internet was considered low tech and hacky, so a lot of people here didn't think it would do much (myself included). We missed the customer value of universalness . . . because we were focused on the technology shortcomings. I think a research group will always tend to have that same bias."

Gates lifted his protection of Myhrvold. In his 1998 deposition, a government lawyer asked, "Was he one of your top executives?"

"He was an executive," Gates responded. "I'm not sure what you mean by top executive. He didn't manage any of the large products that we offer."

"Was he sort of Microsoft's resident strategic thinker?"

"No."

"Did you value his advice?"

"Not over the advice of people who are more directly involved in their businesses," Gates said.

Ballmer didn't object when Myhrvold decided to take a long-term leave, in part to hunt dinosaur fossils. "If a guy wants to go study paleontology, that's what he should do," Ballmer told me.

Ballmer was running the company from Red West—"Red Ink," some people called it—the company's satellite offices west of the main Redmond campus. Red West houses MSN and the rest of Microsoft's collection of Internet and media operations. In November 1998, Ballmer helped Pete Higgins, the affable fifteen-year veteran who had failed to turn around the Internet efforts, decide it was time to go. It wasn't just the losses in interactive media, which totaled hundreds of millions of dollars each year. It wasn't just that Microsoft's attempts to compete with AOL were so ineffectual. (While AOL's customer base shot to more than 14 million, MSN's paying subscribers dropped below 2 million, at which point Microsoft stopped publicly reporting the figures.)

It was that no one seemed to know what business Microsoft was in.

The company's media efforts were star-crossed from the beginning, caught between Microsoft's heritage as a software company and the different dynamics of the media business. In 1995, Microsoft bundled the MSN software with every copy of Windows 95, prompting estimates it would quickly gain 9 million users. That never happened.

Instead, MSN lurched through a series of strategy reversals and execution problems. As launched in 1995, the online service was a proprietary mall, much like AOL at the time. Within a year, MSN dropped its proprietary format in favor of the Web. In 1997, MSN was lavishly relaunched with expensive television-style entertainment "shows." None of them were ready for prime time. By 1998, Microsoft was focused on shopping guides and services, such as the Expedia travel service and CarPoint, an automotive product, as well as the MSNBC cable and Internet news joint venture with NBC.

With no immediate replacement for Higgins, Ballmer took over the snarled MSN operations himself. He set aside his normal bombast in order to educate himself about the Internet business, which he freely admits he didn't know much about. It was Web 101.

He was never enamored of Microsoft's forays into what the Internet industry dryly calls "content." The media business didn't seem suited to Microsoft's strengths. The forays into electronic commerce created the perception that Microsoft was in competition with its traditional software customers. "We're not a bank! We're not a bank!" Ballmer had yelled in his role as sales chief. "We'd like to sell you some NT servers!"

Now he began to disentangle Microsoft from some of its confusing initiatives, agreeing to a spin-off of the Expedia travel service and bringing in Ford, his father's old employer, as a 25 percent investor in CarPoint, the auto site. Microsoft also held on-again, off-again talks about selling the MSN access business. One of the problems was Microsoft's ambivalence. Ballmer drove the discussion to a decision: Microsoft was in the Internet access business and would invest heavily to add customers.

In spite of itself, MSN had become the third most trafficked destination on the Web. Ballmer was beginning to see MSN through the prism of Microsoft's traditional platform business. What was at stake with MSN was control of the Internet "user experience." The measure of success was no longer the programming interfaces software developers used, as it was in the early days of Windows. Now it was about who commanded the attention of millions of computer users as they performed their most common daily tasks. That was the big battle. That was the opportunity Netscape missed and the one AOL was seizing.

As he educated himself, Ballmer began to realize the mistake Microsoft had made in 1997 when it turned away from the challenge of creating a new platform for Internet services, separate from Windows.

To recoup, he turned, once again, to Silverberg. Since the debacle in early 1998, Silverberg had laid low, collecting a retainer from Microsoft that helped ensure he didn't join a competitor. He had been given an office down the hall from Ballmer's in Red West. With Ballmer's new appreciation for his advice, Silverberg became a Steve guy.

Ballmer asked Silverberg to come back full-time, with a sweeping mandate. He would be in charge of all of the company's consumer efforts—MSN, the consumer version of Windows, and Internet Explorer. It was everything Silverberg once had asked for, a job description that was even more expansive than the one he had negotiated with Gates and Maritz before they reversed themselves a year earlier.

Silverberg considered Ballmer's job offer. Ballmer seemed to be "getting it," Silverberg concluded. But he felt that the moment for his return had passed. In the months during which he consulted part-time for Ballmer, Silverberg said he saw internal issues still consumed fully 80 percent of Microsoft's time. If he was going to be a success versus AOL, his team would have to be fully 95 percent focused externally.

"The company is so wrapped up in its shorts that it can't get anything done," he sighed in an e-mail to Ben Slivka, his old ally from the browser and Java battles. Microsoft might still be loaded with brainpower, but it was getting only pennies on the dollar. "So much IQ is wasted," he complained.

The only solution, Silverberg felt, was some kind of company-within-the-company, with its own charter and full autonomy. That was the solution to corporate paralysis prescribed in *The Innovator's Dilemma* by Harvard Business School professor Clayton Christensen, which had become an underground manifesto among Microsoft employees. If he did come back, Silverberg's company-within-a-company needed freedom to pursue its own strategies without paying the "strategy tax" of coordinating with the rest of the company's plans.

"Since the goal is to have a completely reinvented version of Windows, it's clear the team has to be completely separate and independent from Windows," Silverberg wrote in his February 1999 e-mail exchange with Slivka.

Silverberg worried that even Ballmer's prodigious energy might not be enough to overcome Microsoft's deep-seated problems. The root of the problem: Bill Gates. Silverberg feared that Gates's adherence to old PC orthodoxies, and his limited vision of what a reinvented Internet version of Windows might be, would frustrate any excitement he himself might be able to muster. Gates had written several e-mails expressing frustration with MSN's lack of momentum and focus. He seemed to favor a much narrower vision—the online service as simply a PC-support service that would do little more than provide fixes to repair Microsoft's buggy code or provide patches for security breaches.

"I simply do not want to spend my life in meetings struggling with the internal issues, getting pissy mail from Billg," Silverberg wrote. "Or hearing from people who want me to do unnatural and losing things to 'protect' Windows."

As for Slivka, he had recovered from the bruising he had taken at Gates's hands and was once again serving as Microsoft's chief agitator. By 1999, his standing had recovered enough for the company to send him to a photo shoot for a May 1999 *Business Week* cover story. In the caption, he was touted as part of Gates's new "kitchen cabinet of techno-whizzes."

His e-mails accorded Slivka another measure of internal infamy. He was the hands-down winner of the "DOJ Play at Home Game," a mock contest devised by Charles Fitzgerald, one of Microsoft's marketing whizzes, who monitored part of the trial proceedings. To pass the hours in the courtroom, Fitzgerald awarded one point to any employee whose name was on the "cc:" line of an e-mail introduced into evidence. Appearing on the "To:" line won two points. Three points went to the sender of the message. There were additional points for anyone mentioned by name in court and bonuses for those whose e-mails were specifically repudiated by a witness. The contest wasn't even close.

Nonetheless, Slivka's e-mail only grew more pointed. In early

1999, he took his case directly to Gates and Ballmer: The next version of Windows should be a simple machine for connecting to the Internet, explicitly targeting AOL's customers, rather than current users of Windows, he argued. The threat represented by AOL's purchase of Netscape in December 1998 made it all the more important to rally Microsoft's Internet team again. The purchase of Netscape and alliance with Sun Microsystems had given AOL the software development talent to create a full-fledged platform.

It was the same old debate: Could Microsoft's Internet effort be set free to compete, and possibly win, on its own, or must it always be yoked to the weight of Microsoft's Windows legacy?

"We must untangle the charter of the Windows team and what I call the Internet team," Slivka wrote to Gates and Ballmer. He made no attempt to disguise his agenda. "I fear very deeply that trying to win the Internet using Windows is a losing strategy."

Slivka went further. If the *Innovator's Dilemma* book hadn't spurred Gates to change, Slivka made another reading suggestion for the chairman, providing a link to Amazon.com's Web page for James Utterback's book, *Mastering the Dynamics of Innovation.*

That book recounts example after example in which innovations led directly to changes in market leadership. Might Bill Gates turn out to be a latter-day Frederic Tudor, the wealthy nineteenth-century Bostonian known as the "Ice King"? As Utterback recounts the tale, Tudor, harvesting ice from New England ponds, built an empire that supported breweries, meat processors, dairies, and hospitals around the world. Improvements in harvesting and shipping allowed him to cut prices drastically. The booming ice business attracted competitors seeking to displace the Ice King, but the expanding pie made for prosperity all around. The harvested-ice industry of New England reduced the cost per ton from about fifteen dollars to fifteen cents. The 1886 ice harvest was 25 million tons, the biggest ever.

By the mid-1920s, however, the ice-harvesting industry was dead, replaced by manufactured ice producers who took advantage of electric-powered refrigeration.

Impending changes, Utterback wrote, are generally completely knowable. But incumbents "actually resist all efforts to understand them, preferring to further entrench their positions in the older products. This results in a surge of productivity and performance that may take the old technology to unheard-of heights. In most cases, this is a sign of impending death."

Reading Slivka's e-mail on a cloudy Sunday afternoon, Silverberg knew exactly what he was referring to. The dazzling array of features included in Microsoft's traditional software was indeed taking performance to unheard-of heights. But what if nobody cared anymore about all the bells and whistles? Microsoft was falling into the classic innovator's dilemma.

Silverberg wrote back to Slivka: "Regarding the path followed by incumbents as they service ever more complex demands of existing customers, eventually overshooting the needs of the average customer: Can you say 'Office'?" Solutions that were good enough for most people's word-processing and spreadsheet needs were sure to emerge on, say, Linux, or on the Web itself, Silverberg said. "And when they do, watch out."

Slivka was even more blunt in his own response, summoning the example of one of Gates's boyhood heroes, the legendary founder of Digital Equipment whose minicomputers vanquished the mainframe industry only to be overtaken in turn by the PC revolution. "BillG is pulling a Ken Olsen, there's no other way to describe it."

Ballmer was Microsoft's last, best hope. "If SteveB doesn't do something radical with this re-org, I think I'm going to take off six months and then do a startup," Slivka wrote.

Silverberg was similarly excited about reuniting the core of the old Internet Explorer team in a new start-up. "Steve does need to do something radical," he said. But he had little confidence that Ballmer could overcome the resistance from Gates. Silverberg even wondered whether Ballmer's attempts to get him back were genuine. His doubts about Gates's intentions were even stronger. "With Bill, I believe he wants me back, but not the me who I really am, but rather a version of me who would be the obedient soldier (and do all the wrong things!)" he said.

In the end, he turned down Ballmer's job offer. Many of Microsoft's most talented veterans of the browser war departed not long after.

Silverberg wrote Slivka, "I simply do not believe in the path the company is pursuing right now."

HALF-MEASURES

Ballmer's unshakable loyalty to Gates limited him to being, at most, only a partial reformer. In pursuing the reinvention of Microsoft, he repeatedly butted up against Gates's earlier version of the company. He criticized Microsoft's previous regime only obliquely, around the edges, in his comments about new opportunities and past mistakes.

For example, Gates had earlier opposed any change in the time-worn slogan that served as Microsoft's mission statement since the company's founding. The need to replace "A computer on every desk and in every home" had been tentatively broached at the December 1997 presentation that followed the middle managers' retreat. Ballmer himself had thought the slogan sounded like a platitude when he arrived at the company in 1980. He eventually embraced it as a motivational tool. But now his one hundred interviews had convinced him there were large parts of the company's work to which the slogan was no longer relevant. The Web, along with a host of new devices, was changing Microsoft's mission.

"We had to step back and say, 'With all this flux, new risks, changes in the market, was this vision still appropriate to the company?' " Ballmer said. "I guess we decided it wasn't."

The new mission statement adopted in 1999, unwieldy as it is, implicitly recognizes the diminished importance of the PC: "Empower people through great software anytime, any place and on any device."

Ballmer also tried to reshape the company with a sweeping March 1999 "reinvention" he called Vision 2.0. He refused to call his reshuffling of Microsoft's divisions a "reorganization." As the middle managers had suggested, the five divisions would be designed around the needs of particular customer groups, rather than the sometimes arbitrary distinctions between pieces of Microsoft's own technology. The reorganization was touted as a way to free Microsoft's divisions to serve customers without worrying about conflicts with other groups.

"We've got to move, move, move on a lot of different fronts," Ballmer said. The old organization "put Bill and me in the center of too many things. We need six or seven guys to compete with the best in the business."

But when the dust settled, little of substance had changed. Ballmer's instincts were right, but ultimately he was no more willing than Gates to give up Microsoft's vaunted leverage. Slivka met with Ballmer in early 1999 to advocate the notion that software was changing from a product to a service. Once-separate software programs would give way to a sea of interlinked services, all online. To exploit the trend, Slivka argued to Ballmer, Microsoft should "screw Windows, screw Office and staff a group to go out and do the Internet right."

Ballmer upheld the Microsoft orthodoxy that being better wasn't enough. Leverage and lock-ins were necessary to establish an asset with lasting value.

"What advantage would they have?" he asked Slivka. "They'd just be another group of developers."

Many executives inside Microsoft thought Ballmer's reorganization didn't go far enough in untangling the company's many charters. Harel Kodesh, an Israeli-born engineer in charge of Microsoft's efforts on non-PC devices, had undergone an almost religious epiphany. Kodesh had helped develop Windows CE for "consumer electronics" such as handhelds, cell phones, set-top boxes, and the voice-activated "Auto PC" for car dashboards. At first, Kodesh subscribed to Gates's notion that, as with PCs, a uniform operating system across many different electronic devices would attract software developers, who generally target their efforts on the highest-volume platform. Because Windows CE used the same tools and Win32 interfaces as Windows for the PC, Microsoft's dominance in the PC market would give it additional leverage in the non-PC world. Windows CE was a key element in the Windows Everywhere strategy.

But it hadn't worked out that way. Microsoft seemed permanently behind in the handheld market, where Palm was established as the software of choice for "personal digital assistants." And Microsoft was being outflanked by a consortium of cell phone makers, led by Nokia, which established the Symbian joint venture with a British software maker, Psion, to create a specialized operating system for Web-connected cell phones, a potentially huge market.

Kodesh realized that he, and Microsoft, were both on the wrong track. The vaunted Windows leverage had turned out to be a liability. Kodesh had met *Innovator's Dilemma* author Clayton Christensen at a symposium at Harvard. He came back to Redmond with a hundred copies of the book for his thousand-person group. The "information appliance" was exactly the kind of disruptive technology Christensen warned about, Kodesh argued. The new devices needed to be small, cheap, and most of all "cool." That meant they should be precisely tailored to the needs of particular consumers for particular uses. Microsoft's software was like a Swiss Army knife, adequate for many things but optimized for none. It was the only software that could work in handhelds, phones, and set-tops, but it wasn't the best software for any of those categories.

To Kodesh, Microsoft's initiatives were driven by the dictates of the company's technology, rather than the wishes of consumers. An electronics maker like Casio could focus on delivering a product with just the right features for consumers; Microsoft insisted on squeezing PC applications like Word and Excel into the miniature devices.

Kodesh had a radical idea. Microsoft should keep Windows CE for handheld devices but start from scratch on new software for cell phones and all other non-PC devices. Microsoft should start from the other direction, asking manufacturers what they could build for, say, ninety-nine dollars and offering to give them the software they needed, rather than only the software the company already had. The choice was familiar: Would Microsoft embrace the new market for non-PC devices, create an autonomous company-within-a-company to tackle it, and do anything it took to win? Or would it shackle the new devices to its traditional businesses?

In September 1999, Kodesh wrote a memo to Gates and Ballmer under the heading "Starting from Scratch." We need to kill Windows CE for those categories, he argued. Win32 is not an advantage; it's a tax on device design. It served to further Microsoft's strategy but not to help consumers. Given all their other alternatives, electronics manufacturers wouldn't pay the tax. Kodesh wanted to take a small group of developers and work solely on developing the best software for information appliances, unconstrained by the needs of the rest of the company.

Gates rejected the suggestions. "It's very disappointing you feel that way," he told Kodesh. "We don't have time to start from scratch."

Kodesh left Microsoft several months later.

Such policy tensions weren't resolved by Ballmer's reorganization. Ballmer had relieved Gates of some of the decision-making burden, but rather than distribute it broadly, he took it all on himself. The company still operated under central command. Ballmer's management style can be characterized as hub-and-spoke, with Ballmer at the center of nearly every issue. Rather than reach a consensus, he preferred to conduct thousands of one-on-ones, gleaning an idea from one meeting and refining it through dozens of follow-ups. Such a management style can work well in a small organization; in a company the size of Microsoft, it bogged down the decision-making process.

Even more debilitating, managers were losing confidence in their own ability to solve problems. Both Gates and Ballmer managed by detail rather than by overarching strategy. And both were still gripped by a deep need to prove their smarts, to nail the test, to win the game. That leads to inconsistent messages. Even the best managers at Microsoft felt undermined.

The same issue arose repeatedly. "Everybody has gone in and said, 'You need to give people more autonomy,' " said Chris Williams, the human resources vice president. "They agree intellectually, but they have a very difficult time doing it."

In his March 1999 reorganization, Ballmer himself had acknowledged the need to give Microsoft's divisions more autonomy. Companies from AT&T to Hewlett-Packard were "delayering" by spinning off separate businesses into separate, more nimble, customer-responsive, and even innovative companies. Now, some of Microsoft's most astute strategists were beginning to think the unthinkable. At least a year before Judge Jackson's ruling, and wholly separate from antitrust considerations, at least a dozen top managers concluded that Microsoft might well be better off broken up into separate companies. As the difficulties of coordinating Microsoft's dozens of initiatives became a Rubik's Cube of complexity, support grew for a more loosely coupled structure. Different groups needed to be free to serve their customers and pursue competitive strategies without being hamstrung by the Unified Theory of Windows.

Eric Engstrom, a former general manager and one of Microsoft's witnesses in the antitrust trial, told me, "What's most sad is that there is a large body of people inside and outside the company that say 'Break up the company into internal units, so they can compete with themselves.' "

"Markets are good at sorting out winners and losers, but Microsoft no longer operates on a market economy internally," Engstrom said. "There's too much command and control. Microsoft has lost all of its Darwinian forces."

One former vice president told me, "Microsoft needs to be a holding company. Microsoft could have a large, perhaps even controlling interest. But each division would be free to pursue its own strategy." Some common resources—such as the basic research effort—might still be shared. But the new CEO of each spin-off would have the autonomy to cut deals and adopt technology as he or she saw fit.

Slivka went so far as to draft his own breakup plan. "The ideal solution would be for Bill to let a few more flowers bloom," Slivka told me after he left Microsoft. "He could do some internal venture capital. But he seems incapable of that." Therefore, Slivka proposed to dissolve Microsoft into six separate companies: Systems, consisting of Windows 2000 and developer tools; Applications, mostly Office; Wireless, with Windows CE and MSN's mobile services; MSN itself; Home, with the consumer Windows operating system and consumer applications such as Microsoft Money; and Hardware, with the computer mice, keyboards, joysticks, and other peripherals. "You could talk me into putting Hardware and Home together, and Wireless and MSN together. I have Windows 98 and Windows 2000 in separate companies because the target customers are different."

Gates was adamantly opposed to any breakup. Microsoft's major initiatives had always required the energies of the entire company. There was no way to pull apart the pieces as if Microsoft were simply a conglomerate of unrelated businesses. "There is certainly no breakup of the company into smaller companies that I would find acceptable, and we are not anywhere thinking of that as a possibility," he said.

But it was happening anyway. For years, Microsoft had one of the most cohesive management groups in the industry. Then suddenly it fell apart. The rapid dispersal of Microsoft's once-stunning collection of brainpower constituted a slow-motion dissolution more drastic than any court-ordered breakup.

Microsoft was accustomed to losing employees who had gotten rich and were ready to retire. But now a major cause of the exodus was the muddle, not the money. The company seemed to be driving away many of its best and brightest who still had technical contributions to make. The losses went beyond any particular product group. Of the thirty-nine executives ranked vice president or above on a Winter 1997 organizational chart, more than half were no longer with the company by the end of 2000. Of the thirteen middle managers who attended the Power Lab retreat in the fall of 1997, more than half were no longer at Microsoft three years later. Of the eight members of Gates's executive committee in 1997, five were gone.

Microsoft's social calendar began to revolve around farewell parties, where many of those still at the company defensively explained that they, too, planned to leave soon. The most popular literary form seemed to be "goodbye mail," the long, anguished letters departing employees wrote to rationalize their decisions and dissect the company's problems; members of the executive staff received as many as ten each week. One that found a following was from Brandon Watson, who came to Microsoft as a nineteen-year-old intern and returned after earning his MBA.

"This was one of the hardest decisions I have ever made," his good-bye letter began. When he arrived in 1994, he had seen a dynamic company with smart people working on "some very cool and hard problems." Now, he said, "I have seen that we are more concerned with protecting our installed base and giving the cool work to managers who could care less about the work they are doing." Watson challenged the executives to name the company's next "jihad." "If you are inclined to say Windows 2000, I say try again. That is more of a slow moving ground war. . . . If we continue to believe that Windows is the only future of the company, then we are going to lose many people because we are no longer being innovative. Yes, Windows is a key to Microsoft's core business, but the problem is that it is too big, too chaotic, largely overdue and something that is now seen as passe."

Watson's personal frustrations no doubt influenced his analysis. He railed against Microsoft's bell-curve grading system, in which every manager ranked one-fifth of his employees as below average each year to help the company weed out chronic underperformers. The system had indeed generated considerable game-playing: Some employees deliberately chose to work in less-challenging groups, where they knew they could beat the competition; some managers intentionally kept laggards on until the review period in order to have employees they didn't mind cutting. For employees it was a maddening process: "Being told by my manager that even if someone was doing 4.5 work, they could still get a 3 because he 'has to fit the curve' is just about the most backward, frustrating and de-motivating thing I have ever heard in my entire life," Watson wrote.

In conclusion, he said, "The change agents of the 21st Century are going to be young people like me, not 40-something millionaires whose incentive to work hard and think about the big problems has been dramatically reduced. . . . At what point did Microsoft lose its passion, fun and impact at the heart of its leadership team?"

By August 1999, even the thick-skinned Slivka had had enough. He was leaving Microsoft to join Amazon.com. He poured out his reasons in a long exit e-mail to Ballmer.

"The biggest problem is that Bill has not grown enough," Slivka told Ballmer. "He still wants to set technical direction and manage the company the way he used to. Heck, so do you. . . .

"But we're too large and have too many smart people for you guys to do your jobs they way you used to. In trying to maintain your old ways, you squeeze out the innovators and insure that the incrementalists and the politicians are in charge.

"The story I tell myself (since I'm not there to watch), is that you see what really needs to be done to liberate the people of Microsoft. But Bill does not, and does not let you do what you know must be done. You are in the middle between Bill and the rest of Microsoft. It is time for you to do something very courageous, and you know what that is. It will be hard, and Bill will hate you for it, but it is either that or the slow death of Microsoft. Being in the middle is not fun.

"I'm pretty sure that not acknowledging the problem, or taking half-measures, is a sure path to mediocrity. . . . The biggest problem is that Bill wants too much control and thus squeezes out the thought leadership and people leadership that Microsoft most desperately needs."

Ballmer's response was short but plaintive. "I too am probably part of the problem," he wrote to Slivka. "Hard to know what to do."

SILVERBERG'S imminent return had been a constant leitmotif at Microsoft ever since 1997. Now that Silverberg had finally opted out, Ballmer needed someone to run MSN.

Headhunters from the San Francisco office of Heidrick & Struggles talked to all the name-brand Internet players, including Jeff Mallett of Yahoo!, George Bell of Excite, and Jake Winebaum of Disney. None were interested in tackling the challenge of building a new media brand inside a traditional software company. Ballmer came close to landing Mark Booth, the head of the BSkyB satellite network in Europe, but then Rupert Murdoch, the major stakeholder in BSkyB, offered to set Booth up with his own $300 million venture capital firm. Booth also turned Microsoft down.

Traditional media executives weren't comfortable with Microsoft's rough-and-tumble style and lack of luxury perks. Ballmer wasn't really at ease with the media personalities either. Yet there was no single person inside Microsoft with exactly the right combination of skills—media-savvy, deal-making, and complete and utter fealty to Microsoft.

So instead of one person, Ballmer chose three. Ballmer proposed that Maffei, a deal guy, share command of the Internet operations with Brad Chase, a marketing guy, and Jon DeVaan, a software guy. Chase, Silverberg's longtime lieutenant, brought at least a little of the aura of the successful Windows 95 and Internet Explorer efforts and DeVaan, the enormously competent but publicly awkward vice

president in charge of Office, brought solid development experience.

Maffei knew he needed a chance to prove his operational skills if
he had any hope of advancing closer to the top of Microsoft.

But Ballmer's offer didn't fit the bill. Maffei would have only one-
third of the power, and that only until Ballmer brought in a bigger
shot as head of the division above them all.

Being one of "three-in-a-box," as Microsoft called such arrangements, wasn't the kind of promotion Maffei was looking for. Why is
this job better than being chief financial officer? Maffei wanted to
know.

Because if you don't take it, Ballmer told him, I'll bring somebody
else in and that person will do all the deals you're now doing.

And what if Maffei couldn't get along with the bigshot Ballmer
brought in and left the company? Would Ballmer agree to immediately vest all of the Maffei's stock options?

That's not being a team player, Ballmer told him. Maffei declined
Ballmer's job offer.

In the March 1999 reorganization, Ballmer went with two-in-a-
box instead, splitting the responsibility for the Internet operations
between Chase and DeVaan.

Later Ballmer hired a computer industry bigshot to oversee the
whole effort. Ballmer knew Rick Belluzzo, the chief executive of
troubled Silicon Graphics, from his days at Hewlett-Packard, where
he had helped build a multibillion-dollar printer business. Belluzzo
had proved his loyalty to Microsoft when H-P split from the rest of
the Unix industry and agreed to support Windows NT. Now,
Ballmer asked Belluzzo whether he would be able to tune out the
anti-Microsoft rhetoric he was sure to hear from the company's competitors.

"That's easy," Belluzzo assured him. "People have always accused
me of being on the Microsoft payroll. Now I really will be."

As influence shifted to Ballmer, Maffei could see his star beginning
to fade. Ballmer trusts guys with deep sales backgrounds or who have
operated highly profitable businesses. Maffei was neither.

Maffei had been Microsoft's golden boy as long as Gates was the
source of power. Gates appreciated Maffei's sparkling intelligence
and his gambler's heart. Maffei had helped him feel comfortable with
creative financing arrangements. Microsoft's money could help the
company's strategy; the money could also make money. With a few

successful deals, Gates became more willing to take risks. After all, he was playing with the house's money. Some of the returns were spectacular. The $4 million investment in UUNet in 1995, along with the exercise of $12 million in warrants, turned into a stake that at one point was worth more than $500 million.

Among Maffei's other wins: a program to sell "put" warrants to large institutional investors. The warrants give the holders the right to sell Microsoft shares at prices below the current market price—in effect, they are a bet that Microsoft's shares will fall. At first, Gates was only willing to sell warrants so far out of the money that there was little chance they would ever be redeemed. But as he smelled success, his appetite for risk increased. By 1999, Microsoft had collected more than $2 billion from the program.

A complicated stock offering in December 1996 was an even bigger success. Microsoft issued $1 billion in preferred shares, which carried a cap on their appreciation. Microsoft's stock so outperformed the cap the company realized a gain of about $3.5 billion by the time the shares were redeemed.

But if Gates was ready to experiment with financial arrangements, Ballmer was not. He considered them bean-counting at best. At worst, they were flimflam that would backfire in the end.

Associates could sense the tension whenever Ballmer and Maffei were in a meeting together. Ballmer's suspicions of Maffei increased when it became known that Maffei was actively interested in accepting an offer to become chief executive of RoadRunner, a joint venture of Time Warner and MediaOne to provide high-speed Internet access over their cable networks. Microsoft owned 10 percent of Road-Runner, and Maffei sat on its board of directors. Now the rest of the board was looking for someone to ready the service's initial public offering on Wall Street. There was only one catch: As part of Microsoft's investment, Maffei had negotiated a clause giving the company veto power over the hiring of RoadRunner's CEO. Gates exercised his veto. It was Maffei himself who had to convey Gates's decision to the rest of the board.

Ballmer was generally skeptical of the cable deal-making that so consumed Maffei and Gates. The deals didn't generate much in the way of software sales, and they scared away potential partners.

But even Ballmer became swept up in the frenzy that gripped Wall Street in 1999. In March 1999 Comcast made a bid to buy MediaOne, the cable operations built by US West, one of the original Baby Bells. AT&T, the new giant of the cable industry after its purchase of Tele-Communications Inc., was looking to expand further, banking on cable to give it the ability to offer a full bundle of services—local and long-distance telephone, digital television, and high-speed Internet access. AT&T's counteroffer trumped Comcast's original bid. Brian Roberts, the head of Comcast, pleaded with Microsoft to come in on his side.

Roberts, the young and savvy son of Comcast's founder, had established a good relationship with Gates and Maffei in 1997, when he was the only cable titan to take Gates up on his offer to help fund the industry's digital buildout. Now he needed Microsoft's cash to trump AT&T. In fact, he had very little of his own.

Microsoft hadn't made a commitment, but Maffei threw himself into the middle of the action. During a basketball game at Madison Square Garden, Maffei shuttled between his seat with Roberts and another box, where AT&T chief financial officer Dan Somers and Gene Sykes of Goldman Sachs were watching the game. At the same time, Microsoft's own bankers were working out the details of creating a tracking stock to hold the new stake in MediaOne and Microsoft's other media properties, a way to avoid diluting Microsoft's own earnings. Gates himself was on the phone with Steve Case of AOL, who had an interest in making things difficult for AT&T. It was a battle of the titans.

Microsoft was riven with internal debate. Did the company really want to be in the business of controlling cable subscribers? How would the other cable companies react to competition from Microsoft when Microsoft wanted them as customers? More specifically, Maffei knew that if Microsoft backed Roberts, it had better win, because the move would surely alienate AT&T, a major purchaser of set-top boxes.

As the complex negotiations neared a climax, Ballmer changed his mind. He called Maffei to argue that Microsoft should jump in with Comcast to make a counteroffer for MediaOne. But the moment had passed. Two days later, Maffei used the threat of a Microsoft-Comcast alliance to strike a settlement deal with AT&T—a $5 billion investment by Microsoft and a commitment by AT&T to use Microsoft's software in at least 5 million television set-top boxes.

Maffei had become taken with the notion of a tracking stock as a way to get Wall Street to recognize the value of Microsoft's media holdings at a time when stock market valuations were wildly out of whack. In Windows and Office, Microsoft had a real business, generating giant and increasing revenues and huge profit margins on top of that. The Internet businesses were losing money, creating a drag on Microsoft's earnings.

It was all about accounting. Tracking stocks reflected the operations of a segment of a company's business without formally carving out a new company. The beauty of a tracking stock, in Maffei's view, was that it would take the Internet losses off the income statement. Microsoft received a double bonus—the tracking stock could soar, new-economy style, on its profitless Internet revenues; the parent company, valued more traditionally on its profit growth, would be even more attractive without its money-losing Internet operations. Having a separate currency also would make deal-making and recruitment easier. For many employees, Microsoft's shares were no longer a match for the lure of Internet riches.

Gates was game. As proposed in early 1999, the tracking stock would have constituted Microsoft's $1 billion stake in Comcast and its other cable-system investments, its 10 percent holding in Road-Runner, the high-speed Internet access service, and the collection of e-commerce sites, such as Expedia for travel, CarPoint for automobiles, and at the time, Transpoint, a joint venture to process household bills on the Web. The basic Internet access service of MSN, which Gates felt had a more integral tie to Windows, was not to be part of the tracking stock.

Ballmer was more reluctant. It wasn't fair to over-reward some employees, who worked for the money-losing Internet operations, while leaving behind those who stuck with Microsoft's traditional businesses, he thought.

The issue came to a head in the summer of 1999, just before the company's annual conference for Wall Street analysts. In advance of the analysts' meeting, I reported that Microsoft was close to moving forward with the tracking stock plan. The stock price jumped on the news. Ballmer was on vacation. When he came back, he went ballistic in a small meeting, quashing the tracking stock proposal.

GOING SOUTH

Microsoft's knotty compensation problems were getting worse. The company had relied heavily on stock options to minimize its salary expenses. But now there was no way the company's stock was going to do as well in the next three years as it had in the past three. With growth slowing, Microsoft was under pressure to shell out more cash in compensation and to give away larger chunks of options to remain attractive to both current employees and new recruits. Both moves contributed to the further dilution of earnings, weakening the stock even more and increasing the pressure for even larger pay hikes, the beginning of a vicious cycle.

Nonetheless, Ballmer started spreading more wealth around. In April 1999, his new compensation plan called for a 15 percent increase in cash salaries. For years, Microsoft had set its salaries to be in the exact middle of the range for similar jobs elsewhere in the software industry, and the company fell below even that in some job categories. Now, Microsoft would peg its base pay to the sixty-fifth percentile of the software industry, meaning salaries would be above the level in two-thirds of the rest of the industry.

The company used stock options to richly reward many employees without significantly affecting the company's income statement. Historically, the company granted entry-level programmers options on between fifteen hundred and three thousand shares, with annual option grants in the same range. Now, for the particularly prized employees that Microsoft could simply not afford to lose, the company went crazy. The company let it be known that some prized employees were getting two hundred thousand or three hundred thousand or four hundred thousand options. Privately, some employees reported that their offers included options on 2, 3, or 4 *million* shares. Of course, if Microsoft's shares fell below the strike price for the options, it wouldn't matter how many options an employee held; they'd all be under water and worthless.

Analysts in Microsoft's human resources department who have tracked employee complaints against the company's share price have found a perfect inverse correlation. If the stock is high and moving up, the company could turn off the lights and people would never complain. But if it were stagnant and going down, the number of employee complaints about parking, heating, and cafeteria food showed a predictable rise.

Board members and colleagues had long tried to convince Gates that employees at Microsoft were not there for the money. They wanted to work in a place that was exciting, that was winning, they said. They wanted recognition, the satisfaction of seeing their products used by millions, the pride of working for a great company.

Gates wasn't having any of it. They're all going to tell you they're not working for the money, he told Marquardt. They're all lying to you.

BALLMER had good reason to worry about the health of Microsoft's income statement. Nobody can say Microsoft didn't warn investors that slower growth was coming. The company long cried wolf. It was easy to dismiss signs that Microsoft was losing its easy ability to defy gravity. Each quarter, the company had issued cautions to dampen any overenthusiasm by analysts or investors. Each quarter, the company easily surpassed the estimates, and the cycle began again.

In December 1998, the company had again blown away all estimates, reporting profits of nearly $2 billion, 75 percent higher than the year before. But inside the company, the signs were clear.

Microsoft's core markets were increasingly saturated. Through 1995 and 1996, Microsoft had benefited from a huge upgrade cycle, driven by the industry's shift to both Windows 95 and Office 97. Now that cycle was over, and Microsoft's growth was heavily tied to the overall growth of PC sales. The upgrade business generated less revenue than sales to new customers. New products were late and were unlikely to revive growth to the old levels. Worldwide growth was slowing. The PC industry had become mature. The go-go days were over. Growth in Microsoft's operating income, which hit 54 percent in 1999, slowed to 10 percent in 2000 and an estimated 4 percent in 2001.

Wall Street, by and large, ignored the warning signs. As the antitrust case turned into background noise, it was easy to continue to cast Microsoft as the profit-and-cash machine that couldn't be stopped. Cash was piling up at more than $1 billion a month, to nearly $27 billion by December 2000. The rising market made Microsoft's investments look even smarter. The reported value of the company's stock holdings more than quadrupled from two years earlier, to $18.3 billion.

Microsoft's stock hit a peak of $119.125 on December 27, 1999, giving the company a total value of more than $620 billion. Windows 2000 had finally shipped, and Wall Street collectively decided that the antitrust suit was old hat and they preferred the glory days, when Microsoft was on the march to a trillion-dollar market cap.

When the virtuous circle reverses direction, it can quickly become a vicious downward spiral. Though it wasn't yet visible, by the late 1990s the virtuous circle of financial returns that lifted the company throughout the decade had already peaked. In a perverse way, the company's immense profitability started to work against it. Since each dollar of revenue contributed so much to the bottom line, each dollar of lost revenue meant an equally large hit to profits.

The release of Microsoft's earnings statements are a quarterly fire drill for Wall Street analysts and financial reporters. The accounting arcana test the ability of even seasoned observers to ferret out the true measures of the company's performance. By 1999, a close inspection of Microsoft's numbers provided clear signs the bloom was off the rose.

The old adage applies: Follow the money. Microsoft had many ways to polish its quarterly numbers. As only one example, take the $400 million the company set aside in March 1999 to cover upgrade coupons that had been given to buyers of the Office 97 software suite. The coupons, good for a free copy of Office 2000 when it became available, were a common technique to reassure customers they weren't buying obsolete software just when a new version was forthcoming. But a $400 million hit to revenues would reduce earnings by about four cents a share, a significant shortfall that might hit the stock hard.

Microsoft planned to make up the decline with gains from its investment portfolio. In a conference call, Maffei told Wall Street analysts to keep their estimates right where they were. Indeed, when Microsoft reported its results, the gains from its investment portfolio totaled $720 million, nearly double expectations and the highest ever. Microsoft beat Wall Street estimates by three cents a share.

When Microsoft puts funds aside for items such as the $400 million set-aside for the Office upgrade coupons, it uses an account on its balance sheet called the "unearned-revenues" account. The effect is to push into the future a large chunk of Microsoft's revenues. By the end of 2000, the unearned revenue account had grown to nearly $5 billion, or nearly a full quarter of revenues that are available to bolster results in future quarters.

As Office 2000 shipped, the company began to fulfill the upgrade coupons. As it did, it began transferring the $400 million from the unearned-revenue account back to the income statement. Thus, Microsoft's results for the June 1999 quarter were padded by half of the $400 million. That was a major reason the company was—again—

able to blow away Wall Street estimates. When results for the September 1999 quarter also smashed expectations, Maffei attributed the surprise to "awesome" PC demand. But a major factor was another transfer of $150 million from the Office-coupons set-aside.

Many companies similarly burnish their results to keep in the good graces of Wall Street. Microsoft fully disclosed the transfers from the unearned-revenue account. But some suggested there were other transfers that were not as transparent. In June 1999, Microsoft disclosed that the Securities and Exchange Commission had launched an investigation into claims that Microsoft had used hidden reserves to artificially smooth quarterly earnings. A former employee, Charles Panczerkowski, claimed in a lawsuit that he was fired in part because he blew the whistle on Microsoft's practice of using hundreds of millions in reserves to artificially smooth earnings. Former chief financial officer Mike Brown wrote in a 1995 e-mail to Gates, "I believe we should do all we can to smooth our earnings and keep a steady state earnings model." The company denied doing anything improper.

By the end of 1999 and all through 2000, Microsoft was dipping heavily into its investment portfolio to bolster its bottom line. Microsoft was beginning to look just a bit more like a bank and less like an operating company. Operating income actually fell year-over-year for two consecutive quarters, in June and September 2000. For fiscal 2000, the investment gains—which have nothing to do with software operations—totaled $3.3 billion, a 70 percent increase from a year earlier.

For years, the company had steadily increased its operating profit margins. Now, they started to shrink, if only slightly. From a high of 51 percent of revenues in calendar year 1999, operating margins fell to 47 percent in 2000 and an estimated 43 percent in 2001. By January 2001, Microsoft's shares were in the $40s. Even by the standards of the great stock slump of 2000, Microsoft's decline was momentous. It had shed a staggering $360 billion in market value before the share price began to rebound in 2001.

Government lawyers had vowed they would impose a remedy that would cut into Microsoft's profit margins. Now margins were falling even before any court-ordered remedy ever went into effect.

Maffei timed his departure well. With the stock near its peak in December 1999, he accepted an offer to become CEO of a Canadian telecommunications firm building a worldwide fiber-optic network.

He stage-managed the announcement from Jamaica, where he had taken his family, including his parents, for the Christmas holidays. He broke away from his telephone interviews to watch the reports on CNBC describing his departure. Microsoft's shares were down three dollars a share in after-hours trading.

Maffei remained at Microsoft for a couple of weeks into the New Year. In January 2000, he ran into Gates in the hall after the press conference where Gates announced that he was stepping aside as CEO.

"Gee, Bill, look how crazy the market is," Maffei told Gates. "The stock was down three points when I left. Your announcement sent it up two bucks."

Monopolist's Dilemma

Microsoft most likely would never have gotten a second chance to lead the Internet era if Adam Bosworth hadn't been angry enough to quit.

Luckily for the company, the veteran programmer was furious. Back in the spring of 1997, his team, his responsibilities, his authority had been yanked from under him. He wasn't about to be undermined by someone he didn't respect going around his back, telling his own team to ignore his decisions. He was out of there. He sold every share of Microsoft stock he owned—the tax hit be damned.

Bosworth's old boss, David Vaskevitch, had tried to persuade him to stay. The two friends talked late into the night. As general manager of enterprise computing, Vaskevitch was assembling teams for Microsoft's assault on the juicy corporate market dominated by IBM, Oracle, and Sun. His "Vasko-Vision," as his plans were known around Microsoft, called for a stunningly complex architecture, spanning everything from basic software building blocks to sophisticated servers. Vaskevitch needed Bosworth.

Bosworth was considered one of Microsoft's genuine innovators. He prefers the term "entrepreneur," but both terms are in distinction to "shipper," the organizational and motivational powerhouses who can quarterback a massive software project to completion. The best shippers could muster the brute force needed to get projects finished. It was the innovators and entrepreneurs who were needed to get the right ones started.

Bosworth didn't dispute that he had trouble taking direction. He took an engineer's satisfaction in causing discomfort by virtue of his unflinching directness. At the same time, he was prickly and prideful and carried a seemingly permanent chip on his shoulder. Vaskevitch fancied that he was the only one who could manage a problem child like Bosworth.

For all his foibles, Bosworth delivered. His logic was usually sound, his code was good, and his teams were passionate. That he was a leader made him all the more important to the cool, detached Vaskevitch, who for all his influence had attracted few loyal followers. What would it take to get Bosworth to stay?

Bosworth likes to disarm strangers by introducing himself, with a wink, as a "simple country boy from Vermont." In fact, he grew up on Eighty-seventh Street between Amsterdam and Columbus on the Upper West Side of Manhattan. Vermont was for summers and ski sojourns at his family's country house. He was a sophisticated and savvy master of Microsoft's folkways and knew exactly what to ask for.

He told Vaskevitch that there was a way Microsoft could restore his faith. He wanted a fully funded internal start-up and complete freedom to pursue any technology direction he chose. Thirty people, fully loaded with options and benefits, for three years. The cost to Microsoft: about $6 million a year, or $18 million. The money was the least of it. Bosworth wanted total immunity from any and all interference. From anybody. The first infraction, and he was really out of there.

Vaskevitch took the proposal to Gates. Done deal.

There's just one more thing, Bosworth said. Bill has to agree to the deal face-to-face.

It was a long meeting. Gates insisted he hadn't known the details of the dustup over Active Desktop that led to Bosworth's departure from the Internet Explorer 4 effort. Right now, Gates was more interested in calming Bosworth's anger.

His performance had always earned Bosworth a high "Bill score," the unspoken rating of one's standing and influence with Gates. From the time he joined the company, Bosworth insisted on attending his "Bill meetings" alone, without any of his in-between vice presidents. From Bosworth's point of view, the chain of command only got in the way. Intermediaries kowtowed to Gates and enforced, rather than challenged, his bad ideas. Bosworth discovered that if you played him right, Gates actually liked to lose arguments. If you beat him and changed his mind, he listened to you more attentively the next time. This also caused others to listen to you more as well, which led more resources—freedom, head count, attention—to come your way.

Gates committed himself to Bosworth's plan for two fifteen-person teams, fully funded, for three years. Gates had his own nostalgia for the early days of PC software, when a good team was limited to the number that could fit into a VW van. He, too, wanted to keep Bosworth. He agreed to the no-interference pledge.

Bosworth wanted the agreement in writing, in plain English. Vaskevitch sent him an e-mail: "Adam Bosworth can have 30 people to do whatever he wants for three years." Bosworth gave it to his lawyer for safekeeping.

Under other circumstances, the technology Bosworth's team developed would likely have been killed in the cradle. If Gates and Vaskevitch fully understood what Bosworth was going to do over the next three years, they might well have reneged on the deal. The technology Bosworth wanted to pursue represented a clear and present danger to Microsoft's old way of doing things. It weakened the hold of almost all of the heavyweight, tightly coupled approaches that were at the heart of Vasko-Vision. It conferred no competitive advantages on Windows. It promised to deliver ever-shrinking profit margins. Gates liked complex technology; what Bosworth wanted was simple. Microsoft liked to have a proprietary position; Bosworth was basing everything on an open architecture. Microsoft liked its software to work better with Windows; what Bosworth was doing was inherently cross-platform. Gates liked hooks to lock in customers to Microsoft. Bosworth was going to enlist Microsoft's biggest competitors by demonstrating that Microsoft was forsaking any lock-in.

"If Microsoft had any control, we would not have done XML," Bosworth says.

XML, or extensible markup language, is a cousin to HTML, the standard markup language for Web pages. As the popularity of the Web exploded, HTML had overwhelmed most of the proprietary approaches developers had long used to handle text and graphics. XML promised an even more far-reaching shift, not only for software but for commerce itself. HTML was limited to text and graphics. XML provided a common way for software programmers to handle data as well. With simple tags, similar to those used in HTML, XML not only turned the Web into a huge database but made it possible for software applications to work together, regardless of the underlying platform.

Bosworth had laid out the basic rationale two years earlier in his "Internet Applications Manifesto," in which he argued that everything Microsoft was then doing for building software applications was wrong. The memo had explicated the Web's four criteria: simple, flexible, heterogeneous, and loosely coupled. XML fulfilled the mandates Bosworth had identified. Simple—text was simpler than code. Flexible—if some small part was broken, the transaction itself didn't crash. Heterogeneous—XML didn't care whether it was running on Windows or any other operating system. Loosely coupled—like Web browsers and servers—and unlike traditional software—elements of the system could evolve separately.

Bosworth's argument that Microsoft needed to base all of its software on open, public protocols was a tough sell within the company. The software packages Microsoft and the rest of the industry sold to corporations—the customers with the most money to spend on software—were tightly coupled systems. A change in the server software required a change in the client software. When a company upgraded its database server software, it had to roll out new client software to thousands of PC desktops as well. The need for periodic upgrades kept customers making steady licensing payments.

The protocols for transactions between clients and servers were closely held secrets, the proprietary hooks that locked in customers. Oracle, IBM, Microsoft—they were all loathe to share protocols for exchanging data. It was all about control.

On the Web, out of control ruled. Nobody expected to install a new browser every time Amazon.com changed its Web site. On the Web, the kind of control that came from proprietary protocols was turning into a liability, not an advantage. Windows Everywhere was increasingly looking like a nonstarter in a world in which software runs not only on PCs but on all kinds of devices—from tiny handhelds to huge database servers. No company looked likely ever to gain 100 percent of the market. Therefore, interoperability between diverse systems was becoming a key requirement for customers. The company that ensured that everything worked together would have a key competitive advantage. The rules had changed.

Bosworth and his small XML team were going to give Microsoft what it needed, whether the company wanted it or not.

The looming shift in technology strategy gored plenty of oxes, inside and outside of Microsoft. To Bosworth's old friend, Vaskevitch, XML was at best a distraction from the serious work of building enterprise computing systems. Simple text could never be robust or efficient enough for the corporate market he was targeting. To Gates, the technology threatened to put Microsoft on a level playing field, without its cherished lock on customers.

That by June 2000 Microsoft embraced XML and made it the centerpiece of its new Internet platform was the product of serendipity and a stealthy outside-in strategy by Bosworth's small band of zealots. It was, says Jean Paoli, one of Bosworth's key helpers in the effort, a "complot for interoperability"—a conspiracy.

The conspiracy plotters found safe harbor under Bosworth's hard-won guarantee of noninterference. They gained strength when the alternative effort, a semisecret development project under Vaskevitch's direction, collapsed in spectacular fashion. The XML team used bluffs, persistence, and persuasion to win over first Maritz, then Ballmer, and finally Gates to the need to revamp Microsoft's entire software architecture.

Absent the conspiracy, Microsoft would likely have taken a different approach to programming the Internet. The pitch that still worked best with Gates was "You can have it all." He wasn't yet ready for the alternative pitch for the new era: "You have to give up a little to gain a *lot.*" But to his credit, Gates never shut the XML effort down. Microsoft nurtured a disruptive technology in spite of itself, backing its way into what may be its best hope for overcoming the Monopolist's Dilemma.

By the time Microsoft came around, however, Bosworth was gone, one of the many who decided to pursue their innovations independent of Microsoft.

JEAN PAOLI had a passion for "semistructured information." It was a European thing. Working with other French researchers, Paoli helped nurture the roots of what was to become XML for fifteen years before he arrived at Microsoft. From the early 1980s, the predecessor, SGML, or standard generalized markup language, found uses among those customers with massive documentation needs—nuclear engineers, aircraft designers, manufacturers, publishers, and some government agencies around the continent.

But SGML was so complicated that the system never escaped its niche. Then, Tim Berners-Lee, a Brit working at the CERN particle accelerator in Switzerland, stripped it down to its bare bones. He renamed his subset HTML. Berners-Lee released HTML with the rest of his program for sharing research among particle physicists around the globe, as a set of protocols he called the World Wide Web.

The champions of SGML were envious of HTML's success. No major company had ever adopted SGML, yet by 1995, it seemed that every billboard and TV commercial featured a Web address. Simple had won, complex had lost.

But as even Berners-Lee knew, the early Web had severe limitations. HTML was good for presenting text and graphics, but it was like a display case—users could look but not touch or easily manipulate the data. It was easier to surf Web sites than to create them. The early Web was effectively read-only. When I met Berners-Lee in 1995, he told me that the biggest mistake he had made was not designing full two-way interactivity into the original fabric of the new medium.

Berners-Lee moved to MIT to launch the World Wide Web Consortium, or W3C, an industry standard-setting group to protect and expand the interoperability of the early Web. Microsoft adopted the standards body like a drowning man grabbing a life preserver. One way to slow Netscape down was to use industry pressure to draw them into the protracted standard-setting process as well. It was a classic come-from-behind strategy. And Microsoft could win points with the press by wrapping itself in the mantle of the open standards. Thomas Reardon, a hotshot from Silverberg's Internet team, was one of the first people at Microsoft to master the subtle art of "gaming the standards," using the processes of industry standards bodies as part of Microsoft's competitive arsenal.

Reardon was looking for an edge in the "tag war" that had broken out between Microsoft and Netscape. Both sides were introducing and promoting their own specialized extensions, or tags, to HTML to enable more sophisticated Web pages. Both wanted to get the W3C to endorse their new features, or at least not to disallow them.

Paoli met Reardon at one of the first conferences of the World Wide Web Consortium, in Boston in 1995. The two talked for more than three hours. Paoli claimed to have a way to skirt the whole problem of illegal tags and allow Microsoft to legally add whatever tags it needed. SGML enabled any publisher to invent its own tags and publish the new schema; any other publisher could then simply make its own translation. Reardon, excited, sent Paoli out to meet Bosworth.

They met in a lounge in the San Francisco airport. Bosworth was already convinced that the Web's destiny was as a fabric for running applications, not just serving up content on static display pages. That required a way to get data to those applications.

"I know how to move data," Paoli told him. He was hired.

Paoli serenaded Bosworth with the simple but powerful insight at the heart of XML. Simple text, readable by any human, was how computer programs would exchange data with each other. All the sophisticated schemes for stitching software together with complicated binary code were obsolete. It represented a step backward from complexity.

XML tags turned simple text into "semistructured" information. Rather than merely displaying a number, XML tags identified the number as a date, or a price, or an invoice number, or a model number, or a size. That way, similar types of data could be sorted and shared without regard to the software in which it was created. Every industry, from health care to automobiles, would define its own sets of tags, or "schemas," for its own particular categories of information. Any XML-enabled software could read the tags and use the data in its own way.

Four weeks after he joined Microsoft, Paoli became the company's representative to a working group to radically simplify SGML. The group was led by Jon Bosak of Sun Microsystems, Microsoft's fiercest rival. Bosak had been using SGML for its original purpose, to streamline the massive documentation needed for large computer systems. Paoli's old friends in the SGML community wondered what he was doing working for Microsoft, which they considered the black knight of closed formats. Paoli, well aware of Microsoft's lack of credibility in the open standards world, kept a low profile. Even if Microsoft was doing the right thing, the rest of the industry would assume it was the wrong thing. Later, Sun's Bosak felt compelled to start his presentations by disclaiming, "XML is a conspiracy, but not Microsoft's."

Bosworth became an XML convert. His XML skunk works grew to twenty of his thirty people. In the spring of 1997, he, Paoli, and another engineer, Andrew Layman, visited Lehman Brothers on Wall Street, General Motors in Ann Arbor, Michigan, and Intel in Silicon Valley—thirty companies in all—and became convinced that XML solved some pressing problems. Bosworth came home and wrote an XML parser, a small software viewer for reading XML tags. He released it on the Web, complete with open-source code for a

Java version. That was unorthodox in Microsoft's culture, but Bosworth was taking full advantage of his no-interference deal with Gates.

The plotters began to generate bottoms-up support for the new technology within Microsoft. For example, the Internet Explorer team needed a way to do the TV-style "channels" that were to be the main attraction of the Active Desktop in IE 4.0. To enable the channels to "push" content to the desktop, there needed to be a way to identify when Web sites had been updated and to deliver the new material. XML was perfect for the job. Paoli cut back to half time on the XML effort and spent the rest of his time working to ready the XML engine for the browser team. The television-style channels were a flop, but the underlying technology was not. The new "Channel Definition Format" was the first commercial application for XML. The XML engine in Internet Explorer 4.0 could be used for other applications as well. For the first time, XML had mass-market distribution.

Skeptics abounded. Netscape, which had introduced its own specifications for "push" channels, dismissed Microsoft's format. Andreessen pooh-poohed XML as unnecessary and a potential threat to HTML. The innovation worm had turned: HTML, the insurgent technology of 1995, had become the defensive incumbent only a few years later.

Gates's reaction to XML was mixed. "This is text?" Gates asked incredulously when Paoli gave him a demonstration in the summer of 1997. "That's stupid. It's too bulky."

Gates had grown up in the era when computer-processing power was in short supply. His outlook still reflected that scarcity mentality. It was true that XML text was clunky, an order of magnitude less efficient than binary code that had been optimized for a particular machine. But the advantages of interoperability overcame any shortcomings of efficiency. And the march of Moore's Law meant computers had gotten many orders of magnitude faster. There was plenty of excess capacity available to handle the less-efficient text approach.

Gradually, Gates's curiosity overcame his skepticism. He started tracking the work of the XML team with greater intensity. More than perhaps any other senior executive at Microsoft, Gates mastered the technical arcana of XML, the stuff known only to the group's real tech weenies. He was comfortable with the jargon of schemas and mapping and with the alphabet-soup derivatives of XML such as DOM and XSL and XDR and SOAP.

It was the business model implied by XML that made Gates uncomfortable. With open standards, other vendors could use XML to do exactly the same thing. So what was Microsoft's edge? Gates kept pressing Bosworth for an answer to the question: How do we get a competitive advantage?

Bosworth's answer was consistent. Microsoft would win by being the first and the best. While everybody else was still trying to understand XML, Microsoft could be shipping the best implementations. The company would be a leader in interoperability, an increasingly loud demand from customers. Interoperability had worked for Microsoft before. Microsoft's network servers worked well with Novell's, its transaction servers worked well with IBM's. Now, with XML making everything work together, Microsoft could have a technology to lay across everything else. Delivering the newest, most inclusive technology could make Microsoft's software the "superset," absorbing the contributions from other vendors. The idea was to make it easy even for customers with other systems to make Microsoft's technology their next purchase.

Gates understood the value of interoperability, but he wanted a long-term lock. He was looking for a way to have XML work better with Windows than it did with other operating systems.

Gates feels urgency only about initiatives that help him win. In those cases, he'll place his bet and go hard. When he doesn't see any long-term advantage, he's apt to keep a few horses in the race and wait to see how things play out. Without the hooks to Windows, he didn't see much urgency to push XML along. There was no urgent reason, for example, to delay the next release of SQL Server, Microsoft's database software, to add XML support.

Bosworth knew the quickest way to get Microsoft to adopt something new is to make it think the competition will otherwise get there first. He launched a campaign to bring Microsoft's archenemies—IBM, Oracle, and Sun—to the XML party. In February 1998, he called a meeting under the aegis of Jim Gray, one of the industry's éminences grises, a bona fide deep thinker about problems of massive and distributed databases. As part of Microsoft Research, he was removed from the competitive fray of product development. Gray's office at Microsoft's Bay Area Research Center in downtown San Francisco was the closest thing to neutral turf for a Microsoft meeting with executives from IBM, Oracle, and Sun.

At the meeting, Bosworth gave his XML stump speech: Simplicity and flexibility would trump optimization and power in a world where connectivity is the key. Every industry will establish a way for buyers and sellers to meet, even if the companies use wholly different software systems. Business-to-business e-commerce—B2B in Webspeak—was a perfect application for XML. To make XML the standard way of creating Internet applications, Microsoft wanted to join with its rivals in the standard-setting efforts at the W3C so XML would work with everybody's operating system software. There's a $1 trillion opportunity, he said. We have to build the framework together to expand the pie. Then we can compete like hell to grab pieces of it.

His implicit message: Microsoft was jumping on XML bigtime, and the other companies better hurry up or get left behind.

Of course, Microsoft had made no such commitment to XML. But Bosworth's bluff worked. Within a year, IBM and Oracle had embraced XML as well. Sun was a holdout, but Bosworth had what he needed. With Microsoft's competitors in the race, Gates would want to stay out front.

Back in Redmond, Bosworth told Gates that two of Microsoft's biggest competitors were adopting XML. At the same time that Microsoft was facing an antitrust suit brought after ferocious lobbying by IBM, Oracle, and Sun, Bosworth was inviting the very same companies to ramp up their efforts to catch up with Microsoft's lead in XML.

"Am I supposed to be pleased about that?" Gates asked sarcastically.

MUCH OF the rest of Microsoft, contrary to its cherished nimble-as-a-start-up reputation, was bogged down in an excess of democracy. Committees and presentations flourished. The company was in a perpetual reorganization.

Maritz, the highest-ranking technical executive at Microsoft, was preoccupied with preparations for the antitrust trial. In August 1998, he cleared his regular schedule to work full time on trial preparations. When the trial started, he assumed day-to-day oversight of Microsoft's legal strategy, convening a daily war room around his conference table to take the speakerphone call from David Heiner after the day in court in Washington. Maritz's job was to make sure the Microsoft's lawyers had the technical explanations and other resources they needed to go back into court to take another day of drubbing. "The Heiner Report," as it was known, became a daily downer as Microsoft's case steadily went south. Maritz's dry delivery was perfectly suited for the gathering's gallows humor.

As the staff general, it was Maritz's duty to shield his field armies as best he could from the troubles at headquarters. It also became Maritz's duty to shield his superiors. With Gates declining to take the stand, Maritz was the top Microsoft executive to testify in the antitrust trial. It fell to him to defend Microsoft's response to platform threats from Intel, Apple, and Netscape, including the claim he had described Microsoft's plans for Netscape in a meeting with Intel executives by saying, "We're going to cut off their air supply." Maritz denied making the statement.

The legal assignment was one of the most thankless tasks of his career. He suffered only moderate damage under the sharp questioning of Boies, who made his most dramatic points at the expense of other executives. But Maritz was frustrated that he was left to execute a legal strategy he didn't design. He would have done things differently, he told me later, but it was too late to change horses.

Maritz was only too happy to leave it to David Vaskevitch to settle the technology disputes. He put Vaskevitch in effective command of Microsoft's developer division, which directs the evolution of Microsoft's core platforms. Vaskevitch had assumed much of the responsibility for charting Microsoft's path to the Internet.

Vaskevitch's extravagant style is a contrast to Microsoft's spartan aesthetic. Under the egalitarian ethos that has prevailed since the company's early days, almost every employee gets one standard-issue 9x12 office. Vice presidents get a double-wide office, to provide room for a conference table. Vaskevitch's is even larger than a double-wide, lavishly furnished at his own expense with custom woodwork and elegant furniture.

The high esteem in which Vaskevitch holds himself is not universally shared at Microsoft. Underlings made no secret that they considered him an "armchair general" who inspired little loyalty. "If all armchair generals could ship as much stuff as I have, and on time, we'd need more armchair generals," Vaskevitch responds.

Vaskevitch was the chief architect of many of Microsoft's most tightly coupled systems. He shared with Gates a love of complexity. His talks were well-known for their PowerPoint presentations, which set the record for the most flowchart elements crammed onto a single slide. It was said he could keep sixteen-way decision graphs in his head. Vaskevitch's software systems stressed efficiency, richness, and integration—the opposite of simple, flexible, heterogeneous, and loosely coupled.

Vaskevitch had a hard time accepting that the rules of the game had changed just when he was trying to transform Microsoft into a serious contender in corporate computing. He continued to lobby Gates with a plan for the grand integration of all the strands of Microsoft's technology into a consolidated, integrated "enterprise" platform.

He had the ear of the emperor. In recent years, he had clocked more hours on Gates's calendar than anybody but Ballmer. Gates took to telling associates that most of Microsoft's future would be based on Vaskevitch's ideas.

One of Vaskevitch's big ideas was that Microsoft's competitive advantage in enterprise computing would be its control of the standards for the basic building blocks of software, known as objects. Objects are chunks of reusable code that can be snapped together like pieces of Lego. Microsoft's method for deploying objects was known as the Component Object Model, or COM. Microsoft's rivals, particularly Sun, backed CORBA, an alternative way of snapping together software objects. Arcane as it seemed, COM vs. CORBA looked like a key skirmish in the war to dominate the digital platform of the twenty-first century.

Vaskevitch helped convince Gates that the success of COM and its successors were crucial to Microsoft's long term Windows Everywhere strategy. If COM became the standard, Microsoft would hold a tremendous advantage in providing the Web's basic software infrastructure. By defining the way objects snapped together, Microsoft could make COM work better with Windows 2000 and SQL Server, giving it an edge in its challenge to Oracle's database dominance.

The only problem: COM didn't work very well on the Internet. For that matter, neither did the competitors' approach. Both were still slaves to the old rules of tightly coupled systems. Enterprise computing systems still employed the pre-Web approach of exchanging chunks of code between servers and clients. In the old world, complexity was the goal, not the problem.

Gates endorsed Vaskevitch's Big Science approach to the grand unification of all of Microsoft's code in a September 1998 strategy memo, "The Era Ahead." It was the high-water mark of the heavyweight, tightly coupled Windows Everywhere strategy.

It was Gates's first major strategy memo since the 1995 "Internet Tidal Wave" piece signaled his first attempt to turn Microsoft toward the Internet. Microsoft's public relations managers selectively leaked the memo on the condition that it not be quoted directly. With the trial about to begin and a few months after he turned over his day-to-day responsibilities to Ballmer, they felt it was important to demonstrate that he was still engaged in his job.

At the beginning of the memo, Gates was uncharacteristically bullish. Microsoft was the leading company in the leading industry and its position had never been stronger, he said. But he quickly reverted to bad-news type, bluntly assessing the company's weaknesses. Managing PCs was much too difficult. Managing networks was a mess. Customers didn't want to upgrade. The complexity of the company's interfaces was hurting Microsoft with software developers.

The memo was a laundry list of problems and projects. If there was a dominant theme, it was the chaos of complexity. The company couldn't continue to add lines of code at its historical rate, Gates said. The code base was already too big. Adding features created incompatibilities across the product line. Microsoft didn't even have a clear model for writing applications for Windows. Applications installed themselves by dropping files all over the system, updating components and registries, and making other hard-to-track changes. It was no surprise that uninstall programs were among the best-selling PC software products.

Organizational complexity was no less challenging, Gates said. Microsoft had evolved from a company that shipped many relatively independent products into one that was building a unified platform. Groups had more dependencies on other groups. Gates knew that it was a difficult change to force teams to rely on and cooperate with each other.

But his answer to the complexity was more complexity. He remained a true believer in ever-deeper integration. His plans for PC integration included voice, handwriting, photos, digital music, and the telephone, as well as services such as messages, scheduling, and finances. Windows integration extended the operating system to all the new devices, from tablet computers to electronic books to Auto PCs. Windows dial tone, or "Wintone," integrated Microsoft's technical support and upgrade services for a subscription fee. All of that would be the "Windows" of the future.

The grand unification strategy took on the trappings of a great campaign. "Forms+," was to be the single, common way to display and transmit data; "Storage+," the single, common way to store and retrieve anything; and "COM+," the single, common way to snap together the Lego blocks of distributed objects. The marketing umbrella over all the effort was Windows DNA—the new Windows platform, according to Gates.

He did tip his hat to the proponents of the more loosely coupled approach. Near the end of the fourteen-page memo, he devoted three paragraphs to XML. Sharing data easily would make the Web a giant database, he said. Microsoft's platform needed to be the best way to add information to that database and build applications that used it, he said. Again, Gates showed he understood the value of the technology. He just wasn't ready to sign on to the new business model.

While Maritz was preoccupied, Vaskevitch had moved to reconcile the religious and personal disputes over Microsoft's strategy by consolidating the warring groups into a single initiative dubbed "Project 42."

The name came from the underground classic *The Hitchhiker's Guide to the Galaxy*. In the book, members of a civilization on a distant planet want to know the answer to the great question of "life, the universe and everything." They create a massive computer, Deep Thought, which spends years working on the problem. Finally it arrives at the ultimate answer to "life, the universe and everything." 42. That was it. 42. The crowd is disappointed. The problem, the computer points out, is that they hadn't really known the question. To come up with the question, the computer designs an even bigger computer. And that, so the story goes, is the origin of the planet earth.

It was an appropriate lesson. Microsoft's answer to its strategic challenges seemed to be to put everybody in a single group, without a technical vision and without a clear question to answer.

At the beginning, Project 42 had some credibility. Heading the project was James "J" Allard, one of Microsoft's original Internet pioneers. Allard had championed Microsoft's adoption of TCP/IP, the basic protocols of the Internet, and had delivered Microsoft's first Web servers while the Internet Explorer team was delivering the early browsers. Allard was a compelling speaker with the energy, stamina, and people skills to corral the conflicting agendas. His reputation for Internet savvy balanced Vaskevitch's corporate-computing approach.

But Project 42, which grew to more than fifteen hundred people, quickly bogged down. It became the chief venue for airing out all the lingering suspicions and resentments welling up in Microsoft. The old splits between the Windows hawks and the Internet doves had metastasized into dozens of pitched, if arcane, battles. The hawks favored a cascading series of tightly coupled, Windows-only enhancements that would serve as hooks to bind customers to the Windows platform; the doves made interoperability the central design point. Microsoft was trying to unify and rationalize its multiple efforts—that meant a lot of projects were about to get killed. Teams were scared and resentful.

A major goal of Project 42 was to find a way to counter the appeal of Sun's Java technology. More generally, Microsoft was threatened by the trend toward Web-based applications that worked on a simple browser, undermining the importance of Windows. Microsoft was a stalwart defender of the "rich client," the fully featured PC running a complete suite of Microsoft software.

Microsoft's ground war against Java had slowed Sun's advance on the client side. But Microsoft's competitors had simply shifted their tactics. IBM threw more programmers into the Java effort than even Sun had done. The simplicity of Java programming helped it take hold in enterprise computing, where corporations need an easy way to tie together incompatible computer systems.

Jean Paoli assigned half his team to Project 42. At every workshop and committee they pressed the case for XML. Paoli's team doggedly insisted that Java could be beaten only with simple text, not complex code. It was time for Microsoft to play offense, not defense. Microsoft needed to jump to open standards to reveal that Java was controlled entirely by Sun, at least as tightly as Microsoft controlled Windows. Sun was trying to undermine Microsoft's lock, only to replace it with its own lock. Like Windows, Java was heavyweight and tightly coupled. It didn't change the model in any fundamental way. In the end, the winning argument for the XML team was that XML was as disruptive to Java as it was to Windows.

Nonetheless, the infighting and backstabbing of Project 42 exacted a toll. Winners and losers, everyone had had enough. Microsoft was getting to be no fun. As Silverberg had said, the company was wrapped up in its shorts.

Maritz's troops were in virtual revolt against Vaskevitch's leadership. When Maritz was around, he could compensate for Vaskevitch's weaknesses as a manager of people. But with Maritz largely absent, the situation became intolerable. Several highly regarded managers threatened to leave if Vaskevitch was in charge. Even Vaskevitch and Allard had a falling out. Allard took an extended leave of absence and agreed to return to the company only after he got an independent charter to lead the development efforts for the new Xbox, Microsoft's video game console that will compete with Sony's Play-Station.

Vaskevitch acknowledged that his approach often made him unpopular. He was not typical of many of Microsoft's senior executives, who earned their spurs shipping new versions of existing projects. In pushing Microsoft into new product areas, he said, he often faced resistance from developers with a narrow view of the problem. "I'm the only one who sees all the products and how they fit together," he told me. "Some people have trouble with me because I'm the one insisting we have to think about the suspension *and* the brakes *and* the engine *and* the transmission."

Maritz defended Vaskevitch's vision, his intuition, his ability to build technical teams. But he recognized that Vaskevitch was not a natural manager of people. He was neither the kind of leader who supplies reassurance and a shoulder to cry on nor the kind who kicks butt and gets the troops moving, he said.

"None of us are perfect," Maritz said. "None of us have all the attributes that you need."

Project 42 was disbanded in May 1999.

Maritz was out of ideas and patience. He was ready to leave Microsoft. Gates had barely thanked him for his work on the trial. But it was the miserable state of the company's technology teams that distressed him most. He was frustrated that the company was no closer to a consensus about what to do.

Maritz had a growing sense that technology was going through a profound generational change. He knew there were fundamental forces at work in the environment. But he wasn't able to formulate what the new world looked like. Microsoft, like any organization, was comfortable with what it knew. It knew how to make money on Windows and Office. Maritz realized that both the business model and the technology would have to change, but it was difficult for him to transform the organization until he could see enough of the contours to make clear what needed to be done. It wasn't clear what the new business assets of the future would be. On the other hand, Microsoft couldn't just wait to act until everything was figured out. By then it would be too late.

Maritz was beginning to think that he didn't have the stomach for the fight. He had other interests: a wife and three children. A $3.5

million house in Bellevue and a weekend place on Camano Island, north of Seattle. *Forbes* magazine had estimated his wealth at $650 million. And the project that stirred the most passion was his 42,000-acre spread on the Luangwa River in eastern Zambia.

He had grown up in the African bush and was increasingly drawn back to it. Maritz's father, an English-speaking Afrikaaner, grew tobacco and later bought a cattle ranch in what was then white-ruled Rhodesia. His English mother had grown up in Kenya. When Rhodesia declared independence from Great Britain after the Ian Smith rebellion of 1965, Maritz's father moved the family to South Africa. "My father didn't see good coming either way, if the black majority took power or the white minority retained power," Maritz says. He encouraged his sons to see education as their passports to the rest of the world.

But now Maritz was drawn back. Ndevu Ranch is a wild place. The unrest in the Congo has made AK-47s available for as little as five dollars apiece. During one of his visits, he contracted malaria. A spitting cobra hit Maritz's wife in the eye on her first visit.

Maritz hopes to turn the spread into a game preserve. Much of the wildlife in the area is teetering on the edge of extinction. Maritz knows that if he wants to preserve the wildlife on his property he needs to aid in the economic development of the area to give the local population an alternative to poaching, the main source of income for the local community. He is rebuilding two schools and a clinic. He has hired several former poachers to help him manage his property and is seeking to buy an adjacent piece of land to be managed by the locals in conjunction with his project. Before a recent meeting to discuss the project, the local chief sent around a note reminding him to bring his favorite bottle of whiskey. Maritz says that the chief is trying to do right by his people. "But he does like his drink, so you have to go see him before about two o'clock."

Returning from a trip to Africa in the summer of 1999, Maritz told Gates he planned to leave at the end of the year. Gates wasn't happy to hear that. He complained about the heavy pressure he was feeling on many fronts. Later, when friends asked Maritz why he stayed on, he was apt to give a one-word answer: "Guilt."

Maritz did feel responsibility for the state of Microsoft's software development organization, which he headed for much of the 1990s. He had never been sure whether or not he made the right call in late 1997, when he came down on the side of defending Windows in the arm-wrestling between Allchin and Silverberg over the fate of the browser team. But he knew that things had not been going well since then. It was clear that developers were increasingly drifting away from Microsoft's message, and that the technologies the company had spent the 1990s developing were no longer relevant to their needs. His attempt to hand off the problem had failed.

He rallied for one last campaign and set out to redeem himself.

It would require a "cathartic, emotional experience," Maritz told me later, before Microsoft fully accepted that it had to leave behind the "Windows paradise" or get left behind itself. He became the strongest advocate for the argument that Microsoft had to leave much of its legacy behind if it were to stake out a leadership position in the new paradigm.

He had long known the problem was bigger than Win32, Maritz said. But now, he could articulate the message. The difference, he later said, was XML. The Internet was becoming more than simply a replacement for the dumb terminals of the mainframe era. It would be a true infrastructure for computing. The resources on the network could cooperate by sharing information, creating a truly programmable information "bus." Microsoft would deploy a new platform for delivering services over the network. By the summer, Maritz had decided that the company would replumb all of its basic infrastructure around XML.

"This is what the company will be about," he told me.

That would take some doing. Ballmer "got it" first. His brief experience running MSN and Microsoft's other Internet properties had awakened him to the transformation under way in the software industry, away from packaged products and toward a service-delivery model. That's what AOL, and increasingly Yahoo!, was doing. Others, such as Oracle and IBM, were also likely to make a run at dominating the new platform for Internet services. Even network operators like AT&T had a shot. Suddenly, Microsoft was back in a wide-open platform battle. Ballmer understood that Microsoft needed to deliver some of those services and create the tools for partners to deliver others.

Ballmer continued to be skeptical of the new strategy, even while delivering his talk at a kickoff event for the new approach in San Francisco. Just as he was hitting his high-volume stride, the hotel's sound system malfunctioned. Ballmer's booming voice made him more than willing to continue without a microphone. But then the loudspeakers came alive with an address to the annual meeting of an association of jewelers, who were meeting in the next ballroom. Ballmer stood by, fuming. After a twenty-minute break, the sound system was fixed and Ballmer continued.

"We'll either be coming through this inflection point with a strong following . . . or we'll be in tough shape," he said.

Maritz's crew was surprised three days later, when Ballmer whole-heartedly embraced the strategy as his new religion in front of fifteen thousand screaming Microsoft employees at the company's annual meeting at Seattle's Kingdome, the last such gathering before the drafty old stadium was imploded with dynamite. He burst onto the stage to the theme from Disney's *Tarzan*. This was it, Ballmer said, what the company was about.

Of course, he also hedged his bets. The old "it"—Windows—doesn't go away, he said. "We're going to be a two 'it' company for a while."

MARITZ'S biggest challenge was Gates himself. As a final contribu-tion to the company, Maritz picked up the dropped mantle of the In-ternet advocates who had long tried to get Gates to lead, rather than resist, the next big shift in technology. If he could turn Gates around, Maritz might be able to leave the company in better shape than he had found it.

Gates wasn't anti-innovation. Since 1997, he himself had advo-cated for the "Megaserver" initiative to store and synchronize users' data on the network so it would be available on any computer. The vi-sion morphed over time, first into "mega-services" and then into Web services, and eventually into an offering dubbed Hailstorm. Gates can claim credit for being among the first in Microsoft to artic-ulate the software shift from packaged products to subscription ser-vices.

But Gates was wrestling with how to turn such innovation into a viable business. The issue, as always, was how to get a lock on cus-tomers once the new features had drawn them in. What is our pro-prietary advantage? he still wanted to know. He was less interested in Microsoft doing the optimal thing for the Internet than he was in its doing the optimal thing for keeping Windows relevant to the In-ternet.

"You're putting us on a level playing field!" he yelled at Maritz. "You're going to kill the company!"

It was a tough problem. High volume, low price is one thing. High volume, no price is quite another. Long term, the Internet loomed as Microsoft's death star. Many Web services were free. All the volume in the world doesn't make up for a price of zero. There was no guarantee of a payback—ever.

As Gates saw it, Microsoft could continue to make money in its traditional businesses if the new Web services drove demand for Windows. In the long meetings that took place to hash out the new message, Gates unabashedly took the "Windows point of view," as he called it. He resisted suggestions that Microsoft begin to leave Windows behind in order to embrace the new Web opportunity. Indeed, Windows was the key to those opportunities, he argued.

To him, driving customers back to the products where Microsoft made its money—Windows and Office—was only natural. That meant making sure that even networked services on the Web took advantage of features in Windows running on individual PCs. Gates was still hard-core on the long-term advantages of a "rich client"— that is, a Windows PC—over the simpler alternatives, from Web browsers to stripped-down handhelds, set-top boxes, and other "information appliances." Gates hated that Yahoo!'s e-mail, or even Microsoft's own Hotmail, looked just as good on a barebones Web terminal as on a souped-up PC.

Creating services that would run equally well on every platform was not an interesting business proposition. Where were the revenues? The cross-platform approach limited the services to the "lowest common denominator" of features that would work everywhere, without taking special advantage of Windows. On the other hand, Windows Only was clearly a nonstarter in the marketplace, which now demanded a level of interoperability. The Web was a bigger universe than Windows. If Microsoft limited itself only to Windows, someone would trump it with an all-Web strategy.

Maritz's team enlisted developers, customers, and other outsiders to convince Gates that Microsoft had no choice but to change. Gates continued to insist that developers be willing to write their applications in simple HTML and then rewrite them to take specific advantage of Windows. At the Professional Developers Conference in San Diego in 1998, they arranged half-hour sessions for Gates to meet with developers. They even let him choose the developers so that he couldn't say they had been preselected or biased. The developers told Gates that it was too expensive to maintain two code bases. If forced to choose, they would have to go with the Web.

Windows' run at the top was over.

This was becoming clear to the "technical leadership team," or TLT, the replacement for the BLT, or business leadership team, which had been too large for the kind of knock-down, drag-out strategy discussions that were needed. For months, the smaller TLT—Gates, Ballmer, Maritz, Muglia, and Belluzzo, the new head of the consumer division—convened nearly every afternoon for four hours, wrangling over the balance between protecting the old assets and building new ones.

Gates generally went along with the notion that Microsoft had to jump, but he had moments of backsliding. The rest of the group treated Gates with kid gloves. He was irritable and easily set off. Windows was still his baby, and he already felt picked on by the government.

Among Microsoft's senior executives, Muglia was known to have a good mental model of Gates, which enabled him to smoothly work his influence. A stalwart company loyalist who worked his way through most of Microsoft's major businesses, Muglia helped Maritz make the argument for jumping ship. Computers, he said, were increasingly used for communication.

In that world, Muglia said, "Windows matters a whole lot less."

Muglia managed the Office franchise, Microsoft's single biggest moneymaker but also the one most at risk as what people did with computers was changing. Hotmail, Microsoft's free Web e-mail service, for example, was no match for the fully featured Outlook e-mail program that Microsoft included in Office. But in the long term, the Web service was likely to improve and become "good enough" for many users.

"Unless we embrace that and are willing to drive forward and cannibalize our business, we'll be toast," Muglia told me. The new businesses were likely to have lower profit margins, he said, but if you defend profits by following existing customers rather than chasing new ones, "you'll die eventually." Windows had been the basis for so much of Microsoft's success that it was instinctively tough to let it go. Platform transitions are risky, but it's riskier to miss them, he argued.

In October 1999, Maritz arranged a two-day briefing for Gates and the rest of the senior executives. The presentations spotlighted new competitors that were staking out the high ground of Web software systems for high-volume business transactions. Microsoft had been so busy putting the finishing touches on the last generation of technology that it was missing the next. Companies such as Web-Methods and BEA, along with Oracle, had emerged as leading providers of Web software and e-commerce systems. The new crop of start-ups was focused right at the sweet spot in the market—interoperability. Companies wanted to be able to reach other companies quickly and securely without worrying about complex compatibility issues. The upstarts led Microsoft in the new market for business-to-business commerce.

Gates was forced to acknowledge that even if he wasn't able to instantly comprehend the full implications of the shift, he could no longer simply block it. He would have to help make it happen.

SHOWDOWN

By the spring of 2000, the dual storylines, legal and technological, that had dominated Microsoft's existence for three years were fully intertwined.

Judge Jackson's scathing findings of fact in November 1999 sent an unambiguous signal that he was ready to issue a harsh final ruling unless Microsoft agreed to a settlement plan. Microsoft's hopes rose when Jackson asked Appeals Court Judge Richard Posner to try to mediate a settlement. Gates and Ballmer, along with Maritz, Allchin, Muglia, and the lawyers, huddled around the speakerphone in the boardroom through the long months of settlement negotiations.

Putting on their TLT hats, the very same executives spent nearly every afternoon working through the business implications of the company's new Internet strategy.

With Posner as an intermediary, dozens of settlement drafts were passed back and forth. Gates even signed one to demonstrate good faith. In the end, it was rejected by the government as inadequate. Posner declared failure.

In April 2000, Jackson ruled that Microsoft violated sections 1 and 2 of the Sherman Antitrust Act. He found that Microsoft had illegally tied its Web browser to Windows. But he rejected the government's charge that Microsoft's contracts with content providers and ISP's had foreclosed Netscape's ability to reach its customers. Indeed, in his conclusions of law, Jackson acknowledged that Netscape had been able to distribute 160 million copies of its Navigator browser and that its installed base had grown from 15 million users to 30 million even while its percentage share of the market had fallen. Those points, which had not been included in his findings of fact, hardly showed a company foreclosed from the ability to distribute its product.

Before Microsoft could get on with its appeal, however, Jackson had one more matter to decide: the appropriate remedies to mitigate Microsoft's anticompetitive behavior.

In the same period, Microsoft's executives were grasping for an approach to keep the company competitive. In January 2000, in his first move as CEO, Ballmer had announced a major event, Forum 2000, for the spring. It was to be a daylong briefing at which the company would provide the details around what the company was then calling Next Generation Windows Services. It hadn't mattered that those details were still unclear. Ballmer liked to schedule big events to create deadlines, focus Microsoft's energies, and force internal debates to closure.

This was a jihad, we were told. With Windows 2000 finally ready to ship, Microsoft was again lifting its head above the horizon to scope the opportunities and the threats ahead, just as it had in December 1995, four months after the launch of Windows 95, when it announced its first turn-on-a-dime Internet strategy.

Software-as-a-service was the new battle cry. Microsoft's old business—selling packaged software and continual upgrades through distributors and resellers—was going away. Instead, software would become more like telephone service. Microsoft would supply the basic dial tone—Wintone—and some of the more valuable services on top of that—just like phone companies offer voice mail, call-forwarding, and conferencing on top of basic telephone service.

Once Gates was convinced to drop his insistence that "Windows" be part of the name, the company settled on a simple umbrella for all the parts of the new effort. The initiative would be known as "Dot Net." The suffix, .Net, could be added to any Microsoft product— for example, Office.Net, MSN.Net—conveying both "Internet-ready" and "Microsoft-centric."

Now, the .Net initiative become the centerpiece of Microsoft's argument that the company should not be broken up.

Up until it happened, Microsoft executives refused to believe that the government would really ask for a breakup of the company. During the settlement discussions, they had become confident that the breakup plan had been taken off the table. But Joel Klein, the Justice Department's antitrust chief, had concluded that other proposed remedies were unworkable and a "structural" solution was needed to

isolate Windows from the rest of Microsoft's activities. Perhaps it was
Ballmer's ill-timed remark that the company had done "absolutely
nothing wrong." Perhaps it was Gates's defiant response back in 1997
to the original preliminary injunction. The trustbusters had reached
the conclusion that the unrepentant company couldn't be trusted to
abide by more limited restrictions on its conduct.

Gates steadfastly maintained that a breakup was unthinkable. Microsoft was not a conglomerate of independent operating divisions; it
was an integral whole in which each part supported and depended on
the others. Any hint of support for the idea of a breakup was considered heresy.

The legal assault helped shut down any discussion inside Microsoft about whether a more loosely coupled Microsoft might actually be in the company's own best interests. The internal advocates of
a more loosely coupled Microsoft had earlier envisioned a liberation
of the company's talents and energies. In broad strokes, the government was aggressively pushing Microsoft in the same direction that
key executives inside the company were gently nudging it—toward a
post-Windows future, and even perhaps a breakup of the company.
But the punitive terms of the government's remedy further undermined the internal reformers. Every manager would be required to
sign a form confirming that he or she knew that violations of the
order were criminal acts. For up to ten years, the company would be
living under a regime of intense scrutiny. Windows itself was treated
like a dangerous criminal.

The "Windows Company" envisioned by the plan would be heavily straitjacketed to restrict its leverage in adjacent markets. The
Apps Company, including the Office and Internet Explorer franchises, as well as most of Microsoft's other assets, would be substantially freer. The government's plan was to create fierce competition
between the two software companies cleaved from the old Microsoft.
Office would evolve into a "platform" competitor to Windows—
much as Netscape's Navigator browser might have done had not
Microsoft blunted that threat. Free to pursue its own strategic advantages, the newly independent company that controlled the Office
franchise would likely make versions available for other operating
systems, such as Linux. Software from Apps Company, according to a
government expert, "will be designed in order to satisfy user needs,
instead of protecting the Windows monopoly."

In an accompanying brief, Robert Greenhill, a veteran investment banker retained by Klein to put Wall Street's imprimatur on the breakup proposal, made the argument in favor of delayering. Separation would allow management teams to focus on their core operations. Separated businesses would have a greater opportunity to grow without the constraints imposed on units of larger organizations. Corporate initiatives and strategies would be free of compromises needed to protect other corporate assets. Employees would have a clearer sense both of strategic goals and of their own compensation incentives.

"Both entities may have a greater opportunity to innovate to the benefit of consumers," Greenhill wrote. "Both entities may be able to react more nimbly to the competitive landscape."

Beyond the breakup, provisions of the proposed order aimed to loosen Microsoft's hold on the rest of the computer industry. The wide range of restrictions would eliminate Microsoft's ability to cut exclusive deals, retaliate against other software or Internet companies, or rig its products to compromise or disable rival software. Specifically, Microsoft would be banned from punishing computer makers that promoted competitors' offerings over Microsoft's and would be required to let them alter Windows in significant ways.

The government's proposal included several tortured solutions that reflected how difficult enforcement was likely to be. For example, the heart of Microsoft's advantage had always been its ability to give away for free any "middleware" product that might develop into a threat, effectively depriving competitors of the revenues needed to sustain the threat.

Middleware is jargon for any software that rides on top of an operating system but has some characteristics of a platform itself. This fuzzy category includes not only Web browsers but audio and video players, e-mail software, instant messenger features, and geeky components such as the Java "virtual machine." Because such software generally works on a variety of underlying operating systems and offers programming interfaces to other software developers, middleware programs have the potential of evolving into full-fledged platforms of their own—that is, competitors to Windows.

The government wanted PC makers and other customers to be able to license Windows without being forced also to take Microsoft's middleware offerings. To make the choice meaningful in the marketplace, the government went even further. The price for bare-bones Windows had to be less than the fully loaded version. Otherwise, there would be no reason not to take the full bundle. How to determine the discount? By calculating the ratio of bytes of binary code in the middleware product to bytes in Windows itself and cutting the price by a proportional amount. This ham-handed approach treated software as a commodity that could be bought and sold by the bushel, like corn or wheat.

And Microsoft would be required to reveal—in a secure facility, only to authorized representatives of PC makers and other software companies, and "for the sole purpose of enabling their products to interoperate effectively with Microsoft Platform Software"—the top-secret source code for Windows.

In a press conference, Gates was sputtering. He called the breakup proposal "very disturbing . . . unprecedented . . . radical . . . arbitrary . . . out of bounds." The company had always operated as a "single integrated company," he said. Microsoft could never have developed Windows, he said, without the ability to integrate new features. "These proposals would block us from doing new product work." Even if Microsoft could innovate, it would have no incentive because, as Gates saw it, the requirement that Microsoft provide access to Windows' source code meant that Microsoft had to give its intellectual property away to other companies. Later, in a full-page ad in the *Wall Street Journal* and other publications, Gates and Ballmer called the provision an "unprecedented confiscation of the company's intellectual property."

More specifically, Microsoft claimed the order would block the new .Net initiative. Preserving its ability to execute the new initiative was Microsoft's primary objective in rejecting many of the Justice Department's more limited settlement proposals. The Internet initiative, more expensive than Boeing's development of the 747 or NASA's first mission to the moon, became Microsoft's primary argument for not breaking up the company. The Internet platform play was the biggest bet-the-company move since Windows itself, Microsoft's very raison d'être, or as Ballmer liked to put it, Microsoft's new "it." The initiative would require all of the company's resources to make it a success.

"Consumers will suffer if Microsoft no longer has the ability to undertake ambitious projects like [.Net]," the lawyers argued in a brief. The initiative, they argued, "promises to transform the way in which consumers use the Internet, to the benefit of the entire economy."

Microsoft expected to be able to fight the breakup plan in a kind of mini-trial, complete with discovery, exhibits, and expert witnesses. Judge Jackson had other ideas. At the end of May 2000, he abruptly ended the trial with the curt declaration "The case has been submitted."

His announcement meant that he would hold no hearings on the breakup proposal. There would be no opportunity for dramatic courtroom appearances by Gates and Ballmer who, having elected to skip the trial, finally offered to take the stand along with fourteen other witnesses to defend the integrity of Microsoft.

Later, Judge Jackson would say that he didn't see the need for due process at all in the remedies phase of the trial. Microsoft was the loser, he said. Did the Japanese get to dictate the terms of their surrender to General MacArthur in 1945?

The stage was set for an exquisite showdown. Forum 2000, the rollout of the .Net initiative, had originally been scheduled for April. It was delayed to May. Then June. The delays were caused in part by the protracted settlement negotiations in the antitrust case and the successive bombshells of Jackson's finding of a violation and the government's proposal for a breakup. But a bigger reason for the delay was Microsoft's inability to settle the internal debates over the extent to which the company should leave behind its Windows legacy for the sake of the new Internet opportunity.

By the time reporters prepared to descend on Redmond for what they were calling "World Domination 2000," Jackson held a fully drafted breakup order lacking only his signature.

With his decision likely to land right on Microsoft's big day, the company blinked. Executives worried that the press would be so obsessed with the looming breakup order, it would be impossible to get any coverage of the technology initiative itself. Forum 2000 was delayed for several weeks more.

On June 7, Jackson adopted, virtually without change, the government's proposed order. He immediately issued a stay of the breakup order. But the conduct remedies were set to go into effect in ninety days, including one requiring Microsoft to "take no action that undermines, frustrates, interferes with, or makes more difficult the divestiture required by this Final Judgment." The .Net initiative would do precisely that, scrambling the divisional lines drawn by the government with a wholesale reorganization of the company around a new platform and set of services involving Windows, Office, and MSN.

The showdown was narrowly averted. Two days before the Forum 2000 event, Jackson issued a surprise ruling. As part of an effort, ultimately unsuccessful, to send the case directly to the Supreme Court, he granted a stay of his entire order. The breakup was already on hold, but now the conduct remedies were indefinitely postponed as well. The stay was the most substantial break that Microsoft had received to date in the entire course of the trial. The company was free to proceed.

On the morning of the event, Brad Chase mingled with reporters and analysts in the reception areas of Microsoft's spanking-new conference center. "Oh won't you sta-a-a-y, just a little bit longer," he sang happily, giving new meaning to the refrain from the 1964 hit by Maurice Williams and the Zodiacs.

Chase was a skillful survivor of Microsoft's internal battles. He had risen with Silverberg in the "Two Brads" days of Windows and Internet Explorer. With Allchin's triumph, he dutifully submerged his personal loyalties and stepped up to the challenge of marketing Windows 2000. Now the reorganization cycle had come full circle and Chase was in charge of MSN, Microsoft's underachieving step-sibling that the old Internet team had in turns derided and coveted. The marketing duo of Chase and Yusuf Mehdi were delivering the beginnings of a turnaround in the competition with AOL and Yahoo!, inviting comparisons to the excitement of Microsoft's success in the early days of the browser war.

Gates opened his Forum 2000 presentation with a story. It had been six months since he had dropped his day-to-day responsibilities as CEO. In his blue open-necked shirt, he came off like a schoolboy who had been caught playing hooky, or rather, like an executive in semiretirement whose job now consisted mostly of reading and thinking, as he told me later.

"We had a meeting a couple months ago where we sat down and said, 'Okay, what is it that we really want to explain here?' " he began. "When I walked into the meeting they had a slide up that said, 'We have to explain CSA.' And I sat down and I thought, 'What does CSA stand for?' And I thought, 'Well, I'll just play along here. It should become clear. You know, I understand what's going on around here.' "

In Gates's story, the mystery became no more clear as the meeting went on. "So I thought, 'Well, I guess I'll have to make a fool of myself and ask what CSA is, because it's clearly this thing we have to explain at this event, so I'd better know what it is.' "

"Well, it turns out that CSA stands for Chief Software Architect," Gates said. "I get to explain how I've spent the last six months since I've been Chief Software Architect."

It was no joke that Gates was far from being the chief architect of the new strategy.

Five years earlier, on Pearl Harbor Day 1995, Microsoft had launched its first Internet strategy, earning the company plaudits and breathless magazine cover stories for its ability to turn on a dime like a scrappy start-up. In hindsight, most Microsoft executives came to describe the browser war, victorious as they had been, as a limited, re-active, defensive, superficial move that didn't really mark a new era of computing, after all.

"That was a straightforward set of steps over an eighteen-month period," Gates said. No big deal, he seemed to be saying. Never mind.

That period had ended with the backlash against Microsoft's In-ternet team and the retrenchment around Windows in 1997. Now, three years later, Gates was coming back around to the broad outlines of the strategy he had rejected then.

Gates was reluctantly moving beyond Windows. Even in its name, the .Net initiative was explicitly broader than Windows. The operat-ing system was only a small part, and not even the most important part, of the new platform.

The browser effort had once again been separated from Windows. David Cole, the "ship-it" lieutenant on the Windows 95 and IE 4 projects, had moved the main browser effort out of Allchin's Win-dows group and over to MSN, just as Silverberg had earlier advo-cated. The effort was not even called Internet Explorer, but MSN Explorer. Windows continued to bundle the basic Internet Explorer browser, but increasingly Microsoft's emphasis was not on inte-gration with Windows but on creation of a comprehensive "Internet Experience" in competition with AOL, with communication, enter-tainment, and shopping services.

And Gates, who in the earlier round had been a late and reluctant convert to the virtues of industry-standard HTML, was now trum-peting the virtues of industry-standard XML. In his speech he em-braced XML, calling it the "base protocol for this new era" and an even more profound change than had been brought by HTML. He wrapped Microsoft's efforts in the mantle of open protocols. A white paper stressed XML was supported by the W3C and "is not a propri-etary Microsoft technology."

Microsoft proclaimed the new initiative to be a "radical new vision." Gates himself said, "You could say it's a bet-the-company thing."

It soon became clear he was still trying to force-fit Microsoft's long-held traditional business model onto the new paradigm.

The ".Net platform," riding on top of XML, was unabashedly proprietary, a Microsoft platform just like the Windows platform, he explained later. "We haven't decided that Microsoft is a zero-revenue company," he told *Red Herring* magazine. "Look, there's been no change in the framework here. What we do is take industry standards and drive them forward. We're doing that with XML"

Gates's PowerPoint slides detailed the company's ambitions. He made an historical analogy to the structure of the Windows market, circa 1995. In that era, Microsoft delivered both a "platform," in the form of Windows interfaces for both programmers and users, and "applications," which ran on top of the platform. There had long been an uneasy tension between Microsoft as a provider of a platform that is open to outside creators of application software and Microsoft as a competitor in the applications market. The tension was resolved by and large in favor of Microsoft, which gained overwhelming dominance in the most valuable categories of applications—word processing, spreadsheets, databases, and presentation software, all bundled together under the brand name Office.

With .Net, Microsoft was again going to deliver both a platform and a set of applications, the only difference being that applications were no longer packaged in shrink-wrapped boxes but would be offered as services over the Internet. Microsoft claimed to be investing $2 billion over three years to help partners and outside developers build and market .Net services.

Companies basing their business on delivering parts of the core infrastructure for Internet-based services can't say they weren't warned about Microsoft's ambitions. Microsoft would of course be building its own applications, in competition with its partners.

Gates offered no guarantees other than the vague assurance that "as a percentage of what gets built, that will be a fairly small portion."

Hardly. His slide show clearly identified the discrete services that Microsoft considered to be integral parts of its "platform."

Microsoft wanted the high-volume services for itself. Among the .Net "building blocks" Gates identified were Identity and Personalization, all the services of authentication, billing, personal information, and legal accountability; Notification and Messaging, the fabric for knitting digital devices into a real-time communication network that would ultimately subsume the telephone; Storage and Delivery, the distribution and retrieval of all kinds of digital goods, from music to photos to software itself; Directory and Search, the core navigational tools for finding networked resources and information; and Calendar and Collaboration, the central repository for coordinating meetings and schedules. Like services in Windows, Microsoft expected other software developers to build Microsoft's features into their own products, driving adoption of Microsoft's platform.

And the company would keep control of all user interface improvements, particularly speech, vision, and handwriting recognition, all of which were integral to the platform.

Gates dismissed those skeptics who doubted Microsoft's claims that it would live by open standards and provide a level playing field for potential partners. But he did nothing to reassure such skeptics that Microsoft really didn't have an ace up its sleeve. He had given up none of Microsoft's "unfettered rights" to bundle new features into Windows. The more the government pushed, the less willing Microsoft was to make an explicit commitment to guarantee open interoperability.

Trust us, the company was once again saying to the public and its customers.

7

Loosely Coupled

THINK LIKE BILL

One down. Two to go.

Work. Entertainment. Communication. Three vast categories of human activity, all increasingly mediated by software. Over the next twenty years, as the digital transformation of the global economy works its inexorable logic, the software interfaces for work, entertainment, and communication will have value beyond imagination.

As Bill Gates sees it, Microsoft already is the leading provider of the software interface for work. The interfaces for entertainment and for communication are still up for grabs.

"Sitting and reading stuff, thinking about where this stuff goes, that's mostly my job," Gates told me when I saw him in his office in Redmond in September 2000. None of his decisions affect next week, or next month, or even next year, he said. He was thinking eighteen to twenty-four months ahead, and out to 2005 and beyond.

Gates was relaxed. He was one of the few people working on the Microsoft campus on the Friday before a long Labor Day weekend. As the season turned to fall, the crisis atmosphere of a few months earlier had been replaced by an extended intermission. In the far Northwest, summer days are long and nights are short; near the equinox, light and dark are delicately balanced, waiting for winter.

The work of the teams of government lawyers who had spent the spring designing the breakup of Microsoft was likewise on stay, pending the appeals. The work of remaking Microsoft could also wait, at least until after Gates's vacation in Australia, where he planned to catch some of the Olympic games in Sydney.

His trademark sarcasm, it seemed to me, reflected more amusement than bitterness. He was long past accepting as commonplace the through-the-looking-glass ironies of Microsoft's situation. From one direction, Microsoft is depicted as a predatory monopolist so dangerous its power can be curbed only by shackling its products like criminals, caging Windows into a locked cell, and snapping ankle monitors on the remainder of the assets during a lengthy probation.

From the other direction, the company is derided as a PC dinosaur doomed to extinction.

Of the two narratives, Gates has always been more upset by the "Microsoft is toast" storyline, which he reluctantly believes will one day prove true, than by the "Microsoft, the unstoppable juggernaut" story, which he has never believed at all.

The real story, of course, has not yet reached "The End." Inside Microsoft, the debates continue, reorganizations come and go, veterans depart and new hires arrive, opportunities emerge and recede, three-year plans are made and revised, results are duly reported every quarter. Outside Microsoft, chips get more powerful, competitors rise and fall, and lawsuits are filed and appealed.

"Every week you're making trade-offs," Gates said. "This goes with this group; make this decision this way. Then, new things happen in the market, and you make decisions that way."

Microsoft is an organism of assets and relationships and people, adapting to and mastering its environment, or not, through thousands, millions of microcosmic decisions. There is no single strategy that works forever, in all circumstances. There is no single way to determine which new thing to pursue, which old thing to abandon. Timing is everything.

Whatever it is, the whole strategy has to fit into his brain. Gates has given up day-to-day control, but his is still the long-term mental model used to synthesize all new information. He is Microsoft's single point of integration. Microsoft remains, uniquely, a projection of Bill Gates.

To the public, he is at once ubiquitous and enigmatic. He is the preeminent global icon of the early digital age, the world's richest man. His face stares out from magazine covers and down from huge video screens at the front of packed conference halls. His smirky half-smile and tinny voice are instantly recognizable. He is the subject of hundreds of articles, dozens of books, and several movies. But he remains opaque. We hear what he says, but before we can connect, he floats away in his protective bubble and is gone.

Inside Microsoft, he is more transparent. The people who work for Gates develop and refine their own detailed models of his thinking, all the better to "think like Bill." For the most part, they have guarded their private models, preferring to let stand Microsoft's official model of Gates. But the trauma of recent years has shaken loose fragments of a more nuanced reality, as gigabytes of e-mail become public and current and former employees and executives begin to tell their own parts of the story. And as Gates himself, little by little, reveals himself.

In the summer of 2000, I refined my own mental model by once again making the rounds of the people who had surrounded Gates as he led Microsoft through its most difficult period.

Nathan Myhrvold now pursues his eclectic personal and professional interests from a spacious warehouse set among auto shops on a back street of Bellevue. In the lobby of Myhrvold's Intellectual Ventures is the shinbone of an Apatosaurus (sometimes imprecisely called a Brontosaurus), the thirty-ton herbivore of the Jurassic period. In the hallway are artifacts from Myhrvold's other collections—a planetarium projector, a dozen nozzles from turn-of-the-last-century fire hoses, adding machines and early typewriters, and in the back a huge head of a *Tyrannosaurus rex*, star of the movie *The Lost World*. He held another dinosaur bone in a photo for the cover of *Forbes* magazine under the headline "The Art of Being Rich."

"It's annoying to Bill that so many people have left or are playing hooky like I am," he told me.

As Myhrvold saw it, the story of Microsoft, and of technology generally, is like the movie *Rashomon*. Different people, with different statuses, different time horizons, and different sensibilities, see it differently. From the trenches, the battle appears helter-skelter. Firing here, scrambling there, trying not to get shot. From the air, however, the strategy is clear, like an attack from the left flank while another battalion sweeps around to the right.

From Gates's aerial view, the technology industry might have some new elements, he said, "but it is also completely predictable." A school of fish, zigging this way and zagging that way, might appear completely random. Watch them long enough and it will become obvious that they do this every afternoon as they migrate from the mouth of the bay to deeper waters.

Programmers and managers fighting the browser war or navigating the complex standoff over Java or plotting the "conspiracy" to embrace XML had the trench-level view. They often sputtered at Myhrvold in frustration, "You old-timer, you just don't get it," after arguing passionately for some initiative and failing to get support.

Myhrvold's response: "Yes I'm an old-timer, and that's why I do get it."

And Gates gets it even better, he says. From his aerial view, he assesses and synthesizes emerging threats and opportunities into a strategy that might at times look mistaken from the trenches.

For example, Microsoft was in a poor position to advocate an Internet platform strategy in 1997. It lacked a reliable, high-performance server system and commanded only a small share of the Web browser market. By the middle of 2000, Windows 2000 finally gave it credibility in server technology. And Microsoft's share of the browser market stood at 86 percent. Gates could more easily embrace architectural schemes he had ridiculed several years earlier.

Through 1998 and 1999 Gates had employed the "stall," a strategy even more difficult and delicate than the uptempo "Internet time" playbook. The power to control the pace of innovation is a competitive advantage at least as crucial as the ability to innovate itself. Relentless innovation may let you stay barely ahead on an ever-accelerating treadmill. The ability to slow innovation lets you arrange the playing field to your own advantage.

Some snowballs do roll down the hill and pick up great speed. Others roll into the trees. The trick is to tell the difference. At one meeting where Gates was required to choose between two contradictory project proposals, advocates on both sides arrived carrying copies of Christensen's *The Innovator's Dilemma*. The ability to distinguish the fad from the trend, Myhrvold said, "is what separates the men from the boys."

IN OUR interview, Gates slipped easily into his favorite public role as society's Chief Digital Seer. By 2005, he said, the "market will be transformed."

Microsoft's latest and biggest bet in its strategy to capture the Entertainment interface is the Xbox, a sleek, black console as powerful as a high-end PC, with a fast Pentium III processor, large memory bank, and ample hard drive. The Xbox gives Gates another chance to gain entry into the nation's living rooms, which he has been seeking for years. High-resolution, fast-twitch graphics will be what gets Microsoft into the market versus Sony's PlayStation 2. But the real sweet spot for Microsoft is multiplayer gaming for the millions of new subscribers to high-speed Internet access. That's a target for all of Microsoft's networking assets, from MSN's services to the WebTV online service to the racks of Windows 2000 servers connecting remotely to millions of Xbox clients.

A large part of the $500 million the company plans to spend to launch the Xbox are subsidies for the hardware. The rest will subsidize outside makers of the games themselves and support retailers with marketing and advertising. The payoff for Microsoft, if any, is in the games themselves. If volume takes off, each title can make as much money as a hit movie. Microsoft will make some games itself and will receive royalties from outside developers who want access to Xbox users. Some part of the investment is defensive, Microsoft's attempt to deny dominance of the consumer entertainment platform battle to Sony or AOL.

For the Communication interface, the primary "form factor" Gates is pushing is not the cell phone, or even the PocketPC, Microsoft's competitor to Palm. Instead, he predicts the winner that will give Microsoft the "high-volume rich client" it covets will be a new entrant, the "tablet PC." In Gates's vision, people will take a wireless touchpad that recognizes speech and handwriting with them wherever they go to serve as a phone, a viewer, and a notepad. "What you see with instant messaging with kids is the beginning of it," he says. "People can edit with you, talk with you, share with you, come in for ten minutes, and do these real-time things." Variations on such hybrid devices are planned by Sony, Honeywell, Siemens, and Intel, among others, and Microsoft's won't be out until 2002 at the earliest.

In five years, as ever, software will be at the center. What Gates calls "magic software" will make all the right things happen, he assured me, both on the vastly more powerful digital devices that are already proliferating and in the vastly more useful "cloud" of networked services. As for today's knotty obstacles and frustrating trade-offs, the commonsense response will be "Of course that problem got solved," he said. "All of that stuff we—the industry—will have been able to do a dramatically better job on."

Instead of "Windows," Gates uses the techie euphemism "rich client." Microsoft executives note that "rich" is one of Gates's fa-

vorite words. Here it means sophisticated software doing local processing on powerful machines in the hands of end-users. The demands of processing video and graphics, recognizing speech and
handwriting, and managing a growing array of smaller digital devices
mean local computer processing and, by extension, Windows, is
going to continue to be important. "Irrespective of anything about
Microsoft, there will be rich clients ten years from now, twenty years
from now," he says.

To Gates, Microsoft is still the Windows company. In 1997, he had
erupted at a presentation of Microsoft's Java strategy, "Hasn't anybody here ever heard of Windows? Windows is what this company is
about!" In 2001, his strategy is essentially the same, though the message has been explicitly broadened to include non-PC devices and,
increasingly, software services delivered over the Internet. If Gates
no longer dreams of achieving "singularity," where the black hole of
Windows sucks in the entire digital world, he is still pursuing an iteration of his long-standing Windows Everywhere strategy.

The shakeout of technology stocks at the turn of the century
only confirmed Gates's thinking. There aren't enough customers to
support all the duplicative development targeted at relatively modest-
sized markets. In the late 1990s, the willingness of Wall Street and
venture capitalists to overinvest, the explosion of research and development, and the widespread notion that every new technology and
hot start-up company would change the world created what Gates
called an "unusual framework." But in the long term, share prices
would reflect that "it's only the integrated solution that has value."

The more digital people's lives become, the more digital devices in
use, the more reason there is for an integrated company like Microsoft, he said. Few companies are as able to make big research-and-
development bets; assemble large engineering teams; write, test, and
debug millions of lines of code; bundle them in packaged suites; and
drive distribution around the globe.

Integration across different digital devices will be as powerful as
was integration across different types of PC hardware, Gates believes. Windows, and DOS before it, jump-started high-volume PC
sales and transformed the lowly personal computer into the platform
for almost every computing task. Likewise, in consumer electronics
and communications, he believes that a dominant software platform
will eventually emerge as a common software layer across many kinds
of hardware, giving software applications developers the common
platform they needed to attain critical mass.

And the ability to deeply integrate code itself remains Microsoft's most potent tactic. In Gates's view, integration between Windows 95 and Office helped drive a spectacularly successful adoption cycle. Then, integration between Windows and Internet Explorer helped Microsoft come from behind to win the browser war.

In the next round, just as classic Windows integrated the features of any application that was used by a large percentage of PC users, so the .Net platform will integrate any of the services that are used by a large percentage of Internet subscribers.

As Microsoft develops its own services for the .Net platform, executives are again making trade-offs between "Runs Everywhere" and "Windows Only." Microsoft has settled on a middle position—"Works Best on Windows"—providing a basic service as a loss leader but inserting hooks to drive customers back to Windows. Gates advocated such hooks in the planning of the .Net initiative. "I've been at a lot of meetings with these guys—call it the Windows point of view—saying, 'Come on, we need these features for the rich client,' " Gates told me. "We have some of that in version one, but the really good stuff there is in version two."

Just as classic Windows handles basic functions like "print," the new Windows, via the megaservices out on the network, will handle "save" and "find" and "buy." Passport, for example, serves as an identification card for automatic sign-in not only to Microsoft's sites but to other Web sites as well. Even though few Web surfers go there directly, Passport is one of the most heavily trafficked sites on the Internet.

Other such services are under development, some of them under an initiative dubbed Hailstorm. A directory service will keep track of people and machines and resources. A "rendezvous" service will provide real-time coordination of machines as well as people. Another service will function as a clearinghouse for managing the "digital rights" of music, movies, and intellectual property of all kinds.

For all of the services, programming for the rich client—Windows—should be no different than programming for the server—also Windows. Gates wants one way that can be used by all of his products, that achieves critical mass, that works best with Windows. For building user interfaces, he wants Microsoft's unified Forms technology to work the same on rich clients and powerful servers. For saving and retrieving data from local hard drives or network caches, he wants Microsoft's unified Storage technology. For exchanging software objects, he still favors using Microsoft's tightly coupled COM technology whenever possible.

Most important, Gates wants one unified code base for Windows. Before the really big positive feedback cycle could take off, Microsoft needed to bring together the Windows NT code that powers Windows 2000 with the older code that stretches back from Windows Millennium Edition to Windows 98, 95, 3.1, and even MS-DOS. The company had not yet been able to make Windows NT compatible enough with older applications and peripheral devices to promote it for home consumers. His decade-long quest for Windows Everywhere had been delayed. Microsoft turned to its unfinished agenda once the browser war was won. "We said to Windows, 'Windows, your goals is to get to this new code base,' " Gates said. The code unification effort tied up considerable resources that could have been deployed elsewhere. But Gates knew the old code base wasn't going to get the company where it needed to go. Microsoft had been hampered by having, in effect, two platforms awkwardly knitted together. The split made every other initiative more complicated.

For Allchin, the failure to deliver such a unified Windows code base was an annoying loose end left over from the massive Windows 2000 effort, which otherwise represented the pinnacle of his career, his contribution to technology. He went back to work on Windows XP, at the time code-named Whistler, an operating system based on Windows 2000 that would finally be deemed simple and compatible enough to market to home consumers.

A few months before I saw Gates, Allchin invited me to dinner at his home. With his wife, Catherine, and one-year-old son, he was about to leave for a four-month sabbatical, to be spent sailing in the Mediterranean. The baronial stone house on the bluff above the lake is within sight of the Evergreen Point floating bridge across Lake Washington, the road to Microsoft. The traffic noise is nearly imperceptible; in the summer, the prevailing breeze carries the sound south.

The Allchins both wanted to live on the Seattle side instead of the more spacious waterfront communities on the east side of the lake. Catherine liked the meandering streets of Laurelhurst, the same neighborhood where Gates grew up, where people walk after dinner and kids play outside. For Allchin, a music hound, the Seattle side, closer to the clubs and the divy waterfront, is just cooler.

Allchin is a long way from the dirt-floor shack in Florida where he grew up. Built in 1925, their house has an austere, European feel, with long halls with marble floors and high ceilings. But Allchin's favorite room is the smallest and the funkiest, the music studio facing the water. Allchin played trumpet on several albums in his younger days. Now it's his dream to cut a CD of his guitar work. Allchin has laid down background tracks for a CD so he can improvise on the guitar leads. He selected his new favorite from his collection of electric guitars, a handmade Paul Reed Smith guitar with an inlaid mother-of-pearl dragon curling up the neck, and plugged it into an amp. The guitar had been made for Santana, the rock legend, who gave it to Gates at a party in San Francisco on the eve of the launch of Windows 2000, where Santana played a benefit concert sponsored by Microsoft. Gates doesn't play guitar, so he gave it to Allchin, who knew what to do with it.

When I visited, Allchin was working on "Aidan's Song" for his son. As he eased into his extended riff, his eyes closed and his body seemed to shed its tension. Allchin was transported. Many software programmers resonate to music, and musicians to software; the two domains share underlying structures in math and logic. But that's not Allchin's connection.

"I don't think of it in terms of math or anything like that," he says. "It's just a way to express yourself in a different way."

He was coy about how long he planned to remain at Microsoft. He was committed at least through the delivery of Windows XP. In the debates inside Microsoft, he still played his role as a Windows hawk, though now somewhat wearily. He hated that the discussion got framed as Windows versus the Internet. He had been one of Microsoft's early advocates for TCP/IP, the basic protocol of Internet plumbing. And he never was stuck on Windows, per se, as long as any new thing that cannibalized Windows made up for the revenues that shareholders were already expecting.

"It was about having a viable business versus giving it away," he told me. "I'm on the have-your-cake-and-eat-it-too strategy," he told me.

As the age-old debate played out in the planning for the .Net initiative, Allchin acknowledged that Microsoft had fallen into its old confusion, Allchin said. "It got quite muddled internally," he said. "I'd raise my hand and say, 'Can I talk about revenues for a minute?'" The presentation at Forum 2000, he said, was so general and abstract that people read into it whatever they wanted to see.

Allchin had simply wanted Microsoft to improve one of the great product franchises in history, Windows, by reserving innovations for the next version of the product. The only way to overcome customers' resistance to upgrading, he said, is to make the next version demonstrably more compelling than the last one. If you borrow the innovation from the next version and provide it to users of earlier versions for free, you remove the incentive to upgrade.

For example, the team building Windows XP was adding technology for new and improved video- and voice-conferencing capabilities. Some of the managers proposed that the client code be offered as well for earlier versions of Windows, the installed base of users. They argued the free distribution would jump-start the popularity of the new feature by quickly enabling millions of users to take advantage of it.

"Don't even come to the meeting," Allchin told the giveaway advocates. "I'm not going to have that conversation with you. I view this as a core selling proposition of the next version. If we give the software away for free and we run the service for free, how much money do we make? This is not deep stuff."

Allchin had no use for free riders. He argued against opening Microsoft's new .Net directory service to users of, say, Linux or even earlier versions of Windows without some kind of payment. Running the services was going to be expensive. He wanted to make it clear to users that they had to upgrade to Windows XP before they could take advantage of the new advanced services.

The advantage for users, he said, is ever more seamless integration. He doesn't mean simply "included with," as some people interpret Microsoft's position. He means fewer concepts, fewer lines of code, simpler. Allchin considers the new services to be simply part of Windows in the same sense he considered the Web browser three years earlier to be simply part of Windows.

He remains convinced that his deep integration strategy, now as in 1997, is the best way to preserve Microsoft's revenues and the most legally defensible to boot.

Allchin is still upset about the trial. Microsoft had hoped his steely intensity and obvious passion would convince Jackson that Microsoft's actions were the healthy functioning of a competitive company. Boies was worried, too.

After Allchin's first day on the stand, Boies found discrepancies in the Allchin's videotape demonstration. For two days, he hung the compromised evidence around Allchin's neck. When Allchin came off the stand, he was pale and exhausted. Months later, Allchin was still rankled that the majority of the hits returned from a Web search under the word "Allchin" concern the botched videotape.

That debacle was only a distraction from the real contradiction that hampered Allchin's credibility. He was unable to explain in public his strategic and legal position without exposing the power struggles inside Microsoft and the depths of its internal confusion. For their own reasons, government prosecutors were similarly loathe to explore the meaning of the split between the Windows and Internet teams. They feared they might undermine the value as evidence of Allchin's impassioned e-mails. This odd and self-serving complicity between defendant and plaintiff prevented one of the most important threads of the Microsoft story from being aired in the trial.

Allchin makes no apologies for having worked, in 1996 and 1997, to force Gates to make a choice between Microsoft's internally contradictory strategies. For two years, Gates had pursued "both." The time had come for "either-or." The competitive threat to Windows, Allchin believed, came not only from Netscape, or Java, but from Microsoft's own Internet team. Microsoft's engineers were good enough that they might have won. But it would have been a Pyrrhic victory. Their success at building an Internet platform without tight ties to Windows would have undermined the source of the revenues and profits on which the rest of Microsoft is built.

Allchin only wishes Microsoft had adopted his "Windows only" browser strategy from the beginning. Justice Department officials concede it could well have made prosecution more difficult. Such a strategy might still have raised antitrust issues, but proving the violations would have been even harder, they say.

"The truth is I just always believed we didn't need to take and do some of the things we did," Allchin said. "My strategy would have just been different."

Now, the company looked forward to at least a partial reprieve from the U.S. Court of Appeals for the District of Columbia. In the earlier consent decree case, the same appeals court had found in favor of Microsoft, ruling that its integration of Internet Explorer into Windows met the legal burden of providing "plausible benefits" for customers. In two days of oral arguments in February 2000, the seven-judge appeals panel expressed deep skepticism about the government's case. The judges criticized Judge Jackson for sounding off to reporters, saying he had revealed a clear bias against Microsoft.

Richard Urowsky, one of Microsoft's lawyers, was so confident about the outcome of the proceedings that at one point he waived his allotted time to rebut Jackson's findings that the company had attempted to monopolize the market for Internet browsers. The charge that Microsoft acted to maintain its operating-system monopoly seemed more likely to stand. If the appeals court did not provide complete vindication, Microsoft looked to have a chance to negotiate a favorable settlement with the new Bush administration, though the nineteen states that are coplaintiffs with the Justice Department still wield considerable power to block any deal.

But even if Gates's decision to hang tough in the end proves legally defensible, the damage has been done, Allchin said. Whatever the outcome of the appeals, he told me, the ordeal had hurt Microsoft's employee morale, executive focus, and relations with the rest of the industry.

"We could have done things better," he said plaintively. "Did we really need to be here?"

LETTING GO

If between 1997 and 2000, Microsoft appeared to be closing in on itself, hindsight may well reveal the opposite: that the period was when Microsoft began what Maritz called the "cathartic, emotional experience of deeply internalizing that we have to get on with it."

From Silverberg and Slivka, to Bosworth and Paoli, to Maritz and Ballmer, and yes, to Joel Klein and David Boies—a succession of people struggled to loosen the tangled ropes that had tied Microsoft in knots. Some battles were won and some were lost, but over time Microsoft has gradually been pried open.

Windows' lock on the digital infrastructure, if ever it had one, has been broken. Microsoft may well tough out a legal stalemate and a business recovery. But the industry has moved on.

As the government prosecutor had suggested, the first sign of erosion of Microsoft's monopoly came from a decline in its profit margins. By the end of 2000, profits were still spectacular, but they had begun to fall. That was enough to convince Wall Street that Microsoft's invincibility had been pierced. The drop in the price of the company's shares preceded the broader market's fall and reflected, at least in part, the loss of the monopoly premium the stock had previously commanded.

Even Microsoft's allies in the computer industry took advantage of their wider ambit. Even without formal remedies, the antitrust trial served as a check on Microsoft's monopoly power, tying the company's hands while competitors and, importantly, open standards and open-source software established deeper roots. The behind-the-scenes uprising by PC makers, who had complained to the government about Microsoft's strong-arm tactics but refused to testify, is the best example. Gateway now has a major partnership with AOL. Microsoft's closest partners, including Dell and Intel among others, have invested in Linux-based start-up companies, and several PC makers offer some of their computers preloaded with the Linux operating system. Of the Linux investments, Ballmer would only say, "They're not helpful." Microsoft's own tracking studies show it continues to lose the loyalty of developers, who have embraced open standards and even open-source software. Even Java, a threat that Microsoft nearly contained in 1997, appears to have reached critical mass as the default programming environment for server-based Web applications.

Windows' very success freed the software industry from the need for a single, monolithic platform. PCs were becoming a smaller part of a bigger universe of billions of digital devices, all connected to a ubiquitous network via a new industry standard, the Internet protocol that no single company controlled. Microsoft became one bright but fading star in a larger constellation, no longer the software world's center of gravity.

Gates could be forgiven for sticking with his original idea, to develop high-volume, low-priced software separate from hardware. But just as Henry Ford's any-color-as-long-as-it's-black approach to automobiles gave way to the market segmentation strategies of General Motors' Alfred Sloan, Gates's one-size-fits-all approach outlived its natural usefulness.

Interoperability, not lock-in, has become the winning strategy.

Gates underestimated the speed with which the rules of software would be rewritten by the new mandates that issue from the universal connectivity of the Web. But once he "got it," he began to take half-steps toward those four key precepts—simple, flexible, heterogeneous, and loosely coupled.

Those mandates will be key to the success of Microsoft's new .Net initiative. Gates is backing new things—Windows XP has a new user interface that finally begins to leave behind the Windows desktop, and with XML, a new loosely coupled architecture for interoperability. Switching to a new user interface could leave Microsoft vulnerable to alternative offerings from competitors. Opting for XML's simple text approach to connecting computers may undermine many of the strategies Gates had adopted as recently as 1997 and 1998 to guide customers toward an all-Microsoft environment.

For Gates, the opening was all about timing. Interoperability between computers that don't have an established relationship with each other and that don't share common software—the essence of loosely coupled—has been a staple of academic computer science for years. "But the market didn't need it," Gates told me in our interview. "Until you got XML as a standard, until the Internet, using HTML for presentation, got to critical mass, until you got this new form of e-commerce, people really didn't need it. Now, they do."

The trend toward interoperability will work in Microsoft's favor, he said. Perfect "interop" breaks down the walls between computer systems. The winner thus becomes the supplier who delivers the highest performance per dollar. Its high-volume, low-price strategy lets Microsoft offer better price/performance than the mainframe sellers, such as IBM, and the Unix vendors, such as Sun, he said. Free software, such as Linux, running on cheap PC hardware, could undercut Microsoft, but putting that aside, "We're the winners as interoperability works," Gates said. "Interoperability is going to work because the world got XML and the tools. It was natural that it would happen anyway. But it does favor us as it comes into being."

It was all about timing. Instead of simply tweaking the old-fashioned desktop, for example, by 2001 Microsoft was ready to offer the new user interface and encourage developers to use it instead of the old Windows shell. Gates himself served on the .Net task force that met weekly to reinvent the "shell" that had been the coveted prize in so many of Microsoft's internal rivalries. Replacing the timeworn Windows desktop had long been a passion for many people at Microsoft. The Web had triumphed in large part because it presented an easier, more intuitive user interface. People quickly grasped the value of the "back" and "home" buttons, among other browser features. Microsoft had tried and largely failed to move the old desktop tasks—opening applications, managing files—onto a new Web interface. Experienced users rejected any change simply because it was unfamiliar. Once again, by serving its existing customer base, Microsoft diminished its ability to innovate. The company retained the old Windows desktop far longer than its useful life.

"Its days are over," argued Steve Capps, a refugee from Apple Computer who worked on the spectacularly successful Macintosh user interface as well as the failed Newton handheld computer. He advocated ditching the Windows desktop in time for the Millennium Edition (cloyingly called Windows Me), the successor to Windows 98. It didn't happen. "Sure enough, the old Windows desktop is there." Capps wasn't surprised. "They're the most successful company in history doing X, so there's a tendency to continue to do X," he said. "Then a yahoo like me comes in and says, 'You should change everything.' They say, 'You did Newton, so screw you.' "

The way out of its dilemma was, again, looser coupling. Windows' old shell could continue to do Windows-type tasks. The new user interface would handle the new uses for computers—e-mail, messaging, photos, music, and the like. "That's a radical-type move," Gates told me. "It's exciting to be on a product like that, because you get a blank sheet of paper. But it's scary because you know your ship date is years out and you wonder whether the thing will get to critical mass."

BY THE TIME Gates was ready to bet on something new, however, many of the people he was counting on to deliver it had already voted with their feet. They decided to let the company fight on without them.

Like the old approach to software, the tightly coupled organizational model of Microsoft itself couldn't scale.

Maritz called it quits in the fall of 2000. His wife, a psychologist, had diagnosed Maritz as an "enabler" of some of the worst habits of both Gates and Ballmer. To the two of them, every idea was the stupidest thing they had ever heard. It was Maritz's job to pick one of the stupid things and make it work. A health scare, which turned out to be a false alarm, heightened Maritz's sense of mortality. Wrestling Microsoft's contradictory imperatives into a coherent strategy suddenly seemed less compelling.

In September 2000, three months after the public presentation of the .Net strategy at the Forum 2000 event, he followed through on the departure plan he had first set in motion more than a year earlier. He was ready to spend time at his ranch in Zambia and with his fam-

ily. Mike Maples, who had retired from Microsoft several years earlier, warned Maritz to temper his wife's expectations; he had to make
clear, Maples said, that leaving the company didn't mean they would
be going to Florence to hold hands and watch sunsets. Within a few
weeks of leaving, Maritz and his wife were indeed in Florence, holding hands and happily watching a glorious sunset. Microsoft continued to call Maritz a consultant but, in reality, once he was gone, he
was gone.

Maritz was cautiously optimistic that he had helped bring Microsoft through the confusion that had paralyzed it. Now the arguments were about how to execute rather than about what to do.
"There isn't an obvious existing model here to follow," he told me a
few weeks before he announced his departure. "It's up to us now. We
really have to get our shit together and do it."

Bosworth's reasons for leaving Microsoft were less ideological or
strategic than temperamental. Against heavy odds, his small XML
team had not only survived but had propagated the technology
through Microsoft. His three-year deal for guaranteed freedom still
had a year to run, but he was again ready to move on. He just wasn't
having fun anymore. "Don't leave now," Gates pleaded with Bosworth near the end of 1999. "We're just betting on your architecture."

Bosworth knew that meant that one of Microsoft's massive mobi-
lizations would soon be under way. Microsoft was staffing up the
XML effort to include more than two thousand people. Bosworth
preferred to lead teams of dozens of people, not hundreds or thousands. He knew he wasn't good at running large teams. Neither
would he be happy as an "architect" simply kibitzing from the side-
lines.

Bosworth once again had an alternative in mind. He told Gates
and Ballmer what it would take to persuade him to pursue his ideas
inside the company. He wanted to turn his XML initiative into a service that handled all of the behind-the-scenes complexity to allow
companies to take advantage of XML. He proposed that Microsoft
go fifty-fifty with him in an internal start-up company.

Other companies were experimenting with such "intrapreneur-
ship," or internal venture capital funds. Funding new ventures by
employees served the joint purpose of gaining early access to innovative technologies and at the same time keeping some of the most entrepreneurial employees from leaving altogether. Like many of

Microsoft's restless entrepreneurs, Bosworth professed no desire to hurt Microsoft, which had done very well by all of them. He says he would have preferred, out of loyalty and affection, to stay at Microsoft.

But there was a deal-breaker. He insisted on complete freedom to use any technology he deemed most suitable, even if that meant, say, bypassing Microsoft's Windows 2000 or SQL Server database in favor of Sun's servers, or the Linux operating system, or databases from Oracle.

Gates said no. There was no way he could acquiesce to such a condition. Bosworth wasn't the first developer to come to him proposing to be "set free" to pursue a start-from-scratch approach incompatible with the rest of the company's product line.

"To what end?" Gates asked in our interview. "Is it to the end of 'That would be fun'? Or is it to the end of doing the right thing for the end-user? You can't ship a product with a different user interface and say, 'Too bad. XYZ wanted to have his own org and do his own thing and that's why you have to learn a different user interface.' Nobody's interested in that."

It was still Gates's job to enforce the integration of Microsoft's product line. Microsoft wasn't a conglomerate or a holding company in which the pieces were unrelated to each other. It wasn't even like a manufacturing operation, where parts and subassemblies could be outsourced from other suppliers.

"That would be very nice, but in terms of the user interface, the management, the security, the integration of how that all comes together, that's a state-of-the-art thing," he said. "You don't build that except with a lot of very smart people here who want to be involved in very high volume software."

Developers began to decamp individually and en masse. Microsoft might have participated financially in the spinouts by former employees, building on the familiarity the alumni had with Microsoft technologies and business strategies to create a network of alliances based on its platform. That would have given Microsoft a stake in the new value being created. Instead, with rare exceptions, Microsoft treated the defectors with hostility.

Microsoft opted for the heavy-handed approach to Bosworth's new effort. Bosworth and Rod Chavez, who had worked closely on Trident and other projects, set up their new company behind a shopping mall in Redmond, less than two miles from Microsoft's campus.

Bosworth's reputation helped the new company, CrossGain, attract more than twenty other engineers and managers from Microsoft. Frustrated by what it considered poaching of employees by Cross-Gain, Microsoft insisted the start-up require any Microsoft employee seeking a job there to inform his supervisor that he was exploring "outside opportunities."

The most prominent defector to CrossGain was its new chief executive, Tod Nielsen. Nielsen, a twelve-year Microsoft veteran, had seemed to be the company's truest and bluest employee. A local boy from Bothell, Washington, Nielsen is gregarious and good-looking and had fashioned himself into one of the company's most visible cheerleaders. As vice president for developer relations, he had been an evangelist for Microsoft's "platform" efforts. He had made himself an insider, golfing with Gates and volunteering for a months-long stint at the antitrust trial in Washington, where he served as Gates's eyes and ears. As one of Maritz's top lieutenants, he had helped plan the launch of the .Net initiative at Forum 2000. A few weeks before the launch, which had been postponed several times, Nielsen announced he was leaving Microsoft to consider a number of job offers. He soon surfaced at CrossGain.

Relations with Microsoft grew even more chilly when CrossGain announced that part of its $10 million in venture funding came from the investment firm of Jim Barksdale, the former CEO of Netscape, who had testified for the government and against Microsoft in the antitrust trial.

The real breaking point was CrossGain's adoption of Oracle, Sun, and Linux technology, rather than Microsoft's Windows 2000 and SQL Server database, as the platform for its product offerings, to make it easier for developers to deliver software applications on the Web. The freedom to choose a different platform had been Bosworth's deal-breaker demand of Gates. Now, CrossGain made no secret of its technology choices: Its Web site advertised job openings for Linux and Oracle programmers. The start-up was choosing the technology that would help it get its products out most quickly. To Microsoft, it was an embarrassing snub. Bosworth, the XML pioneer, and Nielsen, the Windows evangelist, had seemed to abandon the company's platform and embrace its competitors' as soon as they left the payroll.

Microsoft retained powerful leverage over its former employees, each of whom was barred by contract from competing with the company for one year after departure. Microsoft executives and attorneys made clear they were ready to enforce the non-compete clauses against the defectors to CrossGain. At a meeting with CrossGain's principals, Paul Flessner, Microsoft's senior vice president in charge of SQL Server, defined competition in the broadest possible terms. On a piece of paper on the conference room table, he drew one circle, denoting company A, and another for company B. Any software that allowed A to exchange data with B competed with Microsoft, he said, even if Microsoft didn't yet have technology with the features Cross-Gain was offering.

According to sources close to CrossGain, Flessner offered a way out of the dispute. Microsoft was willing to let slide the non-compete clauses if CrossGain agreed to adopt and showcase SQL Server, not Oracle, as its technology platform. Flessner stopped short of insisting the CrossGain use Microsoft's technology exclusively. CrossGain's engineers began a technical review to determine the feasibility of moving to a dual platform. Before a deal was finalized, Ballmer reviewed the terms. He was adamant that Microsoft be tough in upholding the non-compete provisions. Flessner told CrossGain his earlier position had been too soft. The way CrossGain executives understood the new terms, they would have had to effectively dump Oracle's platform and adopt Microsoft's. Nielsen and Bosworth determined the switch would require extensive re-engineering and cost CrossGain crucial months. Some of the technology Microsoft was pushing didn't even exist yet. There was no way CrossGain could accept the terms.

Microsoft's official position is that it was simply enforcing non-compete provisions that are standard in the industry. "Tod, Adam, and other former employees who left for CrossGain were all well compensated for their work at Microsoft," one official told me. "Tod and Adam in particular were senior executives intimately involved in Microsoft business strategy, with full access to and knowledge of Microsoft intellectual property. When they left Microsoft, they started CrossGain—a company that competed directly with Microsoft's present and future products." He said Microsoft did not insist on exclusive arrangements and gave CrossGain "every opportunity" to resolve the dispute.

Several members of CrossGain's board of directors wanted to call Microsoft's bluff and take it on in court. Microsoft would back down to avoid the embarrassing spectacle of appearing to crush a fledgling effort by some of its most prominent former employees, they argued.

They promised to raise a legal defense fund from Microsoft's many enemies. Other board members argued that any victory over Microsoft would be a Pyrrhic one. A small company like CrossGain had to stay focused on shipping software, not fighting lawsuits.

Instead of fighting it out in court, in January 2000, CrossGain moved to preempt Microsoft's legal leverage. At an emotional company meeting, Nielsen fired all the employees who had come from Microsoft, more than one-quarter of CrossGain's staff. Nielsen, Bosworth, and Chavez resigned. All the employees could return to work at the expiration of their one-year non-compete clauses, for most only a matter of a few weeks or months. In the meantime, CrossGain would have to get along without them. But the company would be free to make its own technology choices.

Bosworth went to the Australian island of Tasmania to take a strenuous trek to work off his frustration. Nielsen retreated to the golf course and spent time overseeing construction of a vacation home in Palm Springs, California, a sunny refuge from drizzly Seattle. He still considered himself a proud alumnus of Microsoft, but he was deeply shaken by the company's hardball tactics. After defending the company from its critics for years, he had seen for himself the darker side of Microsoft. Microsoft hadn't dangled any irresistible partnership opportunities in front of CrossGain; it had simply tried to bully the small start-up. Nielsen laid out the situation in an e-mail to his board of directors. One director, Mitchell Kertzman, the chief executive of Liberate Technologies, a maker of interactive TV software, had tangled with Microsoft many times and recognized the behavior. He sent Nielsen a succinct reply: "Now you know."

IN the newly fractured software industry, a half-dozen or more all-out platform battles now rage in key markets. Plenty has replaced scarcity as the prevailing paradigm in computing: in processing power, venture capital investment, and connectivity bandwidth, where the problem at least in the long-haul networks is no longer shortage but glut. Even in what were once niche markets, volume has reached the critical mass needed to generate strong positive feedback cycles. That gives competitors the ability to carve out defensible positions, if they remain fast and smart. The result is that the winner-take-all stakes of the early PC industry have given way to the Win, Place, and Show payouts of the networked economy.

The most striking pattern in the list of new platform competitions is that Microsoft's position is that of challenger, not leader, in most of them. Microsoft has retained dominance in the markets for PC operating systems and, with Office, for productivity application suites. In the other markets, Microsoft's "good twin" is coming up from below, playing the role of price-busting innovator and bearing out the proposition that software markets work best when Microsoft is the insurgent, not the incumbent.

In Web-based services, AOL is number one, Yahoo! is runner-up, and MSN is in third place. Each has a different approach, keeping the competition keen. In database software, Oracle is the incumbent, dominating the high end of the market. IBM retains a large share, but other historical competitors have largely fallen away, leaving Microsoft's SQL Server as the most formidable challenger. In handheld computers, Palm's leading market share is healthy. The keepers of the Palm operating system have avoided the trap that Apple fell into. They have liberated the software from its tight coupling with Palm's own hardware offerings. As a result, Palm's platform is proliferating on devices produced by Sony, Handspring, and others. Microsoft's PocketPC software is the challenger, driving improvements in features like color graphics and wireless connections.

In streaming media technology, RealNetworks has maintained a substantial lead, despite Microsoft's integration of its own Media Player into Internet Explorer and thus into Windows. The leading format for digital music is not Microsoft's, or even RealNetworks', but MP3, an open industry standard. The codec (short for compression/decompression), which strikes fear into the hearts of record industry executives, confers no strategic advantage on any particular hardware or software maker.

Strong competitors are also established in the nascent markets for software for interactive television and Web-enabled cell phones. Several major cable operators, including ones that have received large investments from Microsoft, have opted for software from Liberate, a spin-off from Oracle. Major cell-phone manufacturers, led by Nokia, are investors in the Symbian joint venture to produce an operating system for mobile Web services. Palm is also a player in the market.

In servers, the story several years ago was simple: Windows NT systems running on Intel PCs were coming up from below to overtake the more expensive hardware/software bundles from Unix vendors such as Sun, IBM, and Hewlett-Packard. Now, Sun is the clear winner among Unix vendors, Windows' growth is stalled, and the real momentum is with Linux, one of the signature successes to emerge from the primordial soup of global Internet connectivity. Linux is not the only open-source success. In one specific server market, Web servers, the Apache open-source software project has long held the market-share lead.

As a challenger, Microsoft asserts itself as a force for openness. It is a matter of strategy, not morality. For example, in instant messaging, a core technology for online and wireless communications. Microsoft's pitch is simple—all instant-messaging users should be able to send and receive messages to all other users. AOL, with two of the leading instant-messaging services, has the bulk of customers worldwide. As the incumbent, AOL has dragged its feet on promises to make its technologies interoperable. Microsoft, in contrast to its claim that opening its own code amounted to an "unprecedented confiscation of the company's intellectual property," pushed government regulators to force AOL to open its instant-messaging code as a condition for approval of the acquisition of Time Warner. Government officials welcomed Microsoft's aggressive stance as the best long-term check on AOL Time Warner's own monopolistic ambitions. One FCC official told the *Wall Street Journal*: "There's only one player who can beat 'em: Microsoft."

BALLMER'S ascension to chief executive has allowed for a looser coupling between Gates and the rest of Microsoft. Gates is letting go of his tight control, though not always willingly.

Publicly, Gates is effusive with praise for Ballmer. "Now the buck stops with him, about how we organize, what sorts of business trade-offs do we make and all that," he told me. "In some sense, it's a more systematic way of looking at new businesses we're in, and the existing businesses we're in, than we've ever had before."

Privately, Gates has grumbled about the company's softening financial situation. The financial strains have occasionally forced tensions between the two men into the open. In one product review session in the fall of 2000, a team leader requested a budget increase to add more people for a key project. Gates, slipping into his old role, approved the request.

Ballmer quickly and publicly vetoed him. "I'm running the company now," Ballmer said. "We can't keep spending and spending with no payoff in sight."

Gates exploded. He accused Ballmer of short-selling the company and failing to make long-term investments. Senior executives had seen blowups between the two old friends in smaller meetings, but never in front of so many lower-level employees.

"Bill is always going to have a hard time letting go," said David Marquardt, a member of Microsoft's board. "Steve is going to rip it out of his hands."

Ballmer was taking on a Herculean task. He had staked his tenure on the .Net initiative, but the initial response was disappointing. The sell-off in Microsoft's stock from its peak in December 1999 shook the company's confidence. The .Net planning team hoped for a solid stock rally to overcome the internal resistance to the inevitable organizational dislocations to come. If the stock rallies to above eighty dollars a share, the initiative is viable, I was told before the event. "In the sixties is a disaster." In the months following Forum 2000, the price of Microsoft's shares slid below fifty dollars. The new stock options that had been distributed to bolster morale and increase retention were all under water. At the launch event for .Net, Mich Mathews, Microsoft's vice president of corporate communications, buttonholed me in the hallway and crisply laid out the three possible outcomes for the company. "We can move ahead with this and prosper," she said. "Or we can become IBM, with a good legacy business. Or we can fail at both."

The phrase "become IBM" resonated with meaning. Microsoft, more than any other company save IBM itself, was responsible for dislodging Big Blue from the center of the computing world, the sweet spot where the winner collects a disproportionate share of the rewards. It had been an article of faith that Microsoft would never end up like IBM, cranking out products, servicing customers' accounts, and generating respectable revenues—but relinquishing the strategic center of information technology.

Microsoft was a bellwether for the deceleration of the world economy and the slump in stock prices that caught up with the rest of the technology sector at the end of 2000. Slowing PC sales, sagging advertising revenues, and saturation in Microsoft's core markets combined to force the company to issue a rare announcement that it would fall short of Wall Street's expectations for both the quarter and the fiscal year ending in June 2001. Ballmer ordered cost-cutting and

a reduction in unfilled vacancies. To forestall another wave of departures, he promised another round of pay raises for all deserving employees.

In a letter to employees, Ballmer tried to rally them to the cause of
holding Microsoft together. Microsoft employees had been telling
him that the company seemed much more complex than it used to be.
"Is there just one thing people need to do well?" he asked rhetori-
cally. "Is it just .Net and transforming software into services? Or are
we a conglomerate of many largely independent businesses?"

Ballmer's answer was: both. He was a fierce proponent of razorlike
focus, but now he laid out the seven businesses that were key to Microsoft, the two priorities for all employees, and the three things the
company must do well. The seven businesses were the Windows
platform; the .Net platform; the Office suite of applications; servers
and tools for corporate networks; the MSN online efforts; software
for non-PC devices such as handheld computers and cell phones; and
business applications for small- and medium-sized companies. The
two priorities for all employees were remaining focused on serving
their specific customers and at the same time helping to deliver the
new common platform. "This 'whole-is-bigger-than-the-sum-of-
the-parts' approach has characterized our success for years," Ballmer
said. The three tasks for the company were to execute on the priorities, eliminate unnecessary costs, and focus on the company's people.
The board of directors had considered and rejected a retreat from
parts of that smorgasbord of goals. "Bill and I and the Board believe
that if we execute on these opportunities, it is within our power to
grow profits significantly over the next five years," Ballmer wrote.

Ballmer likes sports trivia, so here's some: In 1938, the Chicago
Bears fumbled the football fifty-six times, a record for ham-
handedness that has never been exceeded. But Da Bears were a
resourceful team. Their offense holds the all-time record for recovering their own fumbles, with thirty-seven. And adding the fourteen
fumbles that their defense came up with that year, the 1938 Bears are
second on the all-time list for most fumbles recovered in a season.

Microsoft is likewise adept at recovering after it has appeared to
drop the ball. Ballmer installed a corps of solid Steve guys atop each
of Microsoft's key businesses. Belluzzo's experience running big businesses at Hewlett-Packard helped him provide "adult supervision" to
Microsoft's consumer efforts. Under him, veterans of the browser
war, including David Cole, Brad Chase, and Yusuf Mehdi, finally
turned MSN into a serious challenger to AOL. In February 2001,

Ballmer promoted Belluzzo to become Microsoft's president and chief operating officer; like Gates, Ballmer wanted to relinquish some day-to-day responsibilities to give himself more time to concentrate on strategy. With Maritz's departure, Muglia, the consummate company man, assumed effective command of the .Net platform efforts. Raikes moved back from the sales operation to take over Muglia's old Office group, completing a full circle back to the applications business, where he had started at Microsoft.

One of the most influential remaining Bill guys, David Vaskevitch, had stepped out of the limelight. At the Forum 2000 event, he stood by himself on the fringes of the crowd as Microsoft executives mingled with analysts and reporters, touting the new .Net initiative. In the aftermath of Project 42, Vaskevitch had gotten a new assignment, moving Microsoft into the market for networked applications for businesses. It was a reversal for Microsoft, which had recruited software partners by stressing that, unlike Oracle, it was a neutral platform supplier with no designs on their customers. But Vaskevitch knew applications were what drove adoption of any new platform, just as, in an earlier era, Office had propelled Windows.

"In the end, Microsoft has always done well with platform shifts. But in the beginning it has always looked as though we would not," Vaskevitch wrote me in an e-mail exchange a few weeks later. "Platform shifts take a long time; we know how to exploit them; the path only becomes clear with time."

CHALLENGE AND RESPONSE

Gates could see clearly the outlines of a new business model—for somebody else's business. In 2000, through his charitable foundation, he set about the transformation of the global pharmaceutical industry.

For his summer vacation, Gates was taking a trunk full of books for a kind of Australian Think Week on global health. He had long been interested in biotechnology, but now he was diving into the nitty-gritty of infant mortality rates, life expectancies, the mathematics of epidemics, and the distribution of wealth. He devoured *The Evolution of Infectious Diseases*, by Paul Ewald, and *The Coming Plague*, by Laurie Garrett, and a pile of thick, chart-laden reports from the World Health Organization.

As he read more and worked through the numbers, Gates was incensed. Eight million children die simply because the country where they happen to be born doesn't have basic, cheap, available health care. Ninety percent of the world's medical research targets problems faced by 10 percent of the world's people, while 10 percent goes to the problems of 90 percent. Malaria alone kills a million children each year. The $50 million the Gates Foundation contributed for development of a vaccine for malaria nearly doubled the world's annual budget for research on the disease.

"I mean, it's almost criminal that more money isn't spent on drugs like that," he said.

It was a market failure. Drug companies refused to invest in the research for diseases that affected only poor countries because they had no rich-country market in which to recoup their initial development costs. If high prices in Europe and the United States can cover research-and-development costs, developing countries need simply cover the very low marginal cost of production. The moderate successes in jawboning drug makers to lower prices for developing countries was possible only for drugs for diseases for which treatments at least exist.

For diseases that solely affect poor countries, treatments and vaccines never get developed in the first place. Drug companies know the pressure will be immense to make effective vaccines, once they are found, widely available at low cost. So they prefer not to find them in the first place. The market is structured to stunt innovation, even innovation that is a matter of life and death.

The pharmaceutical companies' aversion to risk wasn't surprising. Drugs require huge investments in basic science and practical engineering. Initial development costs might run into the hundreds of millions, or even billions, of dollars. Gates recognized the business model. To him, the drug maker's approach was that of the old mainframe computer companies—low-volume, high-price.

Like the software industry, drug development could be pushed toward the high-volume, low-price model. After the expensive design work, the marginal cost of a dose of vaccine is pennies, just like the marginal cost of a copy of software. That makes them uniquely suited for high-volume distribution. "These are almost miracle-type products," Gates said. "They can become available at very low cost to the entire world at large."

Gates had the money to bootstrap the industry's transformation. Call it the antitrust dividend. Before 1998, Bill Gates had given only a few hundred million dollars to charity. In 1999 and 2000, the sizes of the chunks of Microsoft shares Gates turned over to his foundation were staggering. For his forty-second birthday in October 1998, he donated $1 billion. Three months later, in January 1999, he chipped in $3.3 billion. The $5 billion gift in June 1999 was the largest ever by a living donor until August, when Gates gave another $6 billion. When he put in $5 billion more in January 2000, the Gates foundation became the biggest charity in the world. With a $22 billion endowment, the foundation is obligated under tax law to make grants totaling more than $1 billion every year. Suddenly, by a huge margin, he was the most generous philanthropist of all time. He told one interviewer he would gladly give up his fortune to make the antitrust trouble go away.

Whatever the original motivations, Gates engaged global health issues deeply. He hooked up with Dr. Gordon Perkin, an obstetrician and gynecologist who ran a small nonprofit in Seattle that found ways to deliver the kind of cheap, simple, and practical tools needed in the developing world. Perkin became Gates's global health guru. He had worked for the World Health Organization in Thailand, Mexico, Brazil, and Ghana. His organization developed a simple alternative to the Pap smear for diagnosing cervical cancer; a label for vaccine vials that indicates when the dose is no longer usable, reducing waste; and a cheap, single-injection needle that breaks when it is used, so health workers won't reuse syringes.

The organization's board of directors dined with Gates on the top floor of a downtown Seattle hotel. Perkin had Gates practice delivering vaccines by using the Uniject syringe to inject saline solution into a dinner roll. Gates funded Perkin's efforts, then asked his small organization to manage an initial $100 million grant to make common childhood vaccines more readily available. A strong global vaccination effort in the 1970s had reached about 70 percent of the world's children, but funding cuts, political paralysis, and plain loss of will stalled the effort before it reached the poorest countries.

As he dived into the issues, Gates realized he had been embarrassingly naive. He had worried, for example, that improving health care would lead to population growth, creating an additional set of problems for poor countries. The literature convinced him of the counterintuitive reality: In country after country, seven or eight years of improved health conditions and lowered infant mortality leads to lower population growth. The improved health prospects helped reassure mothers they no longer needed to bear five or six children in order to raise two or three to adulthood. Over time, average family size declined.

Gates recognized a positive feedback cycle when he saw it. "It's really kind of a virtuous connection that's quite phenomenal," he said.

In 2000 the Gates foundation put up $750 million over five years to buy vaccines for 25 million children in the seventy poorest countries. It was the first big contribution toward a fund to distribute existing vaccines and guarantee a mass market for the new vaccines for the major killers that were just entering the product pipeline. It was a classic bootstrap. The fund would create a market pull. Additional funding for vaccine research and development would provide a push.

"The only way great vaccines will be created is by working with the pharmaceutical industry and encouraging them to take more risks, knowing that government and philanthropists will work with them to make sure there is a market," Gates told me in an e-mail.

IT WOULD take longer for Gates to realize that Microsoft's Windows monopoly represented its own kind of market failure.

Gates's favorite role is insurgent. It's how he sees himself. He uses the word "revolutionary" freely to describe his ideas and Microsoft's role. That he had become what he had always pledged to avoid—a defensive incumbent—created a dissonance our conversation made clear he hadn't resolved.

"All the things about being revolutionary in terms of a new approach, that's just inherent in every new piece of software," he told me. "It's a field in which if you don't do superrevolutionary things, you become irrelevant pretty quickly. Fortunately, the assumptions we made when we started the company, that the hardware would improve at such a rate, that allowed us to do revolutionary things."

Ballmer seemed to have a more grounded view of Microsoft's historic trajectory. "You can't be an insurgent all your life," Ballmer told me in 1999, as he walked from his hotel to San Francisco's Metreon entertainment megaplex, where he was to launch yet another blockbuster version of Office. "Unless you're unsuccessful."

The psychic costs of Microsoft's retrenchment had not been borne by Gates alone. The "strategy tax" Microsoft imposed to ensure the preservation of the Windows and Office franchises sapped the morale of his development teams. They had felt they could win by building faster, better, more popular software products than the competing team. They were annoyed by Gates's implicit and explicit assumption that Microsoft couldn't compete on the merits on a level playing field.

Compete on the merits. The phrase has so much commonsense appeal. But Gates knew being better was necessary but wasn't enough. Same with being faster. Same with being popular. Even being cheapest wasn't enough. Without a feature that locks in customers, there's little to stop them from switching to a competitor as soon as a better, faster alternative comes along. Then Microsoft would have to come back with something better and faster yet. It would be on an exhausting treadmill. It was easier to live the "comfortable life of a leader" that Brad Chase promised in his "Preserving the Desktop Paradise" memo back in April 1997.

Gates hadn't set the rules of the game. He just played by them better than anybody else. His competitors decried his tactics while wishing they could execute them half as well. In his deposition, Gates had made it a point to demonstrate his mastery of the fine distinctions between the various legal and commercial protections for proprietary interfaces. Gates had simply mastered the rules for establishing a durable competitive advantage in the evanescent world of software. The law was very clear, he said repeatedly during the course of the trial. Microsoft could integrate, and integration was good for customers. If the rules had changed, somebody needed to tell him.

The rules had changed.

In *U.S. v. Microsoft*, the federal courts, with the high-powered assistance of the Justice Department and Microsoft's own army of attorneys and consultants, began to grapple with the key distinction for the future of software competition: that between integration for the benefit of the customer and integration for the strategic advantage of the software provider.

The courts, at first, appeared to be the appropriate venue for making such distinctions. Yet, the legal system's performance has been less than stellar. By 2001, the numbing details of Microsoft's practices were receding into history as the case that began with an initial filing in October 1997 approached its fourth anniversary. Microsoft's competitors treated the courtroom in Washington as simply another front in the geopolitical battle for market dominance. The case, which generated so many bangs, appeared to be ending with a whimper without delivering clear lessons.

Still, it has only become more clear since 1997 that the private decisions that determine the design of the digital infrastructure are public concerns. There are mainstream public policy debates about the social responsibilities of Big Oil, Big Health, and Big Media. It's likewise appropriate to judge Big Software against the common good.

As Lawrence Lessig, the Stanford law professor who played a small but significant role in the antitrust case, put it, software code is law. He describes the digital realm as a "set of instructions written into code that we, or more precisely, code-writers, have authored. This code sets the rules of this space; it regulates behavior in this space; it determines what's possible here and what's not possible."

Forget browsers. Think instead about the implications of Microsoft's announced plans, dubbed Hailstorm, to integrate into Windows its own network services for handling privacy, security, copyright, identity authentication, real-time communications, payments, scheduling, software delivery, and file storage. It's not hard to imagine the dystopic possibilities when a private monopoly exercises unfettered rights to define the architecture of such important zones of our common, global space.

We've already had glimpses of the unintended consequences, global security breaches such as the "love bug" virus in May 2000 that exploited a flaw in Microsoft's Outlook e-mail program. There are intentional consequences as well, such as for the balance between the absolute rights of intellectual property holders and the public's interest in the free expression of ideas. Microsoft is integrating its "digital rights management" platform into Windows. The console gives copyright holders, such as record and software companies, the ability to specify the exact conditions under which its intellectual property can be used, played or copied.

"We're building the operating system for content distribution," said Will Poole, vice president of the digital media division. He acknowledges a potential conflict of interest: Microsoft is itself a major copyright holder. It is an aggressive enforcer of so-called "shrink-wrap licenses" that users agree to with the click of their mouse, accepting conditions far more restrictive than those found in copyright law itself. "The amount of money we lose from piracy is tremendous," Poole said. "We want to invest in technology that secures copyright."

The most effective check on such conflicts of interest is competition, under which each feature is subject to the rigor of comparison with several alternatives. Microsoft's claim of seamless integration may well be an effective selling point, and so be it, but other consumers and the public at large may opt for, say, rock-solid security, or more transparent privacy protections, or digital rights schemes with a more expansive concept of the "fair use" of copyrighted material. Gates's "works best with Windows" strategy presents no problems as long as Windows users can also easily opt for network services that compete with Microsoft's own.

Fortunately, that's the direction in which the world is already moving.

The historical reliance of Microsoft and many other software vendors on tightly coupled and proprietary interfaces represents an increasingly obsolete model of software creation and distribution. The "horizontal" model of the PC industry, which had replaced the "vertical" model of the mainframe industry, is itself being replaced by a "niche" model that precisely targets opportunities for new, quickly evolving products.

In early 1998, long before Jackson issued his breakup order, SRI Consulting tracked the development of the new era in a scenario for a post-Microsoft future. The thoughtful report speculates about a cataclysmic breakup of Microsoft into five separate companies in 2003. The proximate cause was not a court order, but rather a falling stock price that forced the company to hand employees ever larger grants of stock options until there was no more stock to give.

In the SRI scenario, Microsoft's demise opened the way not for dominance by another big player, but for a loosely coupled network of niche software producers. Rather than high-volume, one-size-fits-all software for the benefit of a dominant software provider, the new starting point was the particular needs of individual customers. Software cooperatives formed to assemble libraries of components for reuse and resale. Modular components, produced by freely forming and disbanding teams of programmers, snapped together with interfaces that adhered to simple, public protocols.

"Like small mammals darting among plodding reptiles, the niche producers, both real and virtual companies, form quickly to produce new componentized products," the report rhapsodized. "A highly responsive industry capable of quickly meeting precise customer needs was being born."

The real breakthrough came in the development of a market in interfaces themselves. The time had passed for a single "user interface" or for a set of "application programming interfaces" controlled by a single company. The invisible hand of the market, rather than the heavy hand of centralized command and control, produced a flurry of innovation in human-responsive user interfaces, from speech and 3-D to full-body virtual reality. Other interfaces delivered new abilities for operating systems, databases, networking protocols, and real-time communication and collaboration.

SRI identified the twin tenets of "proactive modularization" and "flexible integration." Software components might start out as separate, but if two or more can work together, they can be easily joined together, perhaps by one of the many online integration services.

Such trends are in motion even without a breakup of Microsoft. Power in information technology is increasingly shifting from suppliers to customers. With that power, customers are increasingly pressing to preserve their ability to swap out components and eliminate unnecessary lock-ins. In the long run, the marketplace demands of hundreds of millions of customers is likely to protect such diversity more effectively than antitrust enforcement. In a competitive market, any attempt to artificially constrain choice through technical incompatibilities or contractual restrictions are punished as a "tax" that customers will resist paying. As long as a credible competitor is challenging a dominant provider, the public's interest in innovation and choice is likely to be well served.

The policy challenge is to preserve the ability for competitors to play that role. To protect choice, speed innovation, lower prices, increase interoperability, and widen social inclusion, what is needed is not retrospective, reactive antitrust enforcement against a single competitor but proactive public policy that covers all competitors and explicitly enhances customer choice. Customers, including hardware makers that license software for resale, need the right and the ability to swap out components from a dominant provider and substitute one from a competitor at every level of the digital infrastructure. For competition on the merits to thrive, interfaces must be pried open and kept open between as many individual components of the digital infrastructure as is possible.

Gates has resisted such a commitment, decrying even the so-called conduct restrictions in Jackson's order on remedies for its antitrust violations. Gates unleashed the forces of commoditization on the computer hardware industry and isn't about to voluntarily succumb to the same dynamic himself. The Internet is indeed a subversive force. From the time it attained critical mass, the Internet has been a great civic resource and a rolling business disaster, sucking the profit margins out of retailing, then music, and then software itself.

Yet, the demand for competition on the merits and a common code of open interfaces is not as radical as it seems. It's what Microsoft itself advocates for AOL's instant messaging system; it's what it has pledged for itself with its use of industry-standard XML in its .Net initiative. It is already Microsoft's—and every company's—optimal strategy in markets in which it is not already dominant. It is how Microsoft's "good twin" plays the game. A common code of open interfaces may be each competitor's second choice, but it is society's first choice.

Microsoft has already taken half-steps toward the new model. In March 2001, Microsoft announced that about one thousand corporate customers would be given access to the source code for Windows 2000, a tip of the hat to the success of the open-source movement. All that's left is for Gates to have the courage of his own core convictions and lead an industry movement toward open interfaces and competition on the merits. Who among his critics could reject such a pledge?

IN THE HEYDAY of the "Pacific Century" bubble in the 1980s, it was fashionable to describe Microsoft as one of the most Japanese of American companies. Gates was the visionary CEO who made the big bets that ensured long-term advantage without regard to quarterly results.

By the time of the dot-com bubble of the late 1990s, the stock market boxed in Gates more than he liked to admit. Perversely, as the company's value skyrocketed, Gates's freedom of maneuver shrank. Gates's strenuous defense of the Windows monopoly was not only prudent, it was the only economically rational choice for a chief executive entrusted to enhance shareholder value. He couldn't be expected to put at risk a franchise that generated nearly $10 billion in revenues a year and staggering profit margins and held a lock on perhaps the economy's single most strategic market.

Gates's ability to make a truly dramatic gesture had been shackled by Wall Street. He was a prisoner of expectations. Microsoft could not escape the reality that confronts any large company that contemplates dramatic change: It was a slave to the Street.

By the same token, a fallen stock price can become a ticket to freedom. By 2001, Microsoft's valuation, though still at mid-1998 levels, had fallen below Wall Street's worst-case estimates for the value of Microsoft's piece parts under Jackson's breakup order. In May 2000, David Readerman of Thomas Weisel Partners calculated Microsoft's breakup value at fifty to fifty-five dollars a share. At its January 2001 low, Microsoft was trading in the mid-forties. In the eyes of investors, it was as if Microsoft's monopoly had already been broken, its value crushed.

Of course, under almost any scenario, Microsoft has a very long tail of revenues and cash that will keep it among the world's most profitable companies for many years to come. And Gates is likely to be the last person to be unhappy with the low share price, which makes it substantially easier to recruit new talent with promises of renewed upside potential for their options. But at every stage of the story, from the pajama party at Hood Canal in the summer of 1997 through the filing of the antitrust suit in May 1998 and the breakup order two years later, and all the way to the stalled growth and sliding stock of 2000, the conventional wisdom, and my own, had always been that things would never go this far or get this bad for Microsoft.

The worst-case scenario that has come to pass might be the best thing that ever happened to Gates. He could jettison the baggage of the Windows monopoly and blame the government for the disruption of Microsoft's profits. He could take the onetime hit, retool the factory, and position Microsoft for wide-open competition on the merits for leadership on the new Internet platform. He could make a magnanimous gesture of revolutionary leadership. He could end the long legal nightmare and liberate Microsoft's own innovation and passion.

He is free.

EACH member of Microsoft's inner circle serves as a projection of a particular part of Gates's own personality. In broad historical terms, it was Brad Silverberg who came to represent Microsoft's idealized vision of itself. Certainly, he has wrapped himself in the mantle of the Internet perhaps more fully than is warranted by the record. Yet, as the advocate for a new Internet platform and a more loosely coupled relationship between the browser and Windows, Silverberg for a brief moment moved Microsoft incrementally closer to a common code of open interfaces.

Silverberg is a typically flawed hero. He can be moody, ambivalent, and egotistical. He was oddly mute during the legal proceedings. If, in the legal terms of the Sherman Antitrust Act, Jackson found Microsoft's tight technical tying of Internet Explorer to Windows amounted to "monopoly maintenance," Silverberg's strategy to use Windows to propel Internet Explorer as the new client platform for the Internet age represented a form of "monopoly extension." It was his army in the Internet Platform and Tools Division, after all, that prosecuted and won the browser war. It was his marketing team that drove the semi-exclusive contracts with providers of Internet content and access. It was his development teams that executed the strategies to prevent alternative interfaces from Netscape and Sun from supplanting Microsoft's own. Microsoft would not have escaped antitrust action if it had stuck with Silverberg's strategy. Indeed, even Silverberg realized the legal troubles might have been even worse.

In any epic, the hero must be banished, even if he represents the empire's own highest calling. After his precarious deal to keep the browser team blew up in January 1998, he remained on Microsoft's payroll as a part-time consultant for nearly two years. He enjoyed snowboarding from helicopters and wrangling his Jeep over granite slabs in the Sierra foothills; he liked planning his vacation house in Jackson Hole, Wyoming. In the spring of 2000, he was ready to go back to work, albeit less than full time. Along with John Ludwig and about a half-dozen other Microsoft veterans, he linked up with several alumni from Craig McCaw's wireless ventures to form Ignition Corporation, a holding company for wireless Internet start-ups. Ignition in turn funded companies such as Avogadro, a wireless software start-up founded by Thomas Reardon, the live wire from the Internet team who himself recruited more than a half-dozen veterans of Microsoft's Internet effort.

As a businessman, Silverberg tried to avoid antagonizing his former employer, where even gentle criticism can be taken as disloyalty. He had many friends still at the company and maintained good relations with Ballmer. But it didn't take much to stir his old juices. In January 2001, he rented the video of the movie *Gladiator*. In the movie, Maximus, a popular general, is tapped by the dying Emperor Marcus Aurelius to redeem Rome's glory and restore the Republic. He narrowly escapes execution by Commodus, the emperor's jealous son, who assumes the throne and has Maximus's wife and son killed. As the synopsis on the movie's Web site says, "Maximus has learned that the one power stronger than that of the emperor is the will of the people. He knows he can only attain his revenge by becoming the greatest hero in all the empire."

Maximus's vision for a greater and more ideal Rome resonated with Silverberg. When the movie was over, he tapped out an e-mail, his synopsis of his own journey.

"In my own small way what motivated me through Windows 95 and then the Internet stuff was a vision for a greater and more ideal Microsoft," he wrote to me. "A big motivation for the Internet Platform and Tools Division was a chance to reinvent Microsoft to be one that carried the mantle of leadership in a more statesmanlike fashion—a more idealized Microsoft that could lead an industry in a confident and more gracious way."

GATES was more likely to see the spectacular rise and precipitous fall of Microsoft as a video game, perhaps Age of Empires, one of the company's most popular titles. The game's scenario begins: "You are the guiding spirit of a tribe. . . . Your goal is to build your tribe into a mighty civilization that can vie for world dominance. . . ."

Gates's passion for such strategy games is plain. He is nostalgic for the early days of Microsoft, when he was almost alone in believing that mere software could establish lasting value. The thrill of being right is the engineer's reward.

"People claim that they discovered you could create a software platform and that would have economic value," Gates told me in our interview. "Well, wait a minute. All you're doing is writing down what we did. You think you discovered it? We knew that, and we did it."

The opportunities for critical mass and big positive feedback loops, Gates said, almost wistfully, "those are very very few. When they happen, yeah, they're spectacular."

The backlash was perfectly predictable, Gates said. He was referring to all the technology wonder companies that had recently been punished by Wall Street, but it was clear he mostly meant Microsoft. "The press acted as if all these companies had discovered the fountain of youth, that growth and profits and breakthroughs—it was never ending." In the rush to make sense of the boom, reporters ascribed great wisdom to technology leaders. "Maybe they knew the answers to more than just even doing technology," Gates mocked. "Maybe they knew all about management. It was the New Age way of organizing. Look at these technology companies, they must know everything. These companies never do anything wrong. They never make missteps. Their growth always increases.

"If you set the bar high enough, then you're ready to write your next story. Which is, 'Who did these guys think they were? We said they were unbelievable and now they're only just fantastic.' "

The real surprise was that some companies were actually clever enough to deal with the immense expectations, the laws of large numbers that inevitably slowed growth rates in the long term, and the need to preserve some assets and discard others in order to keep the company moving forward.

"What a terrible fall from grace it is to be a company that's doing tablet PCs," Gates mocked with heavy sarcasm. "How boring that is. And the next generation of user interface. And improving the productivity of, oh, about a billion people.

"Who's really doing great software? Tell me the start-up who's doing any of the things that really should be done, will be done, to make software dramatically better than it is today.

"That's happening here."

Gates is a student of history. Arnold Toynbee, the English historian, in his twelve-volume *Study of History* concluded that civilizations remain ascendant only as long as they are led by creative elites who respond successfully to challenges. When their leaders' creativity waned, the civilizations decline into stasis and suffer the tyranny of despotic minorities. But decline was not irreversible. Leaders could rise again to successfully respond to new challenges.

Toynbee has been criticized for placing as much value on myth and metaphors as on factual data. In Gates's case, there's no factual data with which to write the final volume. It's not yet clear whether he will rise to the challenge of change, or retrench yet again. He may let go; he may hold tight.

Gates has offered no public unburdening about his private torment as he bore both the weight of expectations and the pain of unrelenting attacks. There has been no catharsis, no sense of what he may have learned, no indication that any "high-order bit" has flipped to fundamentally change his thinking. He has acknowledged no mistakes, save for his regret he didn't more effectively tell Microsoft's story.

So metaphor will have to do.

I say he shoots the moon.

In the card game of Hearts, shooting the moon is the most difficult, most thrilling strategy. Under the rules of the game, the player with the fewest points wins. One point is tallied for each of the 13 hearts and 13 points for the queen of spades. Playing it safe means avoiding taking any of the tricks that contain those cards.

But sometimes, when a player holds a hand so strong—say, aces and kings in hearts and spades and a high club card to control the game's first trick—he forsakes caution for the exhilaration of "shooting the moon." Rather than avoiding the points, he wants them all. For the player who takes all the hearts and the queen of spades, the rewards are high. Instead of 26 points against him, he gets zero points and wins, while those that played it safe are punished with 26 points against them.

The epic quest to define the primary software interfaces for work, entertainment, and communication will require all of Gates's strategic abilities. The infrastructure for the digital age will be based on competition on the merits and a common code of open interfaces. The rules of the game have changed.

Gates has been dealt a strong hand. He's young, visionary, and intellectually honest. He can indeed scale, can indeed grow. He can certainly track the inevitable. I say he shoots the moon. I say Gates rises to the new challenge. I say he goes out a winner.

Key Dates

August 6, 1997	Microsoft agrees to invest $150 million in Apple Computer and pay another $100 million to settle outstanding patent issues.
October 1, 1997	Microsoft releases Internet Explorer 4.0 browser.
October 20, 1997	The U.S. Department of Justice seeks a contempt-of-court citation against Microsoft for violation of a 1995 consent decree that ended earlier antitrust proceedings.
December 11, 1997	U.S. District Judge Thomas Penfield Jackson rejects the petition for a contempt citation but issues a preliminary injunction ordering Microsoft not to force PC makers to bundle Internet Explorer as a condition for licensing Windows.
March 3, 1998	Gates testifies before the Senate Judiciary Committee, chaired by Senator Orrin Hatch (R-Utah).
May 18, 1998	Department of Justice and twenty states file a broad lawsuit charging Microsoft with violations of the Sherman Antitrust Act.
June 23, 1998	U.S. Court of Appeals overturns Jackson's preliminary injunction.
June 25, 1998	Microsoft releases Windows 98.
July 21, 1998	Steve Ballmer promoted to president of Microsoft.
October 19, 1998	The antitrust trial begins.
March 29, 1999	Ballmer announces reorganization of Microsoft into five groups organized around customer needs.
September 21, 1999	Closing arguments end the testimony phase of the trial.
November 5, 1999	Judge Jackson issues his preliminary findings, calling Microsoft a "predatory monopolist."

January 14, 2000	Bill Gates steps aside as chief executive in favor of Steve Ballmer. Gates remains Microsoft's chairman and "chief software architect."
February 17, 2000	Microsoft releases Windows 2000 at launch event in San Francisco.
April 3, 2000	After the failure of mediation efforts, Judge Jackson finds Microsoft in violation of the Sherman Antitrust Act.
June 7, 2000	Judge Jackson orders Microsoft broken into two companies and imposes additional restrictions on the company's conduct. He later stays the remedies pending Microsoft's appeal.
June 22, 2000	Microsoft unveils its ".Net" Internet initiative at Forum 2000 in Redmond.
December 14, 2000	Microsoft announces quarterly earnings will fall short of Wall Street expectations.
February 26–27, 2001	Oral arguments in Microsoft's appeal before the U.S. Court of Appeals in Washington, D.C. A decision is expected in the spring.
Summer 2001	Microsoft plans to release Windows XP, formerly code-named Whistler, the first consumer operating system based on Windows NT.
Fall 2001	Microsoft plans to release Xbox, its new video game console.

Notes

THE BACKBONE of this book is my reporting on Microsoft for the *Wall Street Journal* since 1996 and the voluminous documentation that emerged from Microsoft's various court battles. I have filled out the story with interviews with dozens of past and present Microsoft employees, as well as with additional documentation. In places, I have relied on their accounts to describe meetings and internal discussions at which I was not present. Because many of the sources for this book insisted they remain unidentified, I have omitted attribution for some of these accounts.

CHAPTER 1: TRACK THE INEVITABLE

10 *Gates gloated:* Dvorak, John, "Anti-Microsoft Sentiment Grows," *PC Magazine Online,* September 8, 1998.

12 *"He doesn't care that much about being aligned with Apple":* "conversations with billg last nite," e-mail from John Ludwig to Don Bradford e-mail, August 21, 1997.

13 *As described in a memo by Bruce Jacobsen:* "Notes from a conversation with Bob Muglia," internal memo prepared by Bruce Jacobsen, July 1997.

14 *"The common wisdom":* Kirkpatrick, David, "Microsoft: Is your company its next meal?" *Fortune,* April 27, 1998.

14 *"Everybody in the communications business is paranoid": Ibid.*

14 *the "master of the big lie technique":* Robert Ingle, interview with the author, October 17, 1997.

16 *After dinner, he moved the conversation:* The Hood Canal briefing was "off-the-record" by decree of Mich Mathews, Microsoft's vice president for corporate communications. All substantive information included here has been confirmed through subsequent interviews, e-mail exchanges, and public statements.

18 *Paul Allen, in Microsoft's early days:* Ballmer told *Newsweek's* Mark Whitaker in a June 11, 1997, interview, "Paul wanted to build computers, actually. Bill didn't."

19 *"When we were doing the revolutionary work":* Bill Gates, interview with the author, July 28, 1998.

21 *Company lore has it:* sidebar to Andrews, Paul, "Microsoft ad-

justing its course after a triumphant quarter-century," *Seattle Times*, September 3, 2000, p. A13. Andrews confirms that a 1989 analyst/media briefing book renders the slogan "A computer on every desk and in every home, running Microsoft software." After Microsoft came under investigation by antitrust officials, company lawyers suggested dropping the final clause.

22 *Myhrvold's long memo to Gates:* Zachary, G. Pascal, *Showstopper: The Breakneck Race to Create Windows NT and the Next Generation at Microsoft* (London: Little, Brown and Company, 1994), p. 31.

23 *Of the people he liked to consult:* Gates was responding to a question in a conference call as to why Myhrvold, who had been a member of the executive committee, had not been named to the newly formed Business Leadership Team in Microsoft's March 29, 1999, reorganization. Myhrvold went on a long-term leave several months later and subsequently left the company.

23 *"We DID get the per transaction deal":* "Re: stt/Netscape," e-mail from Barb Fox to James "J" Allard, April 25, 1995.

24 *"I had this radical idea in '86 or '87":* Pontin, Jason, transcript of interview with Nathan Myhrvold, *Red Herring*, February 1998.

24 *Frustrated that Microsoft wasn't effectively explaining:* Myhrvold, Nathan, "Telling It Like It Is," interoffice memo dated July 18, 1993.

24 *the software company that succeeded in setting the standards:* Gates confirmed that he continues to believe in the winner-take-most nature of platform software at the July 27, 2000, Microsoft Financial Analysts Meeting, saying, "The second idea was that the value of the platform would be significant. Within that realm of software, having the platform that optimized hardware, saved developers work, worked to create interoperability between those various things: that would be a fundamental aspect; in fact, [such] an asset that the leading platform would be significantly more popular than the number two platform because of the dynamics of software availability."

24 *"The historical situation is that the market share leader":* Myhrvold wrote that applications software, such as word processors and spreadsheets, generate significant, if somewhat less powerful,

positive feedback cycles than systems software. "The typical figures are something like 60 percent to 70 percent for the leader, 60 percent to 70 percent of the remainder for the runner-up and so forth," Myhrvold explained. Indeed, in terms of units, Office commands only about 70 percent of the productivity application suite market. But it collects more than 90 percent of the revenues in the market; competitors such as Lotus, with SmartSuite, and Corel, with WordPerfect Office, have priced their offerings far below Microsoft's.

26   *"I admit I find it hard to focus lots of resources"*: Gates, "Internet," e-mail to Craig Mundie, Nathan Myhrvold, Rick Rashid, and Russell Siegelman, April 10, 1995.

27   *"This scares the hell out of me"*: Gates, "FW: Think Week (Long!)," e-mail, September 30, 1996.

28   *The PC model:* Gates's e-mail exchange with the author, September 21, 1997.

34   *"Now they have to say, 'Gee, when the Internet era started'*: interview with the author, September 1, 2000.

35   *IBM waited 11 years:* Utterback, James M., *Mastering the Dynamics of Innovation* (Boston: Harvard Business School Press, 1994), p. 192.

35   *Gates noted the irony:* "I worshipped Digital when I was a kid," Gates was quoted as saying after Digital's acquisition by Compaq. "We don't want to live through that."

36   *Gates hung a framed photo:* Schlender, Brent, "What Bill Gates Really Wants," *Fortune*, January 16, 1995.

37   *the "disturbing regularity"*: Utterback, *op. cit.*, p. 162.

37   *"The habits of mind"*: Utterback, *op. cit.*, p. 223.

39   *"As the majority of hobbyists must be aware"*: Gates's "Open Letter to Hobbyists," as quoted in Manes, Stephen, and Andrews, Paul, *Gates: How Microsoft's Mogul Reinvented an Industry and Made Himself the Richest Man in America* (New York: Doubleday, 1993), p. 92.

39   *"It's one of the most unusual markets"*: quoted by Clark, Don, *Wall Street Journal*, March 13, 1996.

40   *"The software industry in the past"*: Gates's interview with the author, July 28, 1998.

40   *"We believe that we ducked the bullet"*: e-mail exchange between Gates and Joachim Kempin, "As promised OEM pricing thoughts," December 17, 1997.

CHAPTER 2: HAWKS AND DOVES

43 *As the massive effort to deliver the software that would be called Windows 2000:* At that time, the operating system was still known as Windows NT 5.0. To avoid confusion, I have generally used a product's final name, even if it was known by a code name at the time.

44 *Dave Cutler, the creator of the original version:* G. Pascal Zachary, *op. cit.*, p. 3.

47 *His 1983 Ph.D. dissertation:* Allchin, James Edward, "An Architecture for Reliable Decentralized Systems," Ph.D. thesis. Georgia Institute of Technology, September, 1983.

50 *Gates described Cairo:* Schlender, Brent, "What Bill Gates Really Wants," *Fortune,* January 16, 1995.

65 *Microsoft had long placed all its bets:* Microsoft tried a cross-platform strategy in the early 1980s, when it was seeking to broaden its product line into software applications such as spreadsheets and word processors. As Jeff Raikes tells the story, Charles Simonyi, who played a key role in Microsoft's early days, laid out a business model that became known as the "Simonyi Revenue Bomb" at a company meeting in 1982. The theory was that the first application for the first operating system required a big investment but costs declined for subsequent applications and additional systems. Over time, more and more applications on more and more systems cause revenues to explode. "On Jan. 20, 1983 we knew we had the wrong strategy," Raikes remembers. That was the day Lotus shipped Lotus 1-2-3, the spreadsheet that made the company, and arguably the personal computer itself, a success. Lotus 1-2-3 wasn't designed to run on all computers, it was designed to run specifically on the IBM PC. "It didn't matter to customers to have the best spreadsheet on all computers. It mattered to customers to have the best spreadsheet on their computer," Raikes says. Microsoft quickly adopted a new motto: "To win big, make the right bet on the winning platform." By the mid-1990s, nearly all of Microsoft's software bets were on the winning platform—Windows.

72 *Internet Explorer usage:* Chase, Brad, "FY98 Planning Memo: Preserving the Desktop Paradise," April 4, 1997. Chase wrote: "This year we are on the map with an approximate 30% browser share with IE." Another report puts IE's market share at 31 percent by June 1997.

73   *"People were suggesting that Office had to work equally well:* Gates's
      e-mail, "HTML 'Openness,' " January 28, 1997.

CHAPTER 3: THE PATH NOT TAKEN

80   *Gates liked to say that if Microsoft went out of business:* Gates, Bill,
      Business at the Speed of Thought, (New York: Warner Books,
      1999), p. 174.

80   *"The company made some of the wrong choices":* Silverberg made
      available to me his e-mail exchange with Michael Martinez of
      the Associated Press, March 22, 2000.

84   *"I just didn't like it":* transcript of deposition of Brad Silverberg,
      admitted in court January 13, 1999.

86   *"IE 4 and Memphis are joined at the hip"* : Bliss, Megan, "Closure
      on Memphis action items from 3YO and Billg Memphis re-
      view," e-mail to Jim Allchin, Carl Stork, Jonathan Roberts, Bill
      Veghte, Moshe Dunie, March 25, 1997.

86   *In September, an IBM executive told McCue:* McCue, Mike, "Mi-
      crosoft license agreement restrictions," internal Netscape
      e-mail, September 5, 1996.

88   *"The concept of unifying the user's desktop":* Trower, Tandy, inter-
      nal Microsoft memo reviewing IE 4.0 user interface, sent to
      Chris Jones, Joe Belfiore, Bill Gates, Paul Maritz, Brad Silver-
      berg, David Cole, and Aaron Contorer, April 25, 1997.

89   *As late as January 1998, he cited Active Desktop:* small group in-
      terview with Gates in San Jose, California, January 27, 1998.

93   *So the team that outmaneuvered Netscape:* A fuller account of the
      stunt is included in Andrews, Paul, *How the Web Was Won* (New
      York: Broadway Books, 1999) p. 321–22.

97   *Elites, or Tops, would control the wealth:* Oshry, Barry, *Seeing Sys-
      tems: Unlocking the Mysteries of Organizational Life* (San Fran-
      cisco: Berrett-Koehler Publishers, 1995), p. xv.

100   *"I want to apologize":* Gates, "Last e-mail," e-mail to Ben Slivka,
      October 26, 1997.

106   *Even after AOL acquired Netscape:* notes taken by a Microsoft
      employee at Microsoft Competitive Review, December 15,
      1998.

107   *"That idea of thinking of it more like a magazine":* Gates's remarks
      at Microsoft Financial Analyst Day, July 24, 1997.

CHAPTER 4: CITIZEN GATES

112   *"almost a god"*: Platt, Kevin, "China's Youth Entranced by Bill Gates," *Christian Science Monitor,* December 12, 1997.

113   *"China's growth should be significant"*: O'Neill, Mark, "Microsoft chairman says China has key future role; Computer fans out in force to see 'King' Bill," *South China Morning Post,* p. 1, December 12, 1997.

114   *Microsoft signed the consent decree:* Microsoft's Memorandum in Response to the DOJ Petition Seeking to Hold Microsoft in Contempt of the Consent Decree, November 10, 1997, p. 13.

115   *"His last paragraph"*: transcript of deposition of Jim Allchin, March 19, 1998.

115   *"There were a lot of things"*: transcript of deposition of Paul Maritz, April 3, 1998.

116   *"We had a discussion"*: transcript of deposition of Jim Allchin, March 19, 1998.

117   *"We think it's a pretty balanced decision"*: Hiltzik, Michael A., "Judge Halts Web Browser Strategy of Microsoft," *Los Angeles Times,* p. A-1, December 12, 1997.

117   *Over the weekend:* Clark, Don, "Microsoft Is Unlikely to Be Hurt by Ruling," *Wall Street Journal,* December 15, 1997.

121   *"It's very painful when you go home"*: Anthony Bay, speaking at Forrester Forum in London, quoted in *Computerworld,* June 2, 1998.

121   *He hadn't prescribed the particulars:* The exact wording of the order is as follows: "FURTHER ORDERED, *sua sponte,* that Microsoft Corporation, its officers, agents servants, employees, attorneys, and all others in active concert or participation with them, are hereby enjoined, and shall cease and desist from and after the date hereof, from the practice of licensing the use of any Microsoft personal computer operating system software (including Windows 95 or any successor version thereof) on the condition, express or implied, that the licensee also license and preinstall any Microsoft Internet browser software (including Internet Explorer 3.0, 4.0, or any successor versions thereof) pending further order of Court."

122   *"I found their compliance"*: Jackson in interview with Stuart Taylor Jr., *Newsweek,* June 19, 2000.

122   *"We did exactly what the order said"*: Gates in "A Conversation

with Bill Gates Hosted by the Tech Museum, San Jose, California, January 27, 1998."

123   *The wording of the key phrase:* Microsoft, the Justice Department and Judge Jackson agreed that "developing" also included "licensing," in that if Microsoft was permitted to develop an integrated product, it was also permitted to license it.

125   *As Allchin saw it:* Allchin, Jim, "New org," e-mail to Yusuf Mehdi and Brad Chase, February 17, 1998.

129   *Gates prided himself on not spending "one second":* Gates's appearance on *The Charlie Rose Show,* March 4, 1998.

129   *"You have to be ready to take the criticism":* Gates at World Economic Forum, Davos, Switzerland, January 29, 1998.

130   *During Walters's visit to Hood Canal:* Andrews, Paul, "Bill Gates sings for Barbara Walters," *Seattle Times,* January 29, 1998.

140   *PointCast, for example, agreed:* "Marketing, license, distribution and promotion agreement" between Microsoft and PointCast, December 7, 1996

140   *In October 1997, a Microsoft representative threatened:* Wadsworth, Steve, "Microsoft," e-mail to Jake Winebaum, October 16, 1997.

141   *Gates underlined the importance of driving PC customers:* Gates, Jennings and other Microsoft executives, "Re: Wind98 Schedule Update," e-mail string, February 14–15, 1998.

141   *"The PR groups thought it would be controversial":* transcript of Gates's deposition, September 2, 1998.

143   *In reality, however, Gates was obsessed:* Corcoran, Elizabeth, "Microsoft Chief Deeply Stung by Charges, Associates Say," *Washington Post,* p. E1, December 29, 1998.

146   *In an internal strategy paper, IBM outlined:* "Network Computing Software Division Strategy," July 30, 1998.

146   *"to preserve, improve, and reinforce":* Bork, Robert, *The Antitrust Paradox,* (New York: Free Press, 1995).

151   *"If we look back, I think it's clear":* Gates appearing on *Good Morning America,* June 8, 2000.

CHAPTER 5: VICIOUS CYCLE

155   *Cisco Systems, which dominates the market:* Thurm, Scott, "Microsoft's Behavior is Helping Cisco Learn How to Avoid Trouble," *Wall Street Journal,* June 1, 2000.

155   *Jackson's scathing findings of fact:* Jackson, Thomas Penfield,

"Court's Findings of Fact," November 5, 1999. The findings on Gates's dealings with Intel are on pp. 50–52; with IBM, on p. 60; and with Apple, on p. 173.

157   *The public relations team prepared Microsoft employees:* Pinette, John, "Wednesday interview with Ken Auletta," e-mail correspondence. February 26, 1999.

158   *"Bill is both happiest and most productive":* The interview with Buffett was conducted by David Hamilton of the *Wall Street Journal,* who graciously provided his notes.

159   *"Which they did!":* Pontin, Jason, "Bill Gates Unplugged," *Red Herring,* September 2000.

160   *Ballmer played a small but key role:* Andrews, Paul, "How the Web was Won," *op. cit.,* p. 37.

160   *The weekly pickup basketball game:* The team names refer, of course, to the Harlem Globetrotters and their long-suffering patsies, the New Jersey Generals.

163   *Ballmer's report, with Gates at his side:* Foley, Mary Jo, "Ballmer Sounds the Alarm," *Smart Reseller News,* February 22, 1999.

168   *Two memos were prepared:* Valloppillil, Vinod, "Open Source Software: A (New?) Development Methodology," August 11, 1998. The documents were annotated and posted on the Web by Eric Raymond, a perceptive participant/chronicler of the open source phenomena and author of *The Cathedral and the Bazaar* (Sebastopol, CA: O'Reilly & Associates, 1999), expanding upon an essay first published in May 1997.

172   *"If you look at the Internet phenomena":* De Vaan, Jon, "Re: regaining industry leadership," e-mail, December 31, 1996.

178   *the slogan sounded like a platitude:* Ballmer's remarks at Microsoft Financial Analysts Day, July 22, 1999.

CHAPTER 6: MONOPOLIST'S DILEMMA

200   *Later, Sun's Bosak felt compelled:* Bosak, Jon, "Four Myths about XML," *IEEE Computer,* October 1998, pp. 120–22.

212   *The old "it"—Windows:* Greene, Jay, "Microsoft's Big Bet," *Business Week,* October 30, 2000.

217   *Software from Apps Company:* Declaration of Rebecca Henderson, who filed a brief on behalf of the government's proposed remedy.

220   *Later, Judge Jackson would say:* Wilke, John R., "For Antitrust

Judge, Trust, or Lack of It, Really Was the Issue," *Wall Street Journal*, June 8, 2000, p. 1

222 *A white paper stressed XML:* "Microsoft.Net: Realizing the Next Generation Internet," June 2000.

223 *"We haven't decided that Microsoft is a zero-revenue company":* Pontin, Jason, "Bill Gates Unplugged," *Red Herring*, September 2000.

CHAPTER 7: LOOSELY COUPLED

246 *"There's only one player":* Sandberg, Jared, "Rivals Face Battle with AOL Time Warner, Despite Deal's Conditions," *Wall Street Journal*, January 15, 2001.

248 *a record for ham-handedness that has never been exceeded:* The record was tied in 1978 by the San Francisco 49ers.

249 *"I mean, it's almost criminal that more money isn't spent":* Gates at Digital Dividends conference, Seattle, October 18, 2000.

254 *We've already had glimpses of the unintended:* Gomes, Lee, "Love Bug Prompts Security Experts to Poke at Microsoft's Weak Points," *Wall Street Journal*, May 24, 2000.

255 *SRI Consulting tracked the development:* Jacobson, Bob, "After Microsoft," SRI Consulting, first quarter, 1998.

257 *In May 2000, David Readerman:* Buckman, Rebecca, "Go Figure: In Valuing a Split Microsoft, Analysts Offer a Wide Range of Numbers," *Wall Street Journal*, May 2, 2000.

Acknowledgments

THROUGH my years on the Microsoft beat, the people of the company have provided thousands of hours to give me a graduate-level education in the real business of software. Some of their cooperation has been officially sanctioned and some not, but I found everybody to be unfailingly helpful and respectful. Each encounter has deepened my understanding of the company and the industry, and I am deeply grateful. Some people deserve special thanks, but to avoid any awkwardness, I have conveyed them privately. Among the current and former employees of the company that I thank are Jim Allchin, Orlando Ayala, Robbie Bach, Steve Ballmer, Richard Barton, Anthony Bay, Bob Bejan, Rick Belluzzo, Adam Bosworth, Steve Capps, Brad Chase, Rod Chavez, Jennifer Chayes, Larry Cohen, David Cole, John Cordell, Jon De Vaan, Moshe Dunie, Eric Engstrom, Jim Ewel, Charles Fitzgerald, Chase Franklin, Bill Gates, Rob Glaser, Michael Goff, Paul Gross, Steve Guggenheimer, Dave Heiner, Pete Higgins, Phil Holden, Penny Ingersoll, Karl Jacob, Sam Jadallah, Jim Kinsella, Harel Kodesh, Saul Klein, Matt Kursh, Lewis Levin, John Ludwig, Greg Maffei, Paul Maritz, Jerry Masters, Yusuf Mehdi, Sylvia Meraviglia-Crivelli, Ed Muth, Bob Muglia, Craig Mundie, Nathan Myhrvold, Mike Nash, John Neilson, Bill Neukom, Peter Neupert, Tod Nielsen, Mauro Not, Jean Paoli, Steve Perlman, Chris Peters, Will Poole, Jeff Raikes, Rick Rashid, Thomas Reardon, Jonathan Roberts, Ian Rogoff, Brad Silverberg, Steve Sinofsky, Charles Simonyi, Ben Slivka, Charles Stevens, Linda Stone, Patty Stonesifer, Rick Thompson, Martin Tobias, Rich Tong, Michael Toutonghi, James Utzschneider, Brian Valentine, Vinod Valloppillil, David Vaskevitch, Davide Vigano, Hank Vigil, Ben Waldman, Dwayne Walker, Brandon Watson, David Weld, Chris Williams, Deb Willingham, and Cornelius Willis. Any omissions are purely inadvertent.

Mich Mathews and her corporate public relations staff were helpful even in difficult moments. I give my thanks to Jim Cullinan, Mark Murray, Tom Pilla, John Pinette, Greg Shaw, Adam Sohn, Vivek Varma, and all the others. Trevor Neilson at the Bill and Melinda Gates Foundation has also been helpful.

The people of Waggener Edstrom, Microsoft's outside PR agency, have helped make countless arrangements and have strived to maintain a balance between the prerogatives of the press and the interests of their client. Marianne Allison was an advocate for this project in its infancy, for which I am tremendously grateful. Frank Shaw tirelessly arranged many of the interviews for the project and was a friendly companion throughout.

I have relied heavily on the smart insights and reliable information of many Wall Street analysts and industry observers too numerous to mention. But for guiding me through many minefields, I especially need to thank Michael Kwatinetz, David Readerman, and Rick Sherlund.

At the *Wall Street Journal*, I was lucky to have the opportunity to collaborate with the some of the best reporters and editors in the country. On the Microsoft story, I would surely have drowned without the help of Don Clark, Greg Hill, and John Wilke. Many other colleagues in San Francisco, Washington, and New York helped keep us on top of the story, and me out of trouble, for which I thank them. Paul Steiger, Dan Hertzberg, and Steve Yoder were gracious and accommodating in granting me a leave of absence to complete the project.

John Brockman, my agent, helped jump-start the project. At The Free Press, I thank Liz Maguire for her early faith in the book and Rachel Klayman for seeing it through under trying circumstances. Ruth Coughlin, who edited the manuscript, was a serene and calming antidote to deadline pressure. Brian Selfon's help with innumerable details was invaluable and highly appreciated.

Several people helped make my frequent trips to Seattle a pleasure. In particular, Brewster Kahle and Mary Austin, along with Anne Johnston, Eric Schultz, and Dorothee Soechting, generously provided a quiet retreat and warm hospitality. Sarah Block improved my social life and, along with Rob Glaser, heightened my appreciation for the Seattle Mariners and Safeco Field.

Deanne Moenster and Gabe Nansen provided striking and original graphic designs.

Throughout the last year, I have been blessed to be held in the warm embrace of a loving circle of friends and family. Erik Ninomiya read much of the manuscript in its early form and provided valuable feedback. Karen Gilbert appeared at exactly the right moment to help me through a difficult passage. Ronna Tanenbaum, Sharon Leyden, and Laura Stachel provided enthusiasm and laughter throughout. Michael and Adrianne Bank and Leonore Fine were sharp-eyed readers and unflagging supporters.

Three people in particular saved my sanity and came through for me repeatedly. Peter Leyden provided tremendous insight and is a true collaborator in many of the ideas in the book. Hal Aronson generously shared his rare gifts for listening and for keeping me anchored to first principles and higher priorities.

Cesar Chavez, my partner in life and love, soothed my panic and endured my absences. He also read every word, most of them twice. I don't know whether I would have been able to do this without him, but I do know I wouldn't have been nearly as happy.

Index

About the Author

DAVID BANK has been a staff reporter for the *Wall Street Journal*, based in San Francisco, since 1996. Previously, he covered technology and telecommunications for the *San Jose Mercury News*. His work has appeared in *Wired, Newsweek,* and *Out*. He was a Nieman Fellow at Harvard University and is a graduate of the Columbia University School of Journalism and the University of California at Santa Cruz. He and his partner live in Berkeley, California. This is his first book. Additional information can be found at *www.breakingwindows.net*.